ENCYCLOPEDIA
OF
GARDEN PLANTS
AND
FLOWERS

ENCYCLOPEDIA
OF
GARDEN PLANTS
AND
FLOWERS

LANCE HATTATT

p

This is a Parragon Book
This edition published in 2001

Parragon
Queen Street House
4 Queen Street
Bath BA1 1HE, UK

Conceived, edited, illustrated
and produced by Robert Ditchfield Publishers

Hardback ISBN 0 75255 885 4
Paperback ISBN 0 75255 840 4

A copy of the British Library Cataloguing in Publication
Data is available from the Library.

Typeset by Action Publishing Technology Ltd, Gloucester
Colour origination by Colour Quest Graphic Services Ltd,
London E9
Printed and bound in Indonesia

Half title: Doronicum 'Miss Mason'
Frontispiece: Digitalis purpurea
Title page: *Iris pseudacorus, Meconopsis x sheldonii* 'Lingholm', *Camellia japonica* 'Rubescens Major'
Contents page: *Tulipa* 'Maytime'

Cover design by The Bridgewater Book Company Limited

CONTENTS

INTRODUCTION

General information about the plants that we grow, or wish to grow, in our gardens is never, it would seem, to hand in one place at any one time. Too often it is necessary to delve into several different books in order to find the information we are looking for. This encyclopedia sets out to redress the balance.

Arranged alphabetically according to genus, the name under which species of similar characteristics fall, each entry includes a general introduction in which the principal features of the plants within the genus are described. Here too will be found information on hardiness, resistance to cold, cultivation details where appropriate, as well as, in some instances, suggestions for planting sites. Following this, individual species are listed by botanical name, the genus name appearing first in abbreviated form.

The majority of entries includes a description of habit, leaf and flower. Additionally, mention is made of other features such as form, autumn colour and fruit where relevant. Each entry concludes with an indicator of height and spread. To accompany most of the species described is an attractive picture clearly captioned with full botanical name.

Clearly it has not been possible to list all of the species belonging to a single genus. In many cases these run into a substantial number, in others to several hundred. Where a genus contains only one species, then this has been made clear. In all instances species have been listed for their garden worthiness and general appeal. Most should be relatively easy to obtain from garden centres or specialist nurseries.

Introductory pages comprise information on a wide range of subjects. These include general notes on all plant types – shrubs, trees, climbers, annuals, biennials, perennials, alpines and bulbs – as well as advice on hardiness, growth, soil type and an explanation of the way in which plants are named.

Many of the plants listed in this encyclopedia are poisonous either in part or in all parts. Others may cause an allergic reaction if touched. It must, therefore, be assumed that no part of a plant should be regarded as edible unless this is clearly stated or is understood beyond any doubt whatsoever. Severe dermatitis, blistering or allergic reactions to plants which are touched will affect individuals differently. Account should be taken of this before handling plants. In the event of an adverse reaction taking place, professional medical advice should be sought immediately. If possible, collect a sample of the plant for examination.

Finally, care has been taken to ensure that this encyclopedia is comprehensive. As well as including traditional, familiar plants it also lists those which are less widely known or which may be considered unusual. In this way it presents an opportunity to satisfy traditional tastes and expectations yet at the same time introduce new and exciting possibilities to gardeners.

A midsummer combination of *Stachys macrantha*, *Sisyrinchium striatum* and *Campanula lactiflora*.

SHRUBS and TREES

In any garden situation, out of all plant life it is shrubs and trees which provide most in the way of permanent structure. First and foremost their value is to be found in their form, the framework that they give not only within the garden but to the landscape as a whole. Whether deciduous, shedding their leaves in autumn, or evergreen, where leaves are retained for more than one growing season, their woody trunks and spreading branches contribute a permanent quality, or certainly one of long duration, which is essential to the overall composition of any garden.

LEAF

The attractiveness of leaf will be a determining factor in the choice of shrubs and trees for the garden. Colour plays an important role, as does leaf shape. Green, most widely to be found, will be seen to be variable ranging from the very pale to the very dark. In between lies an enormous colour range to include glaucous, where leaves may be coloured blue-green, grey-green or covered in a white bloom, leaves tinged with another colour, such as purple, red or yellow, or leaves which are variegated where an irregular mixture of pigments has taken place, often the result of a mutation.

Leaf shape will be seen to be as variable as colour. On the one hand they may be linear, long and pencil-thin, and on the other peltate, almost a complete round. Within these two points are to be found strap-shaped, broader and less tapering than linear, lance-shaped, widest below the centre and tapering to a narrow tip, oval, heart-shaped, kidney-shaped, diamond, triangular and spear and arrow-shaped. Some will be lobed, separated from adjacent segments, others palmate, fully divided into leaflets, whilst others will be pinnate, a compound with leaflets arranged in pairs. Leaf edges may be entire, that is to say continuous, toothed, with triangular indentations, spiny, scalloped or wavy.

Prunus 'Okumiyako', a glamorous spring-flowering cherry.

FLOWER AND FRUIT

As importantly, both shrubs and trees are cultivated for the flower colour that they provide through each of the seasons, particularly so in winter. Spring would, of course, be incomplete without the flowers of camellias, daphnes, forsythias, magnolias, *Prunus* and *Sorbus*. Summer sees *Ceanothus*, *Deutzia*, *Laburnum*, *Philadelphus* and the full flush of roses. Autumn is dominated more by fruit than flower with berries of *Callicarpa*, *Cotoneaster*, *Pyracantha* and *Viburnum*, as well as the quinces of *Chaenomeles*, crab apples of *Malus* and heps of roses. Winter brings with it the flowers of *Garrya*, *Hamamelis*, many viburnums and winter jasmine.

AUTUMN COLOUR

Many of the shrubs and trees listed in this encyclopedia are valued for their autumn colour, a process which takes place as the leaves of deciduous plants age, usually on account of a breakdown of pigments, especially chlorophyll. The result can be some wonderful, but short-lived, effects when whole shrubs and trees are alive with reds, yellows and flame colours.

BARK AND STEMS

It is not unusual for both shrubs and trees to be grown for the appearance of their bark and stems. These, most apparent in winter, may be coloured, as in the case of the dogwood, *Cornus stolonifera* 'Flaviramea', or *Prunus serrula* with its shining red bark, patterned as with *Acer capillipes*, peeling, as *Betula albosinensis* var. *septentrionalis*, or textured like the Stone pine, *Pinus pinea*.

The flowers of *Hydrangea anomala* subsp. *petiolaris*, a self-clinging climber.

CLIMBERS

Climbing plants, whether deciduous or evergreen, annual or perennial, are invaluable garden subjects not least for their ability to clothe walls and fences, to soften railings and trellises, to enhance arbours, arches, pergolas and pyramids and to extend the period of interest of both shrubs and trees.

HABIT

In general climbers fall into two categories: those which cling and those which twine, scramble or trail. Plants which cling will, in the main, do so without assistance and support themselves once established. For this they use aerial roots or terminal, adhesive pads. They are at their best when positioned to climb a flat, even surface and will succeed against brick, stone, plaster or wood. They will be less happy on rough surfaces, such as pebble-dash, or in a situation which subjects them to wind movement. *Ampelopsis*, Virginia creeper, *Hedera* (ivy) and *Schizophragma*, closely related to *Hydrangea*, are all self-clinging.

Twining plants, on the other hand, require support up to the height at which they are intended to grow. This may take the form of wires fixed along a wall or fence, against which a plant may be trained, or a stout cane positioned into the lower branches of a shrub or tree which will act as host to a climber and which will then support its coiling tendrils or leaf-stalks. In this category clematis are possibly amongst the best known, together with *Lonicera* (honeysuckle) and *Vitis* (vine).

POSITION

Correct growing conditions will ensure healthy, successful plants and to this end care should be taken to satisfy a plant's natural requirements. Most young plants will establish more satisfactorily if generous quantities of well rotted garden compost or manure are worked into the planting hole and plants are initially kept well watered. Whilst this applies to all plants, it is particularly the case with climbers which, positioned close to a host, such as at the base of a tree trunk or at the foot of a wall, may be outside the reach of normal rainfall. To overcome this problem plant as far away as possible, using a cane to lead the climber towards its host. Water given during dry periods will assist the climber to establish.

SHRUBS AND TREES AS CLIMBERS

Many garden-worthy shrubs and trees will respond well to being trained to grow against a wall or fence, most often producing larger flowers over a longer period as a result. These will not, of course, be of self-clinging or twining habit but will require securing against hosts by means of ties which should be checked periodically. Where shrubs and trees lend themselves to this treatment, then mention is made of this fact in either the description of genus or of species.

ANNUALS, BIENNIALS and PERENNIALS

More than anything else annuals, biennials and perennials are the plants to which we look to provide flower colour for the greater part of the year. Grown with shrubs and trees as part of a mixed border, or alone in the traditional herbaceous border, their vast range of colour, form and texture presents the gardener with enormous challenges and possibilities as well as huge scope for exciting experimentation.

ANNUALS

A hardy annual completes its life cycle in one year. That is to say, grown from seed it will germinate, flower, set seed and die within a single season. Seeds normally are sown in the open ground in the spring, very often in the positions in which they are intended to flower. Half hardy annuals differ only in that they are sown under glass and are transplanted outside once the threat of frosts is past. Many annuals are raised specifically for summer bedding schemes where they may be relied upon to flower profusely over a prolonged period.

BIENNIALS

In contrast to an annual, a biennial requires two seasons. During the first year it is normal for a biennial to produce only foliage. Flowering will take place during the second year, after which the plant will set seed and die. Seed is usually sown in summer in situ except in the case of half hardy and frost tender plants which should be sown under glass and kept frost free until planting out takes place in the second year.

PERENNIALS

Perennial plants will establish and remain in the border for a number of years, most commonly flowering annually, producing seed and dying back to ground level in the autumn. Dormant over winter, new growth is made in the spring. Rhizomatous perennials are those with fleshy, mainly underground stems, usually

The corymbs of *Achillea*.

The panicles of *Astilbe*.

horizontal and branching. Bulbous perennials are those either with a swollen stem at the base, most often below the surface, or with an underground bulb, corm or tuber.

FLOWER SHAPE

Flowers, of whatever plant, vary hugely in terms of form, shape and colour. The structure of a daisy-type flower-head, made up of ray-florets surrounding central disc-florets, will be greatly different from that, say, of an iris which consists of standard, fall and lip. The overall appearance, therefore, of all flowers will differ one from another. They may be single, semi-double, double or fully double, cross-shaped, starry, bell, cup, funnel, trumpet or tubular-shaped.

The racemes of *Dictamnus*.

The umbels of *Chaerophyllum*.

They may be held upright, horizontal or hanging, either solitary, in clusters, corymbs (domed or flat inflorescences of stalked flowers), racemes (inflorescences of stalked flowers coming from an unbranched axis), panicles (branched racemes) or umbels (stalked flowers coming from a single point at the top of the stem).

MONOCARPIC

Some plants, including certain perennials, are considered to be monocarpic. These plants will flower once, set seed and die although it may well be that they will grow for a number of years before flowering. Many *Meconopsis* are regarded as monocarpic.

ALPINES and BULBS

ALPINES

Alpines or rock plants, in terms of cultivated garden plants, are those which are of compact habit and include mat and cushion-forming plants, tiny bulbs as well as dwarf or miniature shrubs and trees. True alpines are to be found growing above the tree line at high altitudes where, on account of their low habit, they are resistant to wind and loss of water. Most will survive in thin, free draining soil and withstand extremes of temperatures but not an excess of wet.

THE ROCK GARDEN

In a garden situation alpines are most often to be found growing in a purposely constructed rock garden. Ideally this should be positioned in an open, sunny situation out of the reach of cold, drying winds and provided with sharp drainage. A top dressing of gravel or horticultural grit will aid this. Rocks or large stones set into the soil to emulate natural outcrops, amongst which are created planting pockets, serve to suggest the plant's original habitat.

THE ALPINE HOUSE

Any unheated, well ventilated glasshouse will serve as a suitable environment in which to grow many moisture-sensitive rock plants. Traditional alpines in an alpine house are cultivated in clay pots, set in sand to assist water retention and to give some protection from frost, on raised benches or staging. Tops of pots are dressed with fine grit to facilitate drainage, to avoid splashing of soil and panning when watering, and for appearance. Summer shading of glass reduces the risk of scorching plants.

TROUGHS AND CONTAINERS

Given free drainage, full sun and reasonably fertile soil, there is no reason why alpines should not be grown in troughs and containers. Indeed, in such circumstances it is easily possible to provide plants with the exact growing conditions for their success. The addition of a slow release fertilizer will be beneficial. Always slightly raise troughs and containers to facilitate drainage.

BULBS

Bulbs, a general term, is used to describe plants whose structure consists of a fleshy storage organ, a bulb, corm, tuber or rhizome, which permits a long period of dormancy, most often underground.

A bulb proper comprises a number of fleshy scales, which may overlap, fixed to a small basal plate. Often the scales, as in the case of *Narcissus* (daffodil), are contained within a thin, papery outer case.

Corms represent enlarged stems, sometimes with leaf scars, and mostly, as with *Crocus*, wrapped in a papery or fibrous case. Corms usually are replaced annually. Tubers, swollen sections of roots or stem, are designed to store food and are, like those of *Dahlia*, solid and most often without scales or outer cases. Rhizomes are essentially creeping stems, dividing as they extend on or below the ground. In appearance they may be thin, as with *Convallaria* (lily-of-the-valley), or thick.

In apparent dormancy bulbous plants are, in fact, completely active. It is during this time that the bulb ripens and flower buds form.

A garden of gravel and stone is an ideal site for low-growing alpine and rock plants.

HARDINESS

Plants listed in this encyclopedia come, very understandably, from all over the world. In their natural environment they are, obviously, completely hardy having adapted to the conditions which prevail in and around their habitat. It is only when they are planted in a completely different situation, and become cultivated plants, that hardiness becomes a factor. The degree to which a cultivated plant is hardy rests entirely on the similarities which exist between a garden setting and the plant's natural habitat. In determining this, account will be taken of climate, soil type and fertility.

Of course plants develop the means by which they may survive. Many will be dormant during the winter, others will lose their leaves, whilst some evergreens will develop smaller leaves with a much reduced surface area. In this way they are able to combat the effects of cold, drying winds. Yet other plants will be deeply rooted, thus avoiding or limiting the damage of penetrating frosts.

By being aware of, and taking notice of the natural environment, it is possible to go some way towards imitating the conditions in which a plant is most likely to thrive and succeed.

DEGREES OF HARDINESS

All of the plants listed in this encyclopedia are described in terms of hardiness. Where a plant is considered to be fully hardy, then no mention is made of this fact either under the principal heading, the genus, or against individual entries, the species. In all other cases the degree of hardiness is stated.

TERMS FOR HARDINESS
Hardy (to −15°C/5°F)
Frost Hardy (to −5°C/23°F)
Half Hardy (to 0°C/32°F)
Frost Tender (to 5°C/41°F)

Frost hardy *Solanum crispum* 'Glasnevin' grows against a warm wall where it is partnered with *Clematis montana* 'Rubens'.

Any attempt to categorize hardiness must be seen as a guide only. Much will depend on situation and the conditions in force at the time.

A plant which is described as hardy will withstand temperatures as low as −15°C/5°F and possibly those which are lower for short periods. A frost hardy plant is generally able to withstand a drop in temperature to −5°C/23°F. Many plants will fall between the two categories of hardy and frost hardy and will, therefore, be seen as borderline. Half hardy plants are those which will survive temperatures down to 0°C/32°F whilst those described as frost tender will only withstand temperatures to 5°C/41°F.

PRECAUTIONS AGAINST COLD

Certain measures may be taken to improve the likelihood of a plant's survival during cold periods. Evergreen plants, likely to be damaged by cold, drying winds, may be afforded the protection of a windbreak, made up of trees, a hedge or fine netting. Working the soil to provide deep, crumbly, well drained growing conditions is a means to improve a plant's ability to root easily and maintain a hold on life. A winter mulch, made up of compost, leaf mould or dead bracken, will give much needed protection to plants with a dislike of winter wet. Borders positioned in warm, sunny sites, possibly within the shelter of a wall or hedge, will greatly reduce the effects of cold and may, in winter in an artificially created micro-climate, allow plants not considered totally hardy to survive.

Lychnis coronaria alba enjoys alkaline soil. Here it makes an effective combination with the blue spikes of *Nepeta*.

HEIGHT and WIDTH

Throughout this encyclopedia the approximate measurements of a plant's height and width have been included. These are to be found following the description of each plant listed. Measurements are given in both metric, appearing first, and imperial. The height is the first measurement followed by that of the width, as for example 1.2 × 60cm/ 4 × 2ft.

It should, however, be pointed out that both height and width will vary enormously from garden to garden. Much will depend on growing conditions, soil and climate, as well as on situation. For example, a plant in a warm, favoured coastal situation is likely to establish more readily and grow more quickly than the same plant in an exposed, wind-swept, cold area. This is especially true of shrubs and trees whose ultimate height and width can prove to be unpredictable. For these reasons the measurements which are given can only be offered as a guide.

SOIL and SITUATION

Unless mention is made otherwise, it should be assumed that the plants described in this encyclopedia will succeed in normal, reasonably drained garden soil in a position which affords a proportion of both sun and part shade throughout the day. Where this is not the case, or where a plant requires a specific condition or situation, then this is stated. This may be given in general terms, as in 'best in full sun', or specific, as with 'for acidic soil in full shade'.

SOIL TYPES

The degree of alkalinity or acidity of soil is measured on a pH scale. This determines what will thrive in what kind of soil condition. A pH of 7.0 indicates a neutral soil and one in which the vast majority of garden plants should succeed. Above this measure soil is alkaline, below acid. Some plants, such as rhododendrons, *Pieris* and summer flowering heathers, will not tolerate lime and will only succeed on acid soils with a low pH. Others, like bearded irises and peonies, are happiest with some lime content. They will be at their best on soil with a pH above 7.0. Most garden centres sell simple but effective soil testing kits so that it is relatively easy to ascertain soil type with a high degree of accuracy.

PLANT CLASSIFICATION and NOMENCLATURE

Throughout this encyclopedia plants have been listed and arranged alphabetically according to their most recently agreed botanical names. First to appear is the GENUS, the main category into which one or more plants fall. All of the plants within a genus share a wide range of characteristics. A genus which is crossed with another, a hybrid genus, is preceded by a ×, for example: × *Halimiocistus* is a cross between the genera *Cistus* and *Halimium*.

Second to be listed is the SPECIES, the name given to similar individual plants that breed together in the wild to come true. The species name follows a capital letter denoting the genus. Where variants of a species occur naturally, the species is followed by a further name prefixed by 'subsp.' (subspecies), 'var.' (varietas/variety) or 'f.' (forma/form). A cross of species is indicated by ×.

Cultivars, those plants which are selected or raised artificially, either vegetatively or from seed, are given a name contained within single quotation marks following the name of the species, for example: *Campanula persicifolia* 'Telham Beauty'. Where the parentage is unclear or complex, then the name of the cultivar appears immediately following the initial of the genus, for example: *Campanula* 'Birch Hybrid'. Botanical names are recognized and accepted the world over and must, therefore, take precedence over any other names given to plants. However, frequently a common name, appearing in brackets, is given and an index of such names appears on pages 252–256. Unfortunately it has not been possible to include all common names for any given plant in current use. An example of this is *Stachys* which is referred to as Betony, Bishop's wort, Hedge nettle, Lamb's ears, Lamb's lugs, Lamb's tails, Lamb's tongues and Woundwort.

TABLE TO SHOW BOTANICAL NAMES			
Genus	*Acer*	*Euphorbia*	*Paeonia*
Species	*palmatum*	*characias*	*lactiflora*
Subspecies		*wulfenii*	
Varietas/Forma	*dissectum*		
Cultivar		'Lambrook Gold'	'Bowl of Beauty'

Acer palmatum var. *dissectum*

Euphorbia characias subsp. *wulfenii* 'Lambrook Gold'

Paeonia lactiflora 'Bowl of Beauty'

Abelia 'Edward Goucher'

Abelia schumannii

ABELIA

A genus of deciduous and evergreen shrubs grown for foliage and flower. Grow in full sun away from cold winds. Frost tender species should be afforded wall protection.

A. 'Edward Goucher' Semi-evergreen shrub producing fragrant pink flowers over dark green leaves, tinged bronze when young, in late summer. 1.5 × 1.5m/5 × 5ft
A. schumannii Deciduous shrub bearing lightly scented, lilac-pink flowers from late summer into autumn. Light green foliage coloured bronze when young.
2 × 3m/6 × 10ft

Abeliophyllum distichum

ABELIOPHYLLUM

A genus of a single species of deciduous shrub closely related to *Forsythia*. Sweetly scented, white flowers are borne on bare wood in late winter/early spring, to be followed by dark green leaves. Position in full sun. May be wall trained.
A. distichum Spreading shrub flowering in the early part of the year.
1.5 × 1.5m/5 × 5ft

ABIES (Fir)

Genus of evergreen conifers for well-drained soil in sun or part shade. Grown either as shelter belt or as specimen trees.
A. balsamea f. *hudsonia* Dwarf variety of the Balsam fir of irregular conical shape with leaves of mid-green. No cones.
1 × 1m/3 × 3ft
A. koreana (Korean fir) Conical tree with shiny green leaves, the undersides of which are silvery. Violet-blue cones are produced from late spring.
10 × 6m/30 × 20ft
A. pinsapo (Hedgehog fir) Tall growing tree with dark green/blue-grey leaves held rigidly. Cylinder shaped green cones ripen to brown. 25 × 8m/ 80 × 25ft
A. procera (Noble fir) Columnar tree with distinctive silver-grey bark. Glaucous foliage. Green and brown cones on specimens of 6m/20ft tall.
25–45 × 6–9m/80–150 × 20–28ft

Abies balsamea f. *hudsonia*

Abies koreana

Abies pinsapo

Abies procera

Abutilon 'Canary Bird'

Abutilon × *hybridum*

Abutilon × *suntense*

Abutilon megapotamicum

Abutilon vitifolium 'Album'

ABUTILON

A genus of evergreen and deciduous shrubs, small trees, perennials and annuals grown principally for flower colour and, in some instances, variegated foliage. Half-hardy species require the protection of a conservatory or glasshouse; frost-hardy species should be grown against a warm wall.

A. 'Canary Bird' Evergreen shrub/small tree carrying canary-yellow, bell flowers from spring to autumn. Half-hardy. 3 × 3m/10 × 10ft

A. × *hybridum* Evergreen shrub/small tree bearing flowers of orange, red, white or yellow from spring to autumn. Half-hardy. 5 × 2–5m/15 × 6–15ft

A. × *megapotamicum* Evergreen/semi-evergreen shrub with flowers of red, yellow and purple on arching stems in summer. Frost hardy. 2.5 × 2m/8 × 6ft

A. × *suntense* Deciduous shrub of upright habit carrying white to violet-blue flowers in late spring/early summer. Frost hardy. 4 × 2.5m/12 × 8ft

A. vitifolium var. *album* Deciduous shrub with white hollyhock-like flowers in early summer. Frost hardy. 5 × 2.5m/15 × 8ft

ACACIA

Genus of deciduous and evergreen trees, shrubs and climbers grown mainly for flowers and foliage.

A. dealbata (Mimosa) Evergreen tree with fern–like leaves and scented yellow flowers in winter/spring. Half-hardy. 15–30 × 6–10m/50–100 × 20–30ft

ACAENA

A genus of evergreen and deciduous sub-shrubs and perennials of low and creeping habit grown mainly for their foliage and petalless flowers/burrs.

A. 'Blue Haze' Evergreen, carpeting perennial with pinnate leaves of grey-blue. Round flower heads are followed with red-brown burrs from midsummer. 15cm × 1m/6in × 3ft

Acaena 'Blue Haze'

Acanthus spinosus

Acca sellowiana

Acer capillipes

ACANTHUS (Bear's breeches)
A genus of perennials producing spiny bracts over architectural foliage.
A. mollis Perennial of deeply cut, dark green leaves over which rise white flowers with purple bracts in midsummer. 1.5 × 1m/5 × 3ft
A. spinosus Perennial with narrow, oblong dark green leaves finely cut to the middle. White flowers with purple bracts from late spring to midsummer. 1.5 × 1m/5 × 3ft

ACCA (syn. Feijoa)
Genus of evergreen shrubs grown for their unusual flowers and edible fruits produced in warm climates. Frost hardy.
A. sellowiana (Pineapple guava) Shrub with grey-green leaves for a hot, sunny situation. Flowers with purple-red petals and crimson stamens are carried in midsummer. Fruits follow in autumn. 2 × 2.5m/6 × 8ft

ACER (Maple)
A genus of evergreen trees and shrubs, many with palmately lobed leaves, grown principally for foliage, often brilliant in autumn, and interesting bark. Mostly suited to sun or part shade, cultivars of *A. palmatum* may require some protection from cold winds and late frosts. Smaller varieties are well suited to garden cultivation.
A. capillipes (Snake-bark maple) Deciduous tree with trunk and arching branches streaked white and green, hence the name snake-bark. Three pointed lobed leaves are brilliant red in autumn. 10 × 10m/30 × 30ft
A. cappadocicum 'Rubrum' Deciduous tree with young foliage of dark red on red shoots. Five or more pointed lobed leaves. 20 × 15m/70 × 50ft
A. davidii 'Serpentine' (Snake-bark maple) Deciduous tree with white and green striped bark. Leaves generally unlobed up to 10cm/4in long turning orange-yellow in autumn. 15 × 15m/50 × 50ft
A. griseum (Paper-bark maple) Deciduous tree noted for its orange-brown peeling bark. Three palmate leaves colour orange and scarlet red in autumn. 10 × 10m/30 × 30ft
A. japonicum 'Vitifolium' (Japanese maple) Deciduous tree or shrub with shallow lobed leaves turning deep red in autumn. 10 × 10m/30 × 30ft
A. negundo 'Flamingo' (Box elder) Deciduous tree grown for pinnate leaves of light green with broad margins of pink, bleaching white in summer. 15 × 10m/50 × 30ft
A. negundo var. *violaceum* Deciduous tree with distinctive grey-green shoots and tiny purple-violet flowers. 15 × 10m/50 × 30ft
A. palmatum f. *atropurpureum* (Japanese maple) Deciduous tree of deeply cut, burgundy-red leaves colouring to a brilliant flame-red in autumn. 8 × 8m/ 25 × 25ft
A. palmatum var. *dissectum* A slow growing, deciduous tree with deeply cut, many lobed, fresh green leaves colouring gold in autumn. 2 × 3m/6 × 10ft
A. palmatum var. *dissectum* 'Garnet' Deciduous tree with finely cut, lobed leaves of red-purple remaining so into autumn. 2 × 3m/6 × 10ft
A. platanoides 'Drummondii' (Norway maple) Fast growing deciduous tree with broad, lobed leaves edged with cream. 12 × 12m/40 × 40ft
A. pseudoplatanus 'Brilliantissimum' (Mop-head sycamore) A slow growing, deciduous tree with rounded head and lobed leaves which open shrimp-pink, turn dull gold, then green in late summer. 6 × 8m/20 × 25ft
A. shirasawanum 'Aureum' (Golden leafed Japanese maple) Deciduous tree or shrub with many lobed, brilliant yellow leaves colouring red in autumn. 6 × 6m/ 20 × 20ft

Acer cappadocicum 'Rubrum'

Acer davidii 'Serpentine'

Acer japonicum 'Vitifolium'

Acer griseum

Acer negundo 'Flamingo'

Acer negundo var. *violaceum*

Acer palmatum f. *atropurpureum*

Acer palmatum dissectum

Acer palmatum dissectum 'Garnet'

Acer pseudoplatanus 'Brilliantissimum'

Acer platanoides 'Drummondii'

Acer shirasawanum 'Aureum'

Achillea 'Fanal'

ACHILLEA (Yarrow)

A genus of principally deciduous perennials, a number with aromatic foliage. In recent years many new hybrid introductions. Most are tolerant of the majority of soils and conditions.

A. 'Fanal' (syn. 'The Beacon') Perennial with pinnate leaves inclined towards grey-green above which rise flat flowerheads of red, with yellow disc-florets at the centre, in early summer. 75 × 60cm/2.5 × 2ft

A. filipendulina 'Gold Plate' Evergreen perennial with bright yellow flowerheads during summer into autumn. 1.2m × 45cm/4 × 1.5ft

A. millefolium 'Cerise Queen' Spreading perennial of deep pink flowerheads over dark green foliage throughout the summer. 60 × 60cm/2 × 2ft

A. ptarmica 'Boule de Neige' Vigorous perennial producing pure white, double flowerheads in summer. 60 × 60cm/2 × 2ft

Achillea filipendulina 'Gold Plate'

Aconitum napellus

Aconitum vulparia

Aconitum carmichaelii 'Barker's Variety'

ACONITUM (Monkshood)

A genus of perennials and biennials mostly with palmately lobed leaves of dark green. All parts of the plant are poisonous and contact with the skin may cause irritation.

A. carmichaelii 'Barker's Variety' Upright perennial with dark violet flowers in late summer and autumn.
1.5m × 30cm/5 × 1ft

A. napellus Upright perennial with deeply lobed leaves and indigo-blue flowers in mid to late summer.
1.5m × 30cm/5 × 1ft

A. vulparia Upright perennial of creamy-yellow flowers in mid to late summer.
1.5m × 30cm/5 × 1ft

A. volubile Perennial climber requiring the support of a small shrub. Violet-blue flowers from late summer into autumn.
3m/10ft

ACORUS

Genus of aquatic perennials, evergreen and deciduous, grown at the margins of pond or stream for their foliage.

A. calamus 'Variegatus' Deciduous perennial with strap-like, brightly coloured green leaves for shallow water. 90 × 60cm/3 × 2ft

ACTAEA (Baneberry)

Genus of perennials for light woodland or partial shade carrying white flowers in late spring followed by white, red or black berries.

A. rubra (Red baneberry) Perennial with white flowers in spring followed by shiny red berries. 45 × 30cm/1.5 × 1ft

Actinidia kolomikta

Adiantum venustum

ACTINIDIA

A genus in the main of deciduous climbers cultivated for their decorative foliage, sometimes fragrant flowers and edible fruits. Best grown against a wall in full sun.
A. deliciosa (syn. *A. chinensis*) (Chinese gooseberry) Deciduous climber with heart-shaped leaves bearing creamy-white/yellow flowers in early summer. On female plants these are followed with fruits. 10m/30ft
A. kolomikta Deciduous climber grown for distinctive, dark green leaves with pink and white variegation. Scented white flowers in early summer followed by fruits on female plants. 5m/15ft

ADONIS

A genus of annuals and perennials which, in the main, are of alpine habit.
A. amurensis Perennial forming a clump of low growing, pinnate leaves. Deeply cupped, yellow flowers appear in late winter/early spring. For rich, acidic soil in shade. 20 × 30cm/8in × 1ft

Aegopodium podagraria 'Variegatum'

AEGOPODIUM (Ground elder)

Genus of spreading perennials of which only the variegated cultivars are suitable for garden cultivation.
A. podagraria 'Variegatum' Perennial for ground cover with white variegated leaves, toothed at the edges, and umbels of creamy flowers in early summer. 30cm/1ft × indefinite spread

ADENOPHORA (Gland bellflower)

Genus of perennials, not dissimilar to campanulas, tolerant of either sun or partial shade. Flowers, mostly bell-shaped, range from pale to dark blue.
A. bulleyana Upright perennial of narrow leaves over which are carried mid violet-blue flowers in late summer. 1.2m × 30cm/4 × 1ft
A. tashiroi Ground hugging perennial with racemes of violet flowers on spreading stems in midsummer. 50 × 15cm/20 × 6in

Aeonium arboreum

AEONIUM

A genus of half-hardy, evergreen succulents, mainly perennial or biennial, sometimes sub-shrubs, grown mainly for the appearance of their rosettes of fleshy leaves.
A. arboreum Upright, evergreen sub-shrub with rosettes of mid-green leaves and panicles of yellow flowers in late spring. *A. a.* 'Atropurpureum' has purple-black leaves. 2 × 2m/6 × 6ft

ADIANTUM (Maidenhair fern)

Genus of evergreen, semi-evergreen and deciduous half-hardy and hardy ferns for partial or complete shade.
A. pedatum Deciduous, hardy fern with mid-green, pinnate fronds arranged on dark brown or black stems. 30 × 30cm/1 × 1ft
A. venustum Hardy evergreen fern becoming deciduous in temperatures below −10°C/14°F. Triangular-shaped fronds of mid-green, opening bronze in early spring. 15cm/6in × indefinite spread

Aeonium arboreum 'Atropurpureum'

Aesculus × neglecta 'Erythroblastos'

Aesculus parviflora

Aethionema 'Warley Rose'

AESCULUS (Horse chestnut)

A genus of deciduous trees and shrubs many of which colour well in the autumn. Spiny fruits, containing seeds, follow large panicles of flowers in late spring.

A. hippocastanum Large, spreading deciduous tree with palmate leaves and white flowers tinged yellow, then pink, in late spring. Flowers are followed with fruits – 'conkers'. 25 × 20m/80 × 70ft

A. × neglecta 'Erythroblastos' Deciduous tree grown mainly for the pink colour of juvenile foliage. 10 × 8m/30 × 25ft

A. parviflora Deciduous shrub of suckering habit with bronze coloured young foliage. White flowers, borne in summer, are followed by fruits. 3 × 5m/10 × 15ft

AETHIONEMA (Stone cress)

Genus of evergreen or semi-evergreen sub-shrubs, perennials and annuals suitable for an alpine or rock garden. Best grown in a sunny, open situation in well drained soil.

A. 'Warley Rose' Evergreen or semi-evergreen sub-shrub producing racemes of vivid pink flowers in late spring above grey-green foliage. Short lived. 15 × 15cm/6 × 6in

Agapanthus Headbourne Hybrid

Agapanthus campanulatus var. *albidus*

AGAPANTHUS

Genus of half-hardy and hardy, deciduous and evergreen perennials noted for their strap-like leaves and umbels of tubular flowers. Suitable for border or pot cultivation. Grow in full sun in well drained soil. Protect half-hardy varieties from frost.

A. campanulatus var. *albidus* Hardy, deciduous perennial with grey-green leaves over which are carried tall stemmed, white flowers in summer. 1m × 45cm/3 × 1.5ft

A. Headbourne Hybrid A range of hardy, deciduous perennials varying greatly in colour of flower and size. The name derives from selected seedlings raised by the Hon. Lewis Palmer.

A. 'Loch Hope' Hardy, deciduous perennial bearing deep blue flowers from mid to late summer. 1.5m × 60cm/5 × 2ft

Agapanthus 'Loch Hope'

21

Agastache mexicana

Agave americana

Agave americana 'Marginata'

AGASTACHE (Mexican giant hyssop)

Genus of half-hardy and hardy perennials for normal garden soil in full sun. Above grey-green leaves spikes of tubular flowers are carried in summer through to autumn.

A. mexicana Short-lived, half-hardy perennial with lavender-mauve flowers from midsummer into autumn. 60 × 30cm/2 × 1ft

AGAVE

A genus of half-hardy and frost tender perennials and monocarpic succulents grown mainly for foliage effect. Well suited to pot cultivation.

A. americana A monocarpic, frost tender succulent consisting of a rosette of lance-shaped, spiny, grey-green leaves from which, in summer, rise clusters of yellow-green flowers. 45 × 45cm/1.5 × 1.5ft

A. americana 'Marginata' A monocarpic, frost tender succulent with leaves margined pale yellow, whitening with age. 45 × 45cm/1.5 × 1.5ft

Ageratum houstonianum

Ajuga reptans 'Burgundy Glow'

Ajuga reptans 'Catlin's Giant'

AGERATUM (Floss flower)

A genus of half-hardy annuals and perennials flowering in summer into autumn.

A. houstonianum cultivars A compact annual with blue, pink and white flowers from midsummer until the first frosts. 30 × 30cm/1 × 1ft

AGROSTEMMA (Corn cockle)

A genus of hardy annuals of rather lax habit for cultivation in full sun.

A. githago Hardy annual with magenta flowers in summer. 60 × 30cm/2 × 1ft

AILANTHUS

Genus of deciduous trees and shrubs the most common of which, *A. altissima*, is best cultivated as a specimen tree.

A. altissima (Tree of heaven) Large deciduous tree with panicles of small green flowers in summer followed by fruits. 25 × 15m/80 × 50ft

Ajuga reptans 'Pink Surprise'

AJUGA (Bugle)

Genus of annuals and carpeting, evergreen and semi-evergreen perennials for a partially shaded situation. Tolerant of most soil conditions.

A. reptans 'Burgundy Glow' Ground covering, evergreen perennial with silver-green leaves shaded wine-red. Whorls of deep blue flowers in late spring. 15 × 60cm/ 6in × 2ft

A. reptans 'Catlin's Giant' Ground covering, evergreen perennial with distinctive, large leaves of dark metallic purple. Larger than average blue flowers in late spring.

A. r. 'Pink Surprise' has pink flowers. 15 × 60cm/6in × 2ft

Akebia quinata

Alcea rugosa

AKEBIA (Chocolate vine)

Genus of semi-evergreen and deciduous climbers cultivated for foliage, flower and fruit. Completely hardy although late frosts may damage early spring flowers.
A. quinata Semi-evergreen climber with dark green leaves, the reverse of which are blue/green. Racemes of purple-brown flowers appear in early spring to be followed by elongated fruit.
10m/30ft

ALCEA (Hollyhock)

Genus of biennials and short-lived perennials grown for their many coloured flowers. For a sunny situation in most well drained soils. Foliage is prone to hollyhock rust.
A. rosea 'Nigra' Perennial of upright habit producing tall flower spikes of chocolate-red flowers in early summer.
1.5m × 60cm/5 × 2ft
A. rugosa Upright perennial with open cup-shaped flowers of palest lemon.
1.5m × 60cm/5 × 2ft

Alcea rosea 'Nigra'

Alchemilla mollis

Alchemilla conjuncta

Alchemilla erythropoda

ALCHEMILLA (Lady's mantle)

A genus of perennials cultivated in gardens for their attractive foliage and sprays of tiny flowers. Suitable for sun or partial shade in most soils.
A. conjuncta Carpeting perennial of deeply lobed leaves and sprays of tiny, lime-green flowers all summer. 40 × 30cm/16 × 12in
A. erythropoda Perennial forming rounded clumps of shallowly lobed leaves above which are carried round topped sprays of acid-green flowers from late spring until late summer. 20 × 20cm/8 × 8in
A. mollis Perennial forming clumps of light green, shallowly lobed, felted leaves. Flowers, in sprays, appear from early summer into autumn. 60 × 60cm/2 × 2ft

ALISMA (Water plantain)

Genus of deciduous, aquatic perennials for the margins of ponds and streams.
A. plantago-aquatica An aquatic perennial for a large pond or lake. Grey-green leaves are carried on long stems above water. Flowers, of white or white tinged pink, appear in midsummer. Self-seeds freely. 60 × 45cm/2 × 1.5ft

23

Allium aflatunense

Allium beesianum

Allium cernuum

ALLIUM (Onion)

Genus of bulbous and rhizomatus perennials flowering in spring, summer and autumn. Above mainly strap-like leaves, often aromatic, are to be found in season largely spherical flowerheads in numerous colour shades.

A. aflatunense A bulbous perennial with linear basal leaves of mid-green. Above these are carried umbels of starry purple-pink flowers in summer. 1m × 10cm/ 3ft × 4in

A. beesianum A bulbous perennial with linear basal leaves of grey-green. Umbels of star-shaped, blue or white flowers appear in late summer and early autumn. 15 × 5cm/6 × 2in

A. cernuum (Wild onion) A bulbous perennial of vigorous habit. Basal leaves of dark green carry above them drooping flower bells of deep pink in summer. 30 × 5cm/1ft × 2in

A. cristophii A bulbous perennial with strappy leaves of grey-green which die down as the pink-purple flowers open in early summer. Flowerheads are suitable for drying. 60 × 15cm/2ft × 6in

A. giganteum A bulbous perennial with large strap-like, basal leaves of light green which die down before flowering takes place. Flowers, appearing in summer, are star-shaped of purple-pink. 1.5m × 15cm/5ft × 6in

A. hollandicum 'Purple Sensation' A bulbous perennial with strap-like, basal leaves which die down as the rich purple flowers appear in summer. 1m × 10cm/3ft × 4in

A. moly (Golden garlic) A bulbous perennial of lance-shaped, basal leaves carrying open, starry flowers of bright yellow in summer. Suitable for naturalizing in partial shade. 15 × 5cm/6 × 2in

A. oreophilum A bulbous perennial with linear leaves through which rise umbels of mid-pink flowers in early summer. 15 × 5cm/6 × 2in

A. schoenoprasum (Chive) A bulbous perennial cultivated in the main for its edible, hollow green leaves. Pale purple flowerheads appear in summer. 'Forescate' is a named variety. 30 × 5cm/1ft × 2in

A. sphaerocephalon A bulbous perennial with linear, basal leaves. Flowers, in summer, vary in colour from pink to dark red-brown. 60 × 8cm/2ft × 3in

Allium cristophii

Allium giganteum

Allium moly

Allium hollandicum 'Purple Sensation'

Allium oreophilum

Allium schoenoprasum

Allium sphaerocephalon

Alnus cordata

Aloe aristata

Aloe arborescens

ALNUS (Alder)

A genus of deciduous trees and shrubs thriving on poor and moisture retentive soils.

A. cordata (Italian alder) A deciduous tree with heart-shaped leaves and long, yellow catkins opening during the late winter and early spring. Fruits are borne in summer. 25 × 6m/80 × 20ft

A. rubra (Red alder) A deciduous tree with dark green leaves distinctly marked with red veining. Catkins in early spring are followed with fruits in summer. 25 × 10m/80 × 30ft

ALOE

A genus of frost tender evergreen perennials, the majority of which possess succulent leaves. For full sun and free-draining soils.

A. arborescens A tall growing, frost tender perennial with succulent, pointed leaves with toothed edges. Racemes of red flowers in late spring/early summer. 3 × 2m/10 × 6ft

A. aristata A frost tender perennial with lance-shaped, succulent leaves marked with white dots and forming a tight rosette. Orange-red flowers in autumn. 12cm/5cm × indefinite spread

Alstroemeria ligtu hybrid

Alstroemeria 'Cyprus'

Alstroemeria psittacina

ALSTROEMERIA (Peruvian lily)

A genus of frost-hardy and hardy, tuberous perennials for cultivation in sun or partial shade in soil which is not allowed to dry out. Flowers often grown for cutting.

A. 'Cyprus' A frost-hardy perennial producing creamy-white and yellow flowers in summer. 60 × 75cm/2 × 2.5ft

A. ligtu hybrid A name given to hardy seedling perennials arising from crosses between *A. ligtu* and *A. haemantha*. Flowers, produced in summer, vary in colour. 60 × 75cm/2 × 2.5ft

A. psittacina A frost-hardy perennial with flowers of mid-green deeply shaded wine-red in summer. 1m × 45cm/3 × 1.5ft

Althaea cannabina

Alyogyne huegelii 'Santa Cruz'

ALTHAEA

A genus of annuals and perennials, not dissimilar to *Alcea* (hollyhock) but with smaller, stalked flowers in shades of pink to mauve-purple, best suited to cultivation in moisture retentive soil in an open, sunny situation.

A. cannabina A tall growing, upright perennial producing a cluster of small, mid-pink flowers borne on wiry stems from summer through to autumn. 2m × 60cm/6 × 2ft

A. officinalis (Marsh mallow) Upright perennial with pale pink flowers over hairy leaves from summer through to autumn. 2 × 1m/6 × 3ft

ALYOGYNE

Genus of half-hardy and frost tender, evergreen shrubs for cultivation outdoors in a sunny situation in well drained soil.

A. huegelii 'Santa Cruz' A vigorous, evergreen shrub with single, plummy-mauve flowers produced freely from early summer into autumn. 1–2 × 1–2m/3–6 × 3–6ft

Alyssum spinosum 'Roseum'

Amaranthus caudatus

Amaranthus hybridus var. *erythrostachys*

ALYSSUM

A genus of low growing, mound-forming annuals, evergreen perennials and sub-shrubs particularly suited to the rock garden or to trail over retaining walls. For full sun.

A. spinosum 'Roseum' A small, evergreen sub-shrub with tiny silver-grey leaves and pale rose-pink flowers in early summer. 30 × 30cm/1 × 1ft

AMARANTHUS

A genus of half-hardy annuals or short-lived perennials flowering in summer and most often employed in bedding schemes, hanging baskets or containers. Plant or position outdoors in full sun and water well in prolonged dry periods.

A. caudatus (Love-lies-bleeding) An upright half-hardy annual or short-lived perennial grown for its long, tassel flowers of crimson-red carried freely from summer until autumn. 1m × 45cm/3 × 1.5ft

A. hybridus var. *erythrostachys* A bushy half-hardy annual carrying decorative, upright spikes of crimson flowers from summer until autumn. 1m × 45cm/3 × 1.5ft

Amaryllis belladonna

Amelanchier lamarckii

Anagallis monellii

AMARYLLIS

A genus of a single species of late flowering, bulbous perennial for cultivation in a sheltered spot in full sun in well drained soil. Frost hardy.
A. belladonna (Belladonna lily) Trumpet-shaped, fragrant pink flowers in late summer/autumn. Strap-like leaves appear after the flowers. 60 × 10cm/2ft × 4in

AMELANCHIER (Snowy Mespilus)

Genus of deciduous trees and shrubs, many of suckering habit, grown for their early flowers and autumnal colour and fruit.
A. lamarckii An upright large shrub or small tree. Racemes of white flowers in spring are followed with purple-black fruits. 10 × 12m/30 × 40ft

ANAGALLIS (Pimpernel)

Genus of carpeting annuals and evergreen perennials, often short-lived. Most suited to the rock garden.
A. monellii A ground-hugging perennial producing deep blue flowers in summer. From time to time variants of red and pink will occur. 20 × 40cm/8 × 16in

Anaphalis

Anchusa azurea 'Loddon Royalist'

Andromeda polifolia 'Compacta'

ANAPHALIS (Pearl everlasting)

A genus of perennials, some evergreen, many with grey-green foliage and papery, white flowers which may be cut and dried. Grow in sun.
A. margaritacea A clump forming perennial of grey-green, narrow, tapering leaves over which are carried corymbs of white flowers in midsummer and early autumn.
60 × 60cm/2 × 2ft

ANCHUSA (Alkanet)

Genus of annuals, biennials and short-lived perennials for a sunny situation. Small species, like *A. cespitosa*, are suitable for the rock garden or containers.
A. azurea 'Loddon Royalist' A strong-growing perennial with hairy, lance-shaped leaves and flowers in early summer of dark blue. 1m × 60cm/ 3 × 2ft

ANDROMEDA (Bog rosemary)

A genus of small, evergreen shrubs for acid soil in full sun or partial shade. Suitable for a peat bed or acidic rock garden.
A. polifolia 'Compacta' A compact, many stemmed, evergreen shrub of grey-green leaves and mid-pink flowers in late spring and early summer. 30 × 20cm/1ft × 8in

ANDROSACE (Rock jasmine)

A genus of annuals, biennials and mainly evergreen perennials for the alpine house, rock garden or containers.
A. carnea A cushion forming, evergreen perennial with mid-green, awl-shaped leaves and clusters of yellow-eyed, pink flowers in late spring/summer.
5 × 8cm/2 × 3in
A. chamaejasme A mat forming, evergreen perennial with silky leaves carrying white flowers, flushed pink with age, each with a yellow eye, in late spring/summer. 5 × 20cm/2 × 8in
A. lanuginosa A ground hugging, evergreen perennial with trailing stems carrying grey-green leaves and pale pink, yellow-eyed flowers in midsummer. 5 × 30cm/2in × 1ft

Androsace lanuginosa

Anemone appenina

Anemone blanda 'White Splendour'

ANEMONE (Windflower)

A genus of hardy and half-hardy perennials, some with tubers or rhizomes, ranging from those which are suitable for the open border to those which are appropriate for the rock garden. Flowering from mid-spring until autumn, according to type, there are species for a large range of soil conditions and situations.

A. apennina A hardy, creeping perennial, increasing by rhizomes, for a partially shaded situation. Mainly blue, occasionally white, flowers appear in spring. Summer dormant. 20 × 30cm/8in × 1ft

A. blanda 'White Splendour' A hardy, creeping perennial, increasing by tubers, for sun/part shade. Large white flowers, the backs of which are lightly flushed pink, appear in spring. 15 × 15cm/6 × 6in

A. × hybrida (Japanese anemone) A spreading, hardy perennial with basal leaves above which are borne tall stems carrying pink flowers in late summer/autumn. Many named cultivars with single, semi-double and double flowers in a range of colours. For sun/part shade. 1.2–1.5m/4–5ft × indefinite spread

A. nemorosa 'Alba Plena' A double white form of the creeping, hardy perennial wood anemone flowering in spring and early summer. For part shade. 15 × 30cm/6in × 1ft

Anemone nemorosa 'Robinsoniana' A creeping, hardy perennial for part shade with lavender-blue flowers in spring and early summer. 15 × 30cm/6in × 1ft

A. sylvestris (Snowdrop anemone) A rapidly spreading, hardy perennial bearing half-hanging, white flowers in late spring/early summer. For sun/part shade. 30 × 30cm/1 × 1ft

Anemone × hybrida

Anemone nemorosa 'Alba Plena'

Anemone sylvestris

Anemone nemorosa 'Robinsoniana'

Angelica archangelica

Anisodontea capensis

Antennaria dioica

ANGELICA (Archangel)

Genus of perennials and biennials for moist, fertile soil. Grown principally as architectural plants or, in the case of *A. archangelica*, for culinary and medicinal purposes.

A. archangelica A tall growing, monocarpic perennial which produces rounded umbels of citrus-yellow flowers on heavily ribbed stalks in midsummer. Once flowering is over, the plant will set seed and die. 2 × 1.2m/6 × 4ft

ANISODONTEA

Genus of evergreen half-hardy shrubs and perennials grown in full sun for flowers in the colour range of pale pink to dark red-purple.

A. capensis (syn. *Malvastrum capensis*) Upright shrub carrying pink-red flowers from summer to autumn. Half-hardy but will withstand periods of cold to −5°C/23°F. 60 × 45cm/2 × 1.5ft

ANTENNARIA (Cat's ears)

Genus of evergreen and semi-evergreen carpeting perennials for cultivation in full sun in the rock garden or at the front of a border.

A. dioica Low growing, semi-evergreen perennial with grey-green leaves and corymbs of pink or white flowerheads from late spring into early summer. 5 × 45cm/2in × 1.5ft

Anthemis punctata subsp. *cupaniana*

Anthemis tinctoria 'Alba'

ANTHEMIS

Genus of annuals and perennials, many grown as much for their finely cut, aromatic foliage as for their daisy-type flowers. Most require free draining soil in full sun.

A. punctata subs. *cupaniana* Carpeting perennial with grey-green leaves carrying white flowers in early summer. 30cm × 1m/1 × 3ft

A. tinctoria 'Alba' Perennial with mid-green leaves, the undersides of which are grey. Flowers, made up of creamy petals and dark yellow centres, appear for many weeks in summer. Named cultivars include 'E.C. Buxton', 'Grallach Gold' and 'Sauce Hollandaise'. 60 × 60cm/2 × 2ft

Anthericum liliago

ANTHERICUM

Genus of clump forming perennials producing dainty, lily-like flowers in spring and summer. Cultivate in well drained soil in full sun.

A. liliago (St. Bernard's lily) Perennial of clump forming, thin linear leaves and trumpet-shaped white flowers in late spring/early summer. 60 × 30cm/2 × 1ft

A. ramosum Perennial of clump forming, thin linear leaves of grey-green and star-shaped white flowers in late spring/early summer. 1m × 30cm/3 × 1ft

Anthriscus sylvestris 'Ravenswing'

ANTHRISCUS
A genus of annuals, biennials and perennials grown for foliage and flower as well as for culinary purposes.
A. cerefolium (Common chervil) An annual grown for culinary use. 45 × 24cm/1.5ft × 10in
A. sylvestris 'Ravenswing' A biennial or short-lived perennial form of cow parsley with deep purple leaves and white flowers in late spring/early summer. 1m × 30cm/3 × 1ft

Anthyllis hermanniae

ANTHYLLIS
A genus of annuals, perennials and shrubs for dry soils in full sun.
A. hermanniae A small shrub well suited to the rock garden. Masses of golden-yellow flowers in summer. 45 × 60cm/1.5 × 2ft

Aponogeton distachyos

APONOGETON
Genus of frost hardy and frost tender aquatic perennials growing from tuberous rhizomes suited to cultivation in ponds.
A. distachyos (Water hawthorn) A frost hardy, aquatic perennial with floating leaves and small, fragrant flowers in spring and autumn. Evergreen in mild winters. 10cm × 1.2m/4in × 4ft

Antirrhinum majus

ANTIRRHINUM (Snapdragon)
Genus of half-hardy and hardy annuals, perennials and semi-evergreen sub-shrubs cultivated mainly for their tubular flowers. All benefit from cultivation in free draining soil in full sun.
A. majus A short-lived perennial treated mainly as an annual and used extensively in summer bedding schemes. Flower colour varies considerably and ranges from white and yellow, pink and red to magenta and purple. Bicolours are also to be found. In flower from summer until autumn. Dwarf cultivars include the named 'Bells' and 'Chimes'. Up to 1m × 45cm/3 × 1.5ft
A. Coronette Series Short-lived, tall growing perennials flowering in summer in a wide range of colours to include orange, shades of red, yellow and white. 60 × 45cm/2 × 1.5ft

Aquilegia atrata

Aquilegia hybrid

Aquilegia 'Magpie'

AQUILEGIA (Columbine)

A genus of perennials with bell-shaped flowers for cultivation in normally fertile garden soil in sun or partial shade. Alpine species require sharp drainage and some protection from summer sun. Many named hybrids.

A. atrata A perennial distinguished by its flower colour of dark purple/near black with distinctive yellow stamens. Flowers in late spring. Keep cool in summer. 30 × 30cm/1 × 1ft

A. hybrid A perennial strain of aquilegia producing strong plants bearing flowers in a wide range of colours in spring and early summer. 45 × 45cm/1.5 × 1.5ft

A. 'Magpie' An unusually coloured perennial with flower spurs of deep, violet-purple, mauve-pink and white in early summer. 60 × 45cm/2 × 1.5ft

A. 'Snow Queen' A perennial with white spurred flowers in early summer. 60 × 45cm/2 × 1.5ft

A. vulgaris A perennial of variable flower colour for late spring/early summer. Most usually violet-blue, sometimes pink or white. 1m × 45cm/3 × 1.5ft

A. vulgaris 'Adelaide Addison' A strong growing perennial of double blue and white flowers in early summer. 1m × 45cm/3 × 1.5ft

A. vulgaris var. *flore pleno* Palc Blue A double flowered perennial of pale blue for early summer. 60 × 45cm/2 × 1.5ft

A. vulgaris 'Nora Barlow' A perennial of double, spurless flowers shaded pale green, pink and red. 1m × 45cm/3 × 1.5ft

Aquilegia 'Snow Queen'

Aquilegia vulgaris

Aquilegia vulgaris 'Adelaide Addison'

Aquilegia vulgaris var. *flore-pleno* Pale Blue

Aquilegia vulgaris 'Nora Barlow'

Arabis caucasica

Arabis ferdinandi-coburgi 'Old Gold'

ARABIS (Rock cress)

A genus of annuals and evergreen perennials cultivated mainly for the rock garden or for crevices in paths and walls. For full sun and tolerant of dry conditions.

A. caucasica A low growing, evergreen perennial forming loose rosettes of grey-green leaves over which scented white flowers open in spring. 'Flore Pleno' is similar but flowers are double. 15 × 60cm/6in × 2ft

A. ferdinandi-coburgi 'Old Gold' A low growing, evergreen or semi-evergreen perennial forming loose rosettes of green leaves with cream variegation and white flowers in spring. 8 × 30cm/3in × 1ft

Aralia elata 'Variegata'

ARALIA

Genus of deciduous and evergreen trees and shrubs well suited to moisture retentive soil in part shade.

A. elata 'Variegata' (Japanese angelica tree) A suckering, spreading deciduous tree with leaves widely margined creamy-white. Small white flowers, appearing in late summer and early autumn, are followed by tiny black fruits. 10 × 10m/30 × 30ft

Arbutus unedo

Arbutus unedo f. *rubra*

Araucaria araucana

ARAUCARIA

Genus of evergreen, coniferous trees of which *A. araucana* is the only hardy species.

A. araucana (Monkey puzzle tree) A hardy, coniferous tree grown for a series of whorled branches extending geometrically from a central trunk whose bark is dark grey-brown. Triangular-shaped leaves of dark green are sharply pointed. Lower branches tend to be shed on mature specimens. Plant in an open site and afford protection from cold winds. 25 × 3.5m/80 × 12ft

ARBUTUS (Strawberry tree)

A genus of evergreen trees and shrubs noted for strawberry-like fruits and, in many instances, peeling bark. Afford shelter from cold winds and plant in full sun.

A. unedo An evergreen, spreading tree with peeling reddish bark and lily of the valley-type white flowers in autumn. With these appear the ripening, edible fruits of the previous year. Tolerant of chalk. 8 × 8m/25 × 25ft

A. unedo f. *rubra* Similar to *A. unedo* but with pink flowers. 8 × 8m/25 × 25ft

Arctotis × hybrida 'Wine'

Arctotis × hybrida 'Apricot'

Arenaria montana

ARCTOTIS (African daisy)

A genus of frost tender annuals and perennials, sometimes sub-shrubs, grown for their daisy-like flowerheads which are produced throughout the summer and early autumn. Most often employed as an annual in full sun in summer bedding schemes.
A. × hybrida 'Apricot' A bushy, frost tender perennial grown as a half-hardy annual with flowers of rich apricot in summer. 45 × 45cm/1.5 × 1.5ft
A. × hybrida 'Wine' A bushy, frost tender perennial grown as a half-hardy annual with flowers of wine-red in summer. 45 × 45cm/1.5 × 1.5ft

ARENARIA (Sandwort)

A genus of annuals and perennials, some evergreen, of prostrate habit and suited to the rock garden in full sun.
A. montana A spreading, evergreen perennial with grey-green leaves carrying a profusion of cup-shaped, silver-white flowers in late spring and early summer. 5 × 30cm/2in × 1ft

Argyranthemum 'Vancouver'

Argyranthemum 'Jamaica Primrose'

ARGYRANTHEMUM

A genus of frost hardy to half-hardy evergreen sub-shrubs which are most frequently grown for summer bedding schemes or for pot cultivation. For well drained soil in full sun.
A. 'Mary Wootton' A half-hardy sub-shrub with somewhat coarse green leaves over which are carried white, daisy-like flowers in profusion from late spring to early autumn. 75 × 75cm/2.5 × 2.5ft
A. 'Jamaica Primrose' A half-hardy sub-shrub with grey-green leaves and tall stemmed, daisy-like flowers of warm primrose yellow throughout the summer. 1 × 1m/3 × 3ft
A. 'Vancouver' A half-hardy sub-shrub with grey-green leaves and double, anemone-like flowers shaded light and deep pink throughout the summer. 1 × 1m/3 × 3ft

Argyranthemum 'Mary Wootton'

Arisaema candidissimum

ARISAEMA
A genus of hardy and half-hardy tuberous and rhizomatous perennials grown for their pitcher-like spathes which surround a pencil-like spadix. Best suited to humus-rich, acidic or neutral soil in partial shade.
A. candidissimum A tuberous, frost hardy perennial producing a striking, scented, pink and white striped spathe in summer followed by broadly divided leaves. 45 × 15cm/1.5ft × 6in

ARISARUM
A genus of tuberous or rhizomatous hardy and half-hardy perennials mainly grown for their tubular spathes which conceal tiny flowers.
A. proboscideum (Mouse plant) A hardy, rhizomatous perennial forming a carpet of arrow-shaped leaves through which purple-brown spathes appear in spring. 15 × 25cm/6 × 10in

Aristolochia durior

ARISTOLOCHIA (Dutchman's pipe)
A genus of evergreen and deciduous hardy, half-hardy and frost tender climbers, shrubs and perennials producing unusual petalless, mottled flowers. For sun or part shade.
A. durior A deciduous, hardy climber which in summer carries yellow-green flowers. 10m/30ft

Armeria maritima

ARMERIA (Thrift)
A genus of evergreen perennials and sub-shrubs distinguished by strap-like leaves and rounded heads of small flowers in shades of pink or white.
A. maritima (Sea pink) A hummock forming, evergreen perennial carrying rose-pink flowerheads over small, dark green strappy leaves from spring until autumn. Tolerant of poor soil. 20 × 30cm/8in × 1ft
A. maritima 'Bloodstone' Similar with flowerheads of deep, blood-red. 20 × 30cm/8in × 1ft

ARONIA (Chokeberry)
A genus of deciduous shrubs of suckering habit grown for flowers, autumn colour and fruits. Tolerant of most soil types with the exception of chalk.
A. arbutifolia An upright, deciduous shrub producing white flowers, occasionally flushed pink, in spring followed by red berries and flame-red autumn foliage. 3 × 1.5m/10 × 5ft

Artemisia absinthium 'Lambrook Silver'

Artemisia 'Powis Castle'

Artemisia ludoviciana 'Silver Queen'

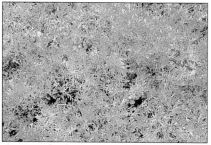

Artemisia schmidtiana 'Nana'

ARTEMISIA (Wormwood)
A genus of evergreen and deciduous shrubs, perennials and annuals grown principally for their aromatic, often finely dissected foliage of green, grey-green and silver. Best in full sun.
A. absinthium 'Lambrook Silver' A woody perennial with aromatic, deeply cut silver foliage and undistinguished yellowish flowers in late summer. 75 × 60cm/2.5 × 2ft
A. alba 'Canescens' A semi-evergreen perennial with finely cut, silver leaves and unnoteworthy yellowish flowers in late summer. 45 × 30cm/1.5 × 1ft
A. ludoviciana 'Silver Queen' A spreading perennial with larger leaves than the type of silver-white, greening with age. Yellowish flowers from midsummer into autumn. 75 × 60cm/2.5 × 2ft
A. 'Powis Castle' A woody perennial forming a bushy plant of feathery, silver leaves. Silver flowerheads are borne in late summer. 60cm × 1m/2 × 3ft
A. schmidtiana 'Nana' A low growing, compact evergreen perennial making a carpet of silvery linear leaves with yellow flowerheads in summer. 8 × 30cm/3in × 1ft

Arum creticum

Arum italicum

Arum italicum subsp. *italicum* 'Marmoratum'

ARUM (Lords and ladies)

A genus of hardy and half-hardy, tuberous perennials for well drained soil in sun or part shade. Grown principally for distinctively marked leaves, large spathes and colourful berries.

A. creticum A tuberous, frost hardy perennial with plain, broad, arrow-shaped leaves and cream or yellow spathes in spring. Position in full sun. 30 × 15cm/1ft × 6in

A. italicum A tuberous, hardy perennial with arrow-shaped leaves veined white and greenish spathes in early summer. Spikes of brilliant orange berries follow. 30 × 15cm/1ft × 6in

A. italicum subsp. *italicum* 'Marmoratum' As the type but leaves are veined pale green or cream. 30 × 15cm/1ft × 6in

ARUNCUS

A genus of perennials for moisture retentive soil in partial shade.

A. aethusifolius A low growing perennial with deeply cut leaves colouring yellow in autumn. Panicles of tiny cream flowers in summer.
25 × 25cm/10 × 10in

A. dioicus (Goatsbeard) A clump forming perennial with toothed, mid-green leaves and panicles of creamy-white flowers in summer. 1.2 × 1.2m/4 × 4ft

A. dioicus 'Kneiffii' A perennial similar to the type but with finely divided leaves and smaller flower plumes.
1.2m × 45cm/4 × 1.5ft

Aruncus dioicus

ARUNDINARIA

A genus of hardy bamboo mainly cultivated as a dense barrier or screen.

A. gigantea A giant bamboo of green-yellow canes and lance-shaped leaves. Periodically throughout the year purple flower spikes are produced. Increases rapidly by means of rhizomes. Needs moist soil and shelter.
10m/30ft × indefinite spread

Aruncus dioicus 'Kneiffii'

Arundo donax var. *versicolor*

ARUNDO

A genus of evergreen, hardy and half-hardy perennial grasses of which *A. donax* is cultivated for its bamboo-like foliage.

A. donax var. *versicolor* A half-hardy reed forming a clump of white-striped leaves of arching habit. 1.5m × 60cm/5 × 2ft

Asarina 'Victoria Falls'

ASARINA

A genus of a single species of evergreen perennial of trailing habit cultivated for flowers which are not dissimilar to those of antirrhinum.

A. 'Victoria Falls' An evergreen, trailing perennial with grey-green leaves and flowers in summer. Prefers sandy soil in part shade. Trailing to 45cm/1.5ft

ASCLEPIAS (Silkweed)

A genus of mainly hardy, evergreen and deciduous perennials, sub-shrubs and shrubs for cultivation in a sunny situation.

A. incarnata A hardy perennial with clusters of rose-pink flowers in summer/autumn. 1.2m × 60cm/4 × 2ft

ASPARAGUS

A genus of hardy to frost tender evergreen and deciduous perennials, climbers and sub-shrubs growing from tuber-like rootstocks. Cultivated principally for foliage.

A. setaceus (Asparagus fern) A half-hardy climber with feathery foliage. Small, white flowers are followed by near-black berries. 3m/10ft

Asperula suberosa

ASPERULA (Woodruff)

A genus of annuals, evergreen and deciduous perennials and dwarf shrubs cultivated in the main for the alpine or rock garden. Some species have a dislike of winter wet.

A. orientalis An annual carrying scented sky-blue, sometimes white, flowers in summer. 30 × 10cm/1ft × 4in

A. suberosa An evergreen perennial carrying tubular pink flowers in early summer. 8 × 20cm/3 × 8in

ASPHODELINE (Jacob's rod)

Genus of biennials and perennials with grass-like leaves and star-shaped flowers for full sun.

A. lutea A clump forming perennial made up of grass-like, blue-green leaves producing long, unbranched spikes of scented yellow flowers in late spring. 1.5m × 30cm/5 × 1ft

ASPIDISTRA

A genus of frost hardy, evergreen perennials grown mainly for their dark, shiny green leaves.

A. elatior (Cast-iron plant) An evergreen, frost hardy perennial most often cultivated as an indoor plant. Lance-shaped leaves are complemented with cream flowers in early summer. 60 × 60cm/2 × 2ft

Asphodeline lutea

ASPHODELUS (Asphodel)

A genus of annuals and perennials for a warm, sunny situation in free draining soil.

A. albus A clump forming perennial with dense spikes of white, occasionally soft pink, flowers in late spring. 1m × 30cm/3 × 1ft

Asphodelus albus

Asplenium scolopendrium

Asplenium trichomanes

ASPLENIUM (Spleenwort)

A genus of evergreen or semi-evergreen hardy to frost tender ferns for humus-rich, moisture retentive soil in part shade.

A. scolopendrium (Hart's tongue fern) A hardy, evergreen fern with strap-shaped, shiny fronds the edges of which are inclined to curve inwards. Cut back old fronds in the early spring. 60 × 60cm/2 × 2ft

A. scolopendrium 'Crispum' As for the type but fronds are distinctly wavy at the edges. 60 × 60cm/2 ×2ft

A. trichomanes A dwarf semi-evergreen fern with tapering fronds and many rounded pinnae. 10 × 10cm/4 × 4in

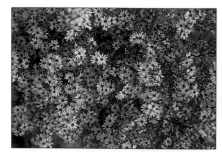

Aster cordifolius 'Sweet Lavender'

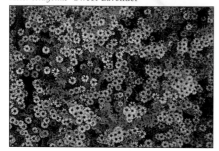

Aster ericoides 'Blue Star'

Aster lateriflorus 'Horizontalis'

Aster luteus

Aster novi-belgii 'Beechwood Charm'

Aster frikartii

ASTER (Michaelmas daisy)

A genus of principally hardy, but some species of frost tender, annuals, biennials, perennials and sub-shrubs with mainly lance-shaped leaves and daisy-like flowers. The majority prefer fertile, moisture retentive soil in full sun or part shade and should be cut back to the ground over winter or once the flowering season has passed.

A. cordifolius 'Sweet Lavender' An upright perennial producing tall-stemmed, arching sprays of lavender-blue flowers in late summer and autumn. Prefers partial shade. 1 × 1.2m/3 × 4ft

A. ericoides 'Blue Star' A clump forming perennial for cultivation in full sun. Blue flowers with yellow disc appear in late summer and autumn. 1m × 30cm/3 × 1ft

A. × frikartii A perennial for full sun producing clumps of dark green leaves and flowers in shades of violet-blue with orange discs from midsummer to autumn. Named cultivars include 'Mönch' with lavender-blue flowers. 75 × 45cm/ 2.5 × 1.5ft

A. lateriflorus 'Horizontalis' A clump forming perennial for a partially shaded situation bearing white and pinky-white flowers with deeper pink discs from midsummer to autumn. 60 × 30cm/2 × 1ft

A. luteus A clump forming perennial producing sprays of tiny, deep lemon flowers in autumn. Plant in full sun. 60 × 30cm/2 × 1ft

A. novi-belgii 'Beechwood Charm' A clump forming perennial with deep-pink flowers from late summer to autumn. 1.2m × 45cm/4 × 1.5ft

A. novi-belgii 'Fellowship' A clump forming perennial with double, mid-pink flowers from late summer to autumn. 1 × 1m/3 × 3ft

A. novi-belgii 'Goliath' A clump forming perennial with lavender-pink flowers from late summer to autumn. 1 × 1m/3 × 3ft

A. novi-belgii 'Harrison's Blue' A clump forming perennial with violet-blue flowers from late summer to autumn. 1 × 1m/3 × 3ft

A. novi-belgii 'Helen Ballard' A clump forming perennial with flowers of dusky-red from late summer to autumn. 60cm × 1m/2 × 3ft

A. novi-belgii 'Sheena' A clump forming perennial with flowers of warm rose from late summer to autumn. 1.2m × 45cm/4 × 1.5ft

A. 'Pink Star' A clump forming perennial with a mass of lilac-pink, thinly rayed flowers from late summer to autumn. 1m × 45cm/3 × 1.5ft

A. sedifolius A clump forming perennial with flowers in a range of colours to include blue-purple, lilac and lilac-pink, each with yellow disc, from late summer to autumn. Plant in full sun. 1m × 60cm/3 × 2ft

A. 'Snow Star' A clump forming perennial producing showers of thinly rayed white flowers from late summer to autumn. 1m × 45cm/3 × 1.5ft

A. thomsonii 'Nanus' A clump forming, low growing perennial with lilac-blue flowers from late summer to autumn. Prefers a partially shaded situation. 45 × 25cm/1.5ft × 10in

Aster novi-belgii 'Fellowship'

Aster novi-belgii 'Harrison's Blue'

Aster novi-belgii 'Helen Ballard'

Aster novi-belgii 'Goliath'

Aster novi-belgii 'Sheena'

Aster 'Pink Star'

Aster sedifolius

Aster 'Snow Star'

Aster thomsonii 'Nanus'

Astilbe × *arendsii* 'Venus'

Astilbe × *arendsii* 'Erica'

ASTILBE
A genus of perennials grown for their divided leaves and panicles of tiny flowers borne in plumes. Best suited to humus-rich, moist/moisture retentive soil in sun or part shade. Unlikely to thrive on chalk.

A. × *arendsii* 'Erica' A perennial of finely-cut, bronze-green foliage producing plume-like flowerheads of mid-pink in midsummer. 45 × 30cm/1.5 × 1ft

A. × *arendsii* 'Granat' A perennial of deep green foliage producing plume-like flowerheads of dark red in midsummer. 60 × 45cm/2 × 1.5ft

A. × *arendsii* 'Venus' A perennial of bright green foliage producing plume-like flowerheads of soft pink in early summer. 1m x 45cm/3 x 1.5ft

A. 'Deutschland' A perennial of bright green foliage producing plume-like flowerheads of purest white in midsummer. 45 × 30cm/1.5 × 1ft

A. 'Montgomery' A perennial of finely-cut, bronze-green foliage producing plume-like flowerheads of dark red in midsummer. 60 × 75cm/2 × 2.5ft

Astilbe × *arendsii* 'Granat'

Astilbe 'Montgomery'

Astilbe 'Deutschland'

Astrantia major

ASTRANTIA (Masterwort)

A genus of perennials forming clumps of lobed leaves over which are produced sprays of papery bracts, often used dried in flower arrangements. For humus-rich, moisture retentive soil in sun or part shade although *A. major* 'Sunningdale Variegated' requires full sun.

A. major A clump forming perennial with deeply lobed leaves and flowers in summer in a range of colours to include green, pink and purple-red. 'Hadspen Blood' is of deepest red. 30cm–1m × 45cm/1–3 × 1.5ft

A. major subsp. *involucrata* A clump forming perennial with extended, papery bracts in summer of green and white flushed pink. Named forms include 'Shaggy' (syn. 'Margery Fish'). 30cm–1m × 45cm/1–3 × 1.5ft

Astrantia major subsp. *involucrata*

ATHYRIUM (Lady fern)

A genus of deciduous, hardy to frost tender ferns cultivated for their attractive fronds. Lady ferns are best suited to moisture retentive, neutral to acid soil in a partially shaded and sheltered situation.

A. filix-femina A deciduous, hardy fern grown for its attractive fronds arranged in the form of an upright, outwardly spreading shuttlecock. There are hundreds of varieties including the Cruciatum Group which have crested pinnae and make a criss-cross lattice pattern. 1.2m × 60cm/4 × 2ft

A. niponicum (Japanese painted fern) A deciduous, hardy fern with fronds of silver-green with deep purple-red midribs. Colouring may be variable. 30 × 30cm/1 × 1ft

Athyrium filix-femina Cruciatum Group

Atriplex halimus

Atriplex hortensis var. *rubra*

ATRIPLEX

A genus of hardy and half-hardy
evergreen or semi-evergreen shrubs, sub-
shrubs, annuals and perennials for
cultivation in free draining soil in full sun.
A. halimus (Tree purslane) A hardy,
semi-evergreen shrub grown for its
attractive, silver-grey foliage.
Insignificant green-white flowers appear
in late summer. 2 × 2.5m/6 × 8ft
A. hortensis var. *rubra* (Red orache) An
upright annual cultivated for its brilliant
red foliage close in appearance to that of
spinach. Dark red flowers appear in
summer. 1.2m × 30cm/4 × 1ft

Aubrieta 'Barker's Double'

AUCUBA (Spotted laurel)

A genus of evergreen shrubs with glossy
leaves, often with variegation, bearing
male and female flowers on separate
plants. Both need to be cultivated for
fruits. Widely grown for the ability to
tolerate poor soil, dry conditions and
shade.
A. japonica 'Gold Dust' An evergreen
shrub with shiny, mid-green leaves
distinctly marked with golden-yellow
specks. Spring flowers of reddish-purple
are followed by brilliant red berries in
the autumn on this female plant.
3 × 3m/10 × 10ft

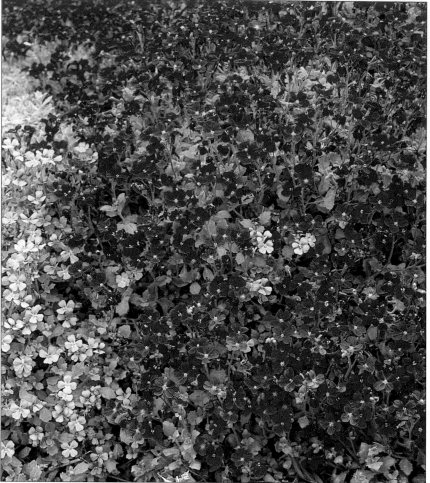

Aubrieta deltoidea

AUBRIETA

A genus of evergreen, low growing perennials most suited to cultivation in full sun
in the rock garden, in paving or to fall over a retaining wall. After flowering, cut
back hard to encourage new growth and to maintain a compact shape.
A. 'Barker's Double' A carpeting, evergreen perennial with a mass of tiny double,
purple flowers, tinted pink, throughout the spring. 5 × 60cm/2in × 2ft
A. deltoidea A carpeting, evergreen perennial producing a mass of tiny single or
double flowers in a broad range of colours in spring. 5 × 60cm/2in × 2ft

Aucuba japonica 'Gold Dust'

Aurinia saxatilis

AURINIA

A genus of biennials or evergreen perennials, closely related to *Alyssum*, most suited to the rock garden or to the front of a border in full sun.
A. saxatilis (Gold dust) An evergreen perennial forming a mound of grey-green leaves above which are carried bright golden-yellow flowers in late spring and early summer. 20 × 30cm/ 8in × 1ft

Azara lanceolata

AZARA

A genus of hardy to half-hardy, evergreen shrubs and small trees with fragrant flowers followed with berries in a hot summer. Suitable for training against a wall. Protect from cold winds.
A. integrifolia A frost hardy, evergreen shrub/small tree with shiny, dark green leaves. Scented yellow flowerheads appear over winter and in early spring. 5 × 3m/15 × 10ft
A. lanceolata A frost hardy, evergreen shrub with dark green leaves and clusters of small, scented yellow flowers in spring. 5 × 5m/15 × 15ft

AZOLLA

A genus of half-hardy to frost tender aquatic ferns cultivated in garden ponds as an aid to the suppression of algae. Overwinter in moist soil in a frost-free environment.
A. filiculoides (Fairy moss) A frost tender, aquatic perennial of pale green fronds for surface coverage in ponds. 1.5cm/ 0.5in × indefinite spread

Azorina vidallii

AZORINA

A genus of a single species of frost tender, evergreen shrub for cultivation in a cool conservatory or glasshouse or, in frost free climates, in free draining, moisture retentive soil in full sun but with some shade during the hottest part of the day.
A. vidallii A frost tender, evergreen shrub with shiny green leaves and hanging, bell-shaped flowers in white or pink in late summer. 60 × 60cm/2 × 2ft

43

B

Ballota pseudodictamnus

Baptisia australis

BALLOTA

A genus of hardy to frost hardy perennials and evergreen sub-shrubs thriving in poor soil in full sun.
B. pseudodictamnus A hardy, evergreen sub-shrub of soft, white woolly stems and oval-shaped, yellow-green leaves producing pink and white flowers in late spring and early summer.
45 × 60cm/1.5 × 2ft

BAPTISIA (False Indigo)

A genus of hardy to frost hardy perennials for cultivation in light, open conditions in sun. Well suited to sandy soil.
B. australis An upright, hardy perennial of dark green leaves and carrying racemes of indigo-blue flowers in the early summer. 1m × 60cm/3 × 2ft

Begonia coccinea

Begonia 'Fire Flush'

Begonia 'Looking Glass'

Begonia semperflorens 'Kalinka Rose'

Begonia sutherlandii

Begonia × tuberhybrida

BEGONIA

A genus of half-hardy and frost tender annuals, perennials, shrubs and climbers of variable habit and grown in the main either for their attractively marked leaves and/or for their colourful flowers. In areas subject to frosts they are principally cultivated as houseplants or as summer bedding. Most succeed in well drained, humus-rich soil in part shade. In general begonias may be divided into seven groups based largely on habit. These are: cane-stemmed, rex-cultorum, rhizomatous, semperflorens, shrub-like, tuberous and winter-flowering.
B. coccinea (Angelwing) A cane-stemmed, frost tender begonia with decorative red and green leaves and racemes of coral-red flowers in spring. Best suited as a house-plant given adequate light. 1m × 30cm/3 × 1ft
B. 'Looking Glass' A cane-stemmed, frost tender begonia with leaves of silver-bronze, olive and deep wine-red and few pink flowers in early summer.
1m × 45cm/3 × 1.5ft
B. semperflorens 'Kalinka Rose' A perennial hybrid, frost tender begonia of succulent stems, green leaves and deep rose flowers in summer. Suitable for pot cultivation in part shade. 60cm × 1m/2 × 3ft
B. sutherlandii A half-hardy, tuberous, trailing begonia with lightly toothed, light green leaves producing tiny, hanging orange flowers throughout the summer.
45cm/1.5ft spread
B. × tuberhybrida A variable, frost tender, tuberous begonia with succulent stems and shiny or dark green leaves. Mainly double flowers are produced in summer.
60 × 45cm/2 × 1.5ft

BELLIS (Daisy)

A genus of ground hugging perennials distinguished by long stalks topped with flowers of mainly pink, pink-red and white.

B. perennis A horizontally creeping perennial with bright green leaves and small daisy flowers from early spring to late summer. Many cultivars are most usually grown as biennials for bedding. 5–20 × 5–20cm/2–8 × 2–8in

BERBERIDOPSIS (Coral plant)

A genus of a single species of frost hardy climber for cultivation against a wall or to twine through a host plant in moisture retentive, humus-rich neutral to acid soil.

B. corallina A frost hardy climber with leaves of dark green, the undersides of which are grey-green, producing clusters of blood-red flowers in summer and early autumn. 5m/15ft

Bellis perennis

Berberis darwinii

Berberis × stenophylla

Berberis thunbergii 'Aurea'

BERBERIS (Barberry)

A genus of deciduous and evergreen shrubs, principally hardy, grown for their foliage, autumn colour, flowers and fruits. Generally unfussy as to conditions, they range from dwarf species and cultivars, most suited to the rock garden, to large shrubs appropriate to many situations.

B. darwinii An upright, evergreen shrub with glossy green, spiny leaves and racemes of vibrant orange flowers in spring, occasionally again in autumn. Flowers are followed with fruit. 3 × 3m/10 × 10ft

B. × stenophylla A spreading, evergreen shrub, often used for hedging, of narrow, spiny green leaves covered in golden-yellow flowers in late spring followed with fruit. 3 × 5m/10 × 15ft

B. temolaica A striking, deciduous shrub of arching habit cultivated for its blue-green foliage. Pale yellow spring flowers are followed with red fruit. 2 × 3m/6 × 10ft

B. thunbergii A rounded, deciduous shrub of fresh green leaves colouring brilliant orange and red in autumn. Pale yellow flowers in spring are followed with red fruit. 1.5 × 2.5m/5 × 8ft

B. thunbergii 'Aurea' A deciduous shrub of brilliant yellow foliage, most pronounced in spring. 1.5 × 2m/5 × 6ft

B. thunbergii 'Rose Glow' A deciduous shrub grown principally for the variegation of its leaves which unfold red-purple and mature with flecks of white. 1.2 × 1.2m/4 × 4ft

Berberis thunbergii 'Rose Glow'

Bergenia Ballawley hybrid

Above right:

Bergenia cordifolia

Bergenia purpurascens

Bergenia 'Silberlicht'

Beta vulgaris

BERGENIA (Elephant's ears)

A genus of mainly hardy, evergreen perennials grown for their large, leathery leaves and spring flowers. Generally unfussy about conditions and situation although most species have a dislike of extreme heat and drought. Bergenias will form sizeable clumps, spreading by means of thick rhizomes which will benefit from division every few years.

B. Ballawley Hybrid A perennial most noted for shiny, mid-green leaves colouring to rich bronze-purple throughout the winter. Red stalks carry crimson flowers during the spring. 60 × 60cm/2 × 2ft

B. cordifolia A perennial with rounded mid-green leaves tinged purple in winter. Red stalks carry pink flowers in various shades in late winter/early spring. 60 × 75cm/2 × 2.5ft

B. purpurascens A perennial with leaves of mid-green colouring deep purple-red in winter. Brown flower stalks carry dark purple-red flowers in spring. 45 × 30cm/1.5 × 1ft

B. 'Silberlicht' A perennial with finely scalloped, mid-green leaves. White flowers, later pink-tinted, appear in spring. 45 × 45cm/1.5 × 1.5ft

BETA (Beet)

A genus of perennials and biennials grown for decorative, ornamental foliage or as an edible crop. Green flowers, not worthy of note, appear in summer.

B. vulgaris subsp. *cicla* A biennial, most often treated as an annual, cultivated for its shiny green leaves, the midribs of which are of brilliant red. 30 × 45cm/ 1 × 1.5ft

Betula albosinensis var. septentrionalis

Betula ermanii

Betula nigra

BETULA (Birch)

A genus of deciduous trees and shrubs cultivated in the main for their attractive bark, spring catkins, both male and female, autumn colour and graceful habit. Birch are tolerant of most reasonably well drained soils in sun or partial shade but are less suited to chalk.

B. albosinensis var. *septentrionalis* A tree of conical habit noted for its peeling bark of orange-brown. Male catkins in spring and yellow foliage in autumn. 25 × 10m/80 × 30ft

B. ermanii (Erman's birch) A tree of conical habit with distinctive creamy-white bark. Male catkins in spring. 20 × 12m/70 × 40ft

B. nigra (Black birch) A tree of conical habit with red-brown, peeling bark, fissured grey-white and black in mature trees, and male catkins in early spring. Foliage colours yellow in autumn. 18 × 12m/60 × 40ft

B. papyrifera (Paper birch) A tree of conical habit with peeling white bark which, when newly exposed, is of pale orange-brown. Male catkins in early spring and autumn colour of yellow and orange. 20 × 10m/70 × 30ft

B. pendula (Silver birch) A tree of narrow, conical habit with peeling white bark becoming cracked at the base of the trunk of mature specimens. Male catkins in spring and yellow foliage in autumn. 25 × 10m/80 × 30ft

B. pendula 'Youngii' (Young's weeping birch) A small, dome-shaped tree with white bark. 8 × 3m/25 × 10ft

B. utilis var. *jacquemontii* (Himalayan birch) A tree of conical habit noted for its distinctive white bark. Autumn foliage. 18 × 10m/60 × 30ft

Betula papyrifera

Betula pendula (autumn foliage)

Betula pendula 'Youngii'

Betula utilis var. jacquemontii

Bidens ferulifolia

Blechnum tabulare

Borago officinalis

BIDENS

A genus of hardy to frost tender annuals, perennials and deciduous shrubs many of which are grown for annual bedding, containers and hanging baskets. All require full sun.
B. *ferulifolia* A short-lived frost hardy perennial with daisy-type, golden flowers carried on slim stems from midsummer until autumn. 30cm/ 1ft × indefinite spread

BLECHNUM (Hard fern)

A genus of mainly evergreen, hardy to frost tender ferns preferring humus-rich, acidic soil in part or total shade.
B. *discolor* (Crown fern) An evergreen, frost hardy fern with dark green fronds forming shuttlecocks. 1 × 1m/3 × 3ft
B. *tabulare* An evergreen, frost hardy fern with tall, spreading fronds of dark green. 1m × 60cm/3 × 2ft

BORAGO (Borage)

A genus of hardy to frost hardy annuals and perennials noted for hairy stems and leaves.
B. *officinalis* A vigorous, hardy annual well suited to cultivation in any reasonably well drained soil and tolerant of dry situations. Blue, starry flowers are produced throughout the summer. 60 × 45cm/2 × 1.5ft

Bougainvillea 'Scarlett O'Hara'

Brachyglottis 'Sunshine' (flowers)

Brachyglottis 'Sunshine' (leaves)

BOUGAINVILLEA

A genus of half-hardy to frost tender, evergreen trees, shrubs and evergreen or part deciduous climbers cultivated for their floral bracts in a range of showy colours. All require to be grown in full sun. Suitable for conservatory or glasshouse.
B. 'Scarlet O'Hara' A strong growing, evergreen, half-hardy climber producing cerise coloured bracts from summer to autumn. 8m/25ft

BRACHYCOME (Swan river daisy)

A genus of frost hardy to frost tender annuals and deciduous and evergreen perennials grown principally as bedding or for containers. All require a sheltered site in full sun.
B. *iberidifolia* A half-hardy annual with scented daisy-like flowers, mainly blue but sometimes violet-pink or white, in summer. 45 × 30cm/1.5 × 1ft
B. Splendour Series Similar to B. *iberidifolia* but flowers in lilac, purple or white with black-eye. 45 × 30cm/ 1.5 × 1ft

BRACHYGLOTTIS (syn. Senecio)

A genus of hardy to half-hardy, evergreen trees, shrubs and perennials grown mainly for foliage and flower, the leaves of many having a felted quality on the undersides. The great majority require well drained soil in full sun.
B. 'Sunshine' A hardy, spreading shrub with hairy-white leaves, the edges of which are lightly scalloped, and golden yellow flowers produced from summer to autumn. 1.5 × 2m/5 × 6ft

BRASSICA

A genus of annuals and evergreen biennials and perennials cultivated mainly as edible vegetables to include cabbage, cauliflower and broccoli. Some grown for their decorative quality. The majority prefer lime-rich soil in a sunny situation.

B. oleracea cultivars A series of ornamental cabbages and kale grown as annuals for foliage effect of pink, red or white leaves. Easily raised from seed. 45 × 45cm/1.5 × 1.5ft

BRIMEURA

A genus of frost hardy bulbous perennials cultivated for their small, bell-shaped flowers not dissimilar to those of a bluebell. Suitable for the rock garden. Needs part shade.

B. amethystina A bulbous perennial with racemes of china-blue to dark blue flowers in spring. Var. *alba* has white flowers. 10–20 × 5cm/4–8 × 2in

BRIZA (Quaking grass)

A genus of annual and perennial grasses grown for their attractive flower spikes, often dried and dyed, as much as for their linear leaves.

B. media (Trembling grass) A hardy perennial grass with fine blue-green leaves and nodding purple-green, later straw, flower spikes from late spring to midsummer. 60 × 30cm/2 × 1ft

BRUGMANSIA (Angels' trumpets)

A genus of frost hardy to frost tender evergreen shrubs and trees grown for their fragrant, trumpet flowers in conservatories or as container plants for outdoor display during the summer months.

B. × candida (syn. *Datura × candida*) A frost tender shrub bearing fragrant trumpets of pale yellow, rarely pink, and white flowers from summer to autumn. 3 × 1.5m/10 × 5ft

B. × candida 'Knightii' (syn. *Datura × candida* 'Plena') Similar to *B. × candida* but with hose-in-hose blooms. 3 × 1.5m/10 × 5ft

BRUNNERA

A genus of hardy perennials grown for their carpeting foliage and forget-me-not type flowers of blue, violet-blue and occasionally white. Best in partial shade in humus-rich, moisture-retentive soil.

B. macrophylla A perennial of hairy, mid-green leaves and light blue flowers in spring. 45 × 60cm/1.5 × 2ft

B. macrophylla 'Dawson's White' (syn. 'Variegata') A perennial of mid-green leaves broadly margined in creamy-white. Light blue flowers in spring. 45 × 60cm/1.5 × 2ft

Brassica oleracea

Brugmansia × candida 'Plena'

Brugmansia × candida

Brunnera macrophylla

Brunnera macrophylla 'Dawson's White'

Buddleja alternifolia

Buddleja crispa

Buddleja davidii 'Dartmoor'

BUDDLEJA (Butterfly bush)

A genus of principally hardy evergreen, semi-evergreen and deciduous shrubs, occasionally trees and climbers. Most respond to cultivation in well drained soil in a sunny situation. *B. davidii* cultivars, flowering on the current season's growth, should be pruned hard in early spring.

B. alternifolia A deciduous shrub with arching branches carrying clusters of scented, lilac flowers in early summer. May be grown as a standard. 4 × 4m/12 × 12ft

B. crispa A deciduous shrub whose arching stems bear woolly-white, hairy leaves. Scented, lilac-pink flowers are produced in midsummer. Frost hardy. Plant in a sheltered spot in full sun. 3 × 3m/10 × 10ft

B. davidii 'Dartmoor' A vigorous, deciduous shrub of narrow grey-green leaves and panicles of red-purple flowers in midsummer to autumn. 3 × 3m/10 × 10ft

B. globosa A deciduous or semi-evergreen shrub bearing globular deep orange and yellow flowers held on stiff branches in early summer. 5 × 5m/15 × 15ft

B. 'Lochinch' A quick growing, deciduous shrub with hairy white, mid-green leaves carrying violet-blue flowers with orange eye from late summer to autumn. 2.5 × 3m/8 × 10ft

B. loricata An evergreen shrub with slender blue-green leaves, the undersides of which are white-felted, carrying small panicles of grey-white flowers in summer. Position in well drained soil in sun. 1.2 × 1m/4 × 3ft

B. × *weyeriana* A deciduous shrub whose arching stems carry clusters of scented yellow to violet panicles of flowers from summer to autumn. 4 × 3m/12 × 10ft

Buddleja 'Lochinch'

Buddleja globosa

Buddleja × weyeriana

Buddleja loricata

Bupleurum angulosum

Buxus sempervirens 'Suffruticosa'

Buxus sempervirens 'Handsworthiensis'

BUPLEURUM (Thorow-wax)

Genus of hardy to frost hardy annuals, perennials and evergreen or semi-evergreen shrubs for well drained soil in full sun.

B. angulosum A hardy, semi-evergreen perennial with tapering blue-green leaves over which are carried clusters of papery yellow-green flowers in midsummer. 30 × 30cm/1 × 1ft

B. fruticosum A hardy, evergreen shrub of spreading habit. Above dark blue-green leaves rounded umbels of small golden flowers are carried on short stems in late summer to autumn. 2 × 2.5m/6 × 8ft

BUXUS (Box)

A genus of mainly hardy, evergreen shrubs and trees grown in the main for their foliage, sometimes variegated, which is dense in habit making it most suitable for clipping either as hedging or as topiary specimens. Insignificant spring flowers. Prefers part shade.

B. sempervirens 'Handsworthensis' A hardy, bushy, upright shrub or tree with extended, shiny green leaves. Well suited as hedging. 5 × 5m/15 × 15ft

B. sempervirens 'Suffruticosa' A hardy, dwarf, slow growing form of common box. Leaves of shiny, mid-green. 1 × 1.5m/3 × 5ft

Calamintha nepeta

CALAMINTHA (Calamint)

Genus of perennials with aromatic leaves tolerant of most situations and thriving in moisture retentive, humus-rich soil. Flowers are attractive to bees.
C. nepeta A spreading perennial of dark green, aromatic leaves carrying flowers of light mauve, occasionally pink, in summer. 45 × 75cm/1.5 × 2.5ft

Calceolaria integrifolia

CALCEOLARIA (Slipperwort)

A genus of some hardy, but mainly frost hardy to frost tender annuals, biennials, perennials and shrubs with distinctive slipper-like flowers. Mainly grown as summer bedding or in glasshouses.
C. Herbeohybrida Group Compact half-hardy biennials, largely raised as container plants for spring/summer. Cultivars in a wide range of bright colours. 20–45 × 15–30cm/8in–1.5ft/6in–1ft
C. integrifolia A half-hardy, evergreen sub-shrub most often grown as an annual. Yellow flowers all summer. 1m × 30cm/3 × 1ft
C. 'Walter Shrimpton' A hardy, evergreen perennial bearing orange-bronze, brown spotted, white banded flowers in summer. 10 × 23cm/4 × 9in

Calceolaria hybrids

Calceolaria 'Walter Shrimpton'

CALENDULA (Marigold)

A genus of quick growing, hardy to half-hardy annuals and evergreen perennials with daisy-type flowers mainly in shades of orange and yellow. Mostly cultivated as annuals for summer bedding.
C. officinalis cultivars Hardy annuals flowering in summer with single or double flowerheads in a range of colours to include apricot, cream, gold, orange and yellow. 30–75 × 30–45cm/1–2.5 × 1–1.5ft

CALLICARPA (Beauty berry)

Genus of hardy to frost tender, evergreen and deciduous shrubs and trees cultivated principally for their small, brightly coloured fruits which are borne at the end of summer.
C. bodinieri var. *giraldii* An upright, hardy, deciduous shrub with tiny pink flowers in summer which are followed by distinctive, glistening, violet-purple fruits. 3 × 2.5m/10 × 8ft

Calendula officinalis

Callicarpa bodinieri var. *giraldii*

Callistemon pallidus

CALLISTEMON (Bottlebrush)

Genus of hardy to frost tender, evergreen trees and shrubs cultivated on account of their bottlebrush-like flowers in a range of colours. Best in full sun in neutral to acid soil.
C. pallidus (Lemon bottlebrush) A spreading, half-hardy shrub with grey-green leaves and creamy-greenish flower spikes from late spring to midsummer. 2–4 × 2–4m/6–12 × 6–12ft
C. rigidus (Stiff bottlebrush) A bushy, half-hardy shrub with dull green leaves and dark red flower spikes in summer. 1–2.5 × 2–3m/3–8 × 6–10ft

Callistemon rigidus

Calluna vulgaris 'Silver Knight'

Calluna vulgaris 'Sir John Charrington'

CALLUNA (Heather, Ling)

A genus of a single species of evergreen shrub of which there are very many named cultivars. Bell-shaped flowers in many shades of pink, purple, red and white appear from midsummer until autumn. Leaves, most often of dark green but sometimes of yellow or gold, are frequently purple tinted in winter. Calluna thrives best in acidic soil in sun and should be cut back in spring.

C. vulgaris 'Silver Knight' An evergreen shrub with silver-grey foliage, tinged purple in winter, and pinky-mauve flowers in summer. 45 × 75cm/1.5 × 2.5ft

C. vulgaris 'Sir John Charrington' An evergreen shrub with golden foliage, tinged orange and red in winter, and mauve-pink flowers in summer. 45 × 75cm/1.5 × 2.5ft

C. vulgaris 'Spring Cream' An evergreen shrub with green foliage touched with cream in spring. White flowers in summer. 30 × 45cm/1 × 1.5ft

Calocedrus decurrens

CALOCEDRUS (Incense cedar)

A genus of hardy to frost hardy, evergreen trees, the hardy species of which lend themselves to cultivation as specimens.

C. decurrens A conifer of columnar habit, spreading more widely in the wild, with dark green leaves and cones ripening to reddish-brown. Foliage is faintly aromatic. 20 × 2m/70 × 6ft

CALTHA (Kingcup, Marsh marigold)

A genus of moisture loving, hardy to frost hardy perennials best suited to the margins of pond or stream in a sunny situation.

C. palustris A hardy perennial for shallow water or boggy soil. Dark green, kidney-shaped leaves are topped with deep butter-yellow, waxy flowers in spring. 45 × 45cm/1.5 × 1.5ft

C. palustris 'Flore Pleno' Similar to *C. palustris* but flowers are double and of a slightly paler yellow tinged with green at the centre. 25 × 25cm/10 × 10in

CAMASSIA (Quamash)

A genus of hardy to frost hardy, bulbous perennials with narrow, basal leaves and racemes of starry flowers in spring and summer. Bulbs should be planted deeply in moist soil.

C. leichtlinii A frost hardy, bulbous perennial carrying racemes of creamy-white flowers on upright stems in late spring. 60 × 10cm/2ft × 4in

C. leichtlinii subsp. *suksdorfii* A frost hardy, bulbous perennial carrying racemes of blue to violet-blue flowers in late spring. 60 × 10cm/2ft × 4in

Caltha palustris

Caltha palustris 'Flore Pleno'

Camassia leichtlinii

Camassia leichtlinii subsp. *suksdorfii*

Camellia 'Cornish Snow'

Camellia japonica 'Kimberley'

Camellia japonica 'Konronkoku'

Camellia japonica 'Mathotiana Alba'

Camellia japonica 'Nobilissima'

Camellia japonica 'Otome'

Camellia 'Inspiration'

CAMELLIA

A genus of hardy to frost tender, evergreen shrubs and trees for neutral to acid soil in a partially shaded situation out of the reach of cold winds and the early morning sun. Camellias are grown for their dark green, most often shiny, leaves and their wide range of flower colour in shades of pink, red, white or yellow. Flowers may be single, semi-double, anemone-form, peony-form, rose-form double and formal double, the result of extensive hybridizing. *C. japonica* and its cultivars are of upright, bushy habit and retain their spent blooms. *C. × williamsii* cultivars are more lax in growth and drop spent blooms. *C. sasanqua* and its cultivars require to be grown in full sun. Variable in size but about 3 × 2–3m/10 × 6–10ft though many are ultimately much larger.

C. 'Cornish Snow' A hardy shrub with leaves of bronze maturing to dark green. Small, single white flowers from late winter to late spring.

C. 'Inspiration' A hardy shrub or small tree producing semi-double flowers of deepest pink from late winter to late spring.

C. japonica 'Kimberley' A hardy shrub producing single flowers of bright crimson from early spring.

C. japonica 'Konronkoku' (syn. 'Kouron-jura') A hardy shrub producing semi-double to formal double black-red flowers from spring over a long period.

C. japonica 'Mathotiana Alba' A hardy shrub producing rose-form double or formal double white flowers in mid and late spring.

C. japonica 'Nobilissima' A hardy shrub producing large anemone-form white flowers shaded yellow from early spring.

C. japonica 'Otome' (syn. 'Pink Perfection') A hardy shrub producing small formal double pink flowers in early spring.

C. japonica 'Rubescens Major' A hardy shrub with rounded leaves of dark green producing rose-form double or formal double flowers of crimson-red in spring.

C. 'Leonard Messel' A hardy shrub with leaves of dull green producing large, semi-double to peony-form flowers of rose-pink in spring.

C. × williamsii A strong growing, hardy shrub with shiny, green leaves producing single pink flowers in spring.

C. × williamsii 'Bartley Pink' A hardy shrub producing semi-double pink flowers in spring.

C. × williamsii 'Donation' A hardy shrub producing semi-double pink flowers from late winter to late spring. Flower colour deepens according to the degree of shade.

C. × williamsii 'Elsie Jury' A tall growing, hardy shrub producing large, peony-form pink flowers throughout the spring.

C. × williamsii 'Galaxie' A hardy shrub producing medium, formal double flowers of pale pink in mid-spring.

C. × williamsii 'Water Lily' A hardy shrub of lanky growth producing large, formal-double flowers of rose-pink from early spring.

Camellia 'Leonard Messel'

Camellia × *williamsii*

Camellia japonica 'Rubescens Major'

Camellia × *williamsii* 'Bartley Pink'

Camellia × *williamsii* 'Donation'

Camellia × *williamsii* 'Elsie Jury'

Camellia × *williamsii* 'Water Lily'

Camellia × *williamsii* 'Galaxie'

55

Campanula alliariifolia

Campanula cochleariifolia var. alba

Campanula cochleariifolia var. pallida 'Miranda'

Campanula garganica

Campanula glomerata

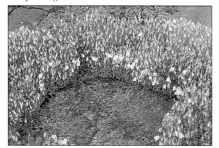

Campanula × hallii

Campanula 'Birch Hybrid'

CAMPANULA (Bellflower)

A genus of hardy to frost tender annuals, biennials and perennials, some evergreen, varying greatly in habit and requirements for cultivation. Most species are easily grown and will flower over a long period. Flowers are most usually bell, tubular or star-shaped and are produced in a wide range of colours to include blue, lilac, mauve, pink, purple, red and white.

C. alliariifolia (Ivory bells) A hardy, clump forming perennial with grey-green, basal leaves and drooping, tubular white flowers from midsummer until early autumn. 60 × 45cm/2 × 1.5ft

C. 'Birch Hybrid' A hardy, ground hugging, evergreen perennial with bright green leaves and open bell flowers of violet-blue in summer. 10 × 45cm/4in × 1.5ft

C. cochleariifolia var. alba (Fairies' thimbles) A hardy, low growing perennial with leaves of a bright green and bell flowers of white in summer. Best in sun. 8 × 30cm/3in × 1ft

C. cochleariifolia var. pallida 'Miranda' A hardy, low growing perennial with bell flowers of slate-blue in summer. 8 × 30cm/3in × 1ft

C. garganica (Adriatic bellflower) A hardy, low growing perennial with mid-green leaves producing racemes of starry flowers, from vivid blue to lilac, in summer. Best in sun. 5 × 30cm/2in × 1ft

C. glomerata (Clustered bellflower) A hardy, rapidly spreading perennial bearing globes of tubular flowers on stiff stems in shades of violet-blue, lavender and white in summer. 45 × 45cm/1.5 × 1.5ft

C. × hallii A hardy, low growing, perennial producing white bell flowers in summer. 5 × 60cm/2in × 2ft

C. isophylla 'Alba' (Italian bellflower) A half-hardy, trailing perennial with leaves of light green and producing open, saucer-shaped flowers of purest white in mid-summer. Well suited to containers and hanging baskets. 20 × 30cm/8in × 1ft

C. lactiflora (Milky bellflower) A hardy, tall growing perennial producing bell flowers of white or light blue, sometimes lavender, lilac-blue or violet, through summer into autumn. Self-seeds freely. 1.2m × 60cm/4 × 2ft

C. latifolia white A hardy, strong growing perennial forming basal clumps of mid-green leaves above which rise tall stems of white, tubular flowers in summer. 1.2m × 60cm/4 × 2ft

C. latiloba alba A hardy, clump forming perennial of mid-green leaves producing tall stems of cup-shaped, white flowers in mid and late summer. 1m × 45cm/3 × 1.5ft

C. latiloba 'Hidcote Amethyst' A hardy, clump forming perennial with cup-shaped flowers of pale amethyst with deeper shading. 75 × 45cm/2.5 × 1.5ft

Campanula isophylla 'Alba'

Campanula latiloba alba

Campanula lactiflora

Campanula latiloba 'Hidcote Amethyst'

Campanula latifolia white

Campanula persicifolia 'Telham Beauty'

Campanula portenschlagiana

Campanula poscharskyana

Campanula pyramidalis

Campanula persicifolia

C. persicifolia (Peach-leaved bellflower) A hardy perennial forming rosettes of bright green leaves over which are carried cup-shaped flowers in varying shades from white to lilac-blue in early and midsummer. 1m × 30cm/3 × 1ft

C. persicifolia 'Telham Beauty' A hardy, spreading perennial with flowers of light blue in early and midsummer. 1 × 1m/3 × 3ft

C. portenschlagiana (Dalmatian bellflower) A vigorous, hardy evergreen perennial forming mounds of mid-green foliage over which are produced tubular, dark purple flowers in mid and late summer. 15 × 45cm/6in × 1.5ft

C. poscharskyana A hardy, spreading perennial with mid-green leaves and panicles of lavender-blue, starry flowers in summer and autumn. 15 × 45cm/6in × 1.5ft

C. punctata 'Rubriflora' A hardy creeping perennial of dark green leaves producing long, drooping bells of dusky pink stained red in early summer. 30 × 45cm/1 × 1.5ft

C. pyramidalis (Chimney bellflower) A frost hardy, short lived, tall growing perennial with pyramidal racemes of lightly scented, pale blue or white flowers from late spring to summer. Most often grown as a biennial. 1.2m × 60cm/4 × 2ft

Campanula punctata 'Rubriflora'

Campsis × tagliabuana 'Madame Galen'

Canna 'Fireside'

Caragana arborescens 'Lorbergii'

CAPSICUM (Chilli pepper)

A genus of frost tender annuals and perennials grown either for their fruit, in green, orange, red or yellow, as houseplants, or in a glasshouse or conservatory. Outdoors cultivate in humus-rich soil in full sun.

C. annuum A frost tender annual or short-lived perennial with single white or yellow flowers in summer and long, conical fruits, chilli peppers. 1.5m × 45cm/5 × 1.5ft

CAMPSIS (Trumpet vine)

A genus of hardy to frost hardy, vigorous climbers grown for their showy, trumpet-shaped flowers. Plant in well drained soil in a sheltered position in full sun.

C. × tagliabuana 'Madame Galen' A frost hardy climber with dark green leaves and orange-red, trumpet flowers in late summer to autumn. 10m/30ft

CANNA (Indian shot plant)

A genus of half-hardy to frost tender herbaceous perennials grown principally for their large paddle-like leaves and showy, tubular flowers in a range of bright colours. Most often used as summer bedding, or for containers, cannas require a position in full sun and water during prolonged dry periods.

C. 'Fireside' A half-hardy perennial with large mid-green leaves and scarlet flowers from midsummer to early autumn. 1m × 30cm/3 × 1ft

CARAGANA (Pea tree)

A genus of deciduous shrubs which are grown for foliage and single pea-like flowers in yellow, white or pink. Brown seedpods are borne in autumn. Best in full sun but tolerant of poor soil in exposed situations.

C. arborescens 'Lorbergii' A deciduous shrub with attractive, light green foliage and small yellow flowers in late spring. 6 × 4m/20 × 12ft

Cardamine pratensis 'Flore Pleno'

Cardamine pratensis

CARDAMINE (Bittercress)

A genus of annuals and perennials for humus-rich, moisture retentive soil in partial or complete shade. Many are suitable for the border, for woodland or for the rock garden. Some annuals are persistent garden weeds.

C. pratensis (Lady's smock) A perennial forming rosettes of grey-green to shiny, dark green leaves with panicles of lilac, purple or white flowers in late spring. 30 × 30cm/1 × 1ft

C. pratensis 'Flore Pleno' A perennial forming a basal rosette from which double, lilac-pink flowers are produced in late spring. 20 × 30cm/8in × 1ft

C. trifolia A low growing perennial with dark green leaves, reddish underneath, and racemes of white or pink flowers in late spring. 15 × 30cm/6in × 1ft

Cardamine trifolia

Cardiocrinum giganteum

Carex comans Bronze Form

Carex pendula

Carex elata 'Aurea'

CARDIOCRINUM (Giant lily)

A genus of hardy to frost hardy bulbous perennials grown for their showy, lily-like flowers. Bulbs, which take several years to develop, are monocarpic, dying after flowering but leaving small bulbils to mature. Plant in rich soil in a sheltered, part shady site and water in dry periods. Cardiocrinums are intolerant of scorching conditions.
C. giganteum A hardy, bulbous perennial with shiny leaves and fragrant, white trumpet flowers in summer.
1.5m × 45cm/5 × 1.5ft

CAREX (Sedge)

A huge genus of mainly hardy deciduous and evergreen perennials thriving in a wide range of conditions and situations. Grown generally for their attractive foliage, often colourful or variegated.
C. comans Bronze Form A thickly tufted evergreen perennial of reddish brown leaves, appearing bronze in winter, and inconspicuous brown flower spikes in early summer. 30 × 75cm/1 × 2.5ft
C. elata 'Aurea' (Bowles' golden sedge) A deciduous perennial forming clumps of deep yellow leaves narrowly margined green. Flower spikes, brown or green according to sex, are carried in late spring and early summer. Thrives best in damp soil. 60 × 45cm/2 × 1.5ft
C. pendula (Drooping sedge) A tufted, evergreen perennial forming clumps of shiny green leaves and having catkin-like, hanging flower spikes in late spring and early summer. Best in damp soil. 1.4 × 1.4m/4.5 × 4.5ft

Carlina acaulis

CARLINA (Carline thistle)

A genus of annuals and perennials made up of basal rosettes and stemless flowerheads. Best in poor soil which is well drained in full sun.
C. acaulis A short-lived perennial grown for its papery flower bracts of off-white, occasionally pink-tinted in summer. Suitable for drying. 10 × 25cm/4 × 10in

CARPENTERIA

A genus of a single species of frost hardy, evergreen shrub cultivated for its slightly glossy, leathery leaves of dark green and its scented flowers. Best in full sun in a sheltered spot. Suitable for wall training.
C. californica A frost hardy, evergreen shrub producing open cup-shaped white flowers with pronounced yellow stamens in early and midsummer.
2 × 2m/6 × 6ft

Carpenteria californica

Carpinus betulus

Caryopteris × clandonensis 'Heavenly Blue'

CARPINUS (Hornbeam)

A genus of deciduous trees grown for their decorative foliage either as specimens or as hedging. Flowers in the form of catkins, both male and female together on the same plant, are borne in spring. Good autumn colour.

C. betulus (Common hornbeam) A large, deciduous tree of mid-green leaves which colour orange-yellow in autumn. Spring catkins are yellow if male, green if female. Often cultivated as a hedge when it may be trimmed to size and shape in late summer. May retain old leaves over winter. 25 × 20m/80 × 70ft

CARYOPTERIS (Blue spiraea)

A genus of hardy to frost hardy, deciduous shrubs and perennials grown for their aromatic foliage and late summer flowers. Best in full sun in well drained soil.

C. × clandonensis 'Heavenly Blue' A hardy shrub with grey-green leaves and deep blue flowers in late summer and early autumn. 1 × 1.5m/3 × 5ft

Cassiope 'Muirhead'

Castanea sativa

Catalpa bignonioides 'Aurea'

CASSIOPE

A genus of small, evergreen shrubs for cultivation in acidic soil in the rock garden or in a peat bed. Best in part shade.

C. 'Muirhead' A low growing, evergreen shrub of dark green leaves arranged flat against whipcord-like stems producing white bell flowers in late spring and early summer. 20 × 20cm/8 × 8in

CASTANEA (Sweet chestnut)

Genus of deciduous trees and shrubs cultivated for their handsome foliage and spiny fruits. Most prefer soil which is neutral to acidic.

C. sativa (Spanish chestnut) A vigorous, deciduous tree with furrowed bark and dark, glossy green leaves. Carries fruits which are edible in autumn. 30 × 15m/100 × 50ft

CATALPA

A genus of deciduous trees principally grown for their attractive foliage, their bell-shaped flowers and, developing in autumn, seedpods. Hardy but position away from strong winds.

C. bignonioides 'Aurea' (Indian bean tree) A deciduous tree cultivated for its bright yellow leaves, opening bronze in spring. 10 × 10m/30 × 30ft

Catananche caerulea

CATANANCHE (Cupid's dart)

A genus of perennials with linear grey-green leaves and single flowerheads composed of strap-shaped florets and papery bracts. For well drained soil in full sun.

C. caerulea A short-lived perennial with grass-like, grey-green leaves producing flowerheads of deepish blue from midsummer into autumn. Unlikely to thrive in heavy clay. 1m × 30cm/3 × 1ft

Ceanothus 'Autumnal Blue'

Ceanothus 'Blue Mound'

Ceanothus arboreus 'Trewithen Blue'

CEANOTHUS (California lilac)

Genus of deciduous and evergreen, hardy to frost hardy shrubs, sometimes small trees, for well drained soil sheltered from the reach of strong, cold winds. Tolerant of lime, but becoming chlorotic on shallow chalk. Grown in the main for profusion of small flowers, mostly blue but also pink and white, appearing in season according to type. May be wall trained.

C. arboreus 'Trewithen Blue' A large, frost hardy, evergreen shrub with rounded, dark green leaves and panicles of mid-blue, scented flowers in late spring and early summer. 6 × 8m/20 × 25ft

C. 'Autumnal Blue' A hardy, evergreen shrub with glossy, bright green leaves and panicles of clear, sky-blue flowers from late summer into autumn. 3 × 3m/10 × 10ft

C. 'Blue Mound' A frost hardy, evergreen shrub with shiny, dark green leaves, grey-green on the undersides, and dark, violet-blue flowers in late spring. 1.5 × 2m/ 5 × 6ft

C. 'Cascade' A frost hardy, evergreen shrub of open habit with shiny, dark green leaves and panicles of lavender-blue flowers borne in profusion in late spring and early summer. 4 × 4m/12 × 12ft

C. × *delileanus* 'Gloire de Versailles' A hardy, deciduous shrub with leaves of dark green and panicles of pale blue flowers from midsummer into autumn. 1.5 × 1.5m/5 × 5ft

C. dentatus var. *floribundus* A frost hardy, outwardly spreading, evergreen shrub with dark green leaves and dense clusters of dark blue flowers in late spring. 1.5 × 2m/5 × 6ft

C. impressus (Santa Barbara ceanothus) A frost hardy, outwardly spreading, evergreen shrub with dark green leaves, heavily veined, and flowers of deep blue in spring. 1.5 × 2.5m/5 × 8ft

C. impressus 'Puget Blue' A vigorous, frost hardy, evergreen shrub with larger leaves than those of *C. impressus* and a profusion of deep blue flowers in spring. 3 × 3m/10 × 10ft

C. × *pallidus* 'Marie Simon' A hardy, deciduous shrub of upright growth and mid-green leaves borne on red stems. Pale pink flowers from midsummer to autumn. 1.5 × 1.5m/5 × 5ft

C. thyrsiflorus var. *repens* (Creeping blueblossom) A hardy, low evergreen shrub of spreading habit with leaves of shiny, mid-green. Dark blue flowers in spring. 1 × 2.5m/3 × 8ft

Ceanothus 'Cascade'

Ceanothus × *pallidus* 'Marie Simon'

Ceanothus × *delileanus* 'Gloire de Versailles'

Ceanothus dentatus var. *floribundus*

Ceanothus impressus

Ceanothus 'Puget Blue'

Ceanothus thyrsiflorus var. *repens*

Cedrus deodara

Cedrus libani subsp. *atlantica* 'Glauca'

CEDRUS (Cedar)

Genus of evergreen, coniferous trees valued for their spreading branches and stately appearance. For any open, sunny site but requiring space in which to develop. Tolerant of chalk.

C. deodara (Deodar) Fast growing coniferous tree making a substantial specimen. Grey-green needle leaves on drooping shoots when young; deep green in maturity. 36 × 10m/120 × 30ft

C. libani subsp. *atlantica* 'Glauca' A substantial coniferous tree with dark bark and grey-green leaves. Slowly ripening cones in autumn.
30 × 30m/100 × 100ft

CELMISIA (New Zealand daisy)

A genus of frost hardy evergreen perennials and sub-shrubs forming rosettes of silver-grey leaves and carrying single daisy-like flowers. For moisture retentive, slightly acidic soil.

C. spectabilis A perennial with narrow, silvery leaves and white daisy flowers, with yellow disc, in early summer.
30 × 30cm/1 × 1ft

CELOSIA (Cockscomb)

A genus of hardy to frost tender annuals, perennials and shrubs grown mainly for their colourful, often plume-like flowers as summer bedding.

C. Plumosa Cultivars Half hardy perennials, usually grown as annuals, with plumes of brightly coloured flowers in summer. 60 × 60cm/2 × 2ft

CENTAURIA (Knapweed)

Genus of hardy to frost hardy annuals, biennials, perennials and sub-shrubs with simple, somewhat coarse foliage and spherical flowerheads.

C. cyanus (Cornflower) Hardy annual producing sprays of daisy flowers in summer of blue, purple, red, pink or white. Tall varieties make good cut flowers. 30cm–1m × 20–40cm/
1–3ft × 8–16in

C. hypoleuca 'John Coutts' A hardy perennial with leaves of light green, the undersides of which are white-green. Rose-pink flowers, slightly scented, are produced in summer.
60 × 45cm/2 × 1.5ft

C. montana f. *alba* A hardy perennial forming mats of mid-green leaves, woolly on the undersides, with white flowerheads from late spring to midsummer. 45 × 60cm/1.5 × 2ft

CENTRANTHUS (Valerian)

A genus of hardy to half hardy annuals and perennials of which *C. ruber* is the only species widely cultivated. For chalk or lime soils in sun.

C. ruber A hardy perennial forming a woody base of slightly fleshy, mid-green leaves. Rounded flowerheads in shades of pink, red and white are produced from late spring to late summer.
1 × 1m/3 × 3ft

Centauria cyanus

Centauria hypoleuca 'John Coutts'

Centauria montana alba

Centranthus ruber

Cephalaria gigantea

Cerastium tomentosum

Ceratostigma plumbaginoides

CEPHALARIA

A genus of hardy to half hardy annuals and perennials cultivated for scabious-like flowers of pale lemon-yellow or white.

C. gigantea (Giant scabious) A tall growing, hardy perennial forming basal clumps of coarse leaves over which rise stems of pale lemon-yellow flowers in summer. 2 × 1.2m/6 × 4ft

CERASTIUM

A genus of annuals and perennials most suited to cultivation in full sun. Those most commonly grown are vigorous, carpeting perennials.

C. tomentosum (Snow-in-summer) A rapidly spreading, low growing perennial with silver-white leaves and small, starry white flowers in late spring and summer. 5–8cm/2–3in × indefinite spread

CERATOSTIGMA

A genus of hardy to frost tender deciduous and evergreen perennials and sub-shrubs cultivated for their clusters of blue flowers. For sun and shelter.

C. plumbaginoides (Hardy plumbago) A hardy, spreading deciduous perennial with bright green leaves, becoming red-tinted in autumn, and brilliant blue flowers in late summer and early autumn. 45 × 30cm/1.5 × 1ft

Cercidiphyllum japonicum (autumn foliage)

CERCIDIPHYLLUM

A genus of a single species of deciduous tree mainly grown for the brilliance of autumn colour. Prefers neutral to acidic soil in sun or light shade. Hardy but shelter from cold winds.

C. japonicum (Katsura tree) A rounded, deciduous tree with mid-green leaves, opening bronze, turning to shades of flame in autumn. 20 × 15m/70 × 50ft

Cercis siliquastrum

CERCIS

A genus of deciduous trees and shrubs with heart-shaped leaves and pea-like flowers grown either as specimen trees, in shrub borders or wall trained.

C. canadensis 'Forest Pansy' A spreading, many stemmed deciduous tree with leaves of a deep red-purple. Pink flowers in spring before leaves emerge. 10 × 10m/30 × 30ft

C. siliquastrum (Judas tree) A deciduous tree with leaves of blue-green colouring yellow in autumn. Deep pink flowers appear on bare stems in spring. 10 × 10m/30 × 30ft

C. siliquastrum f. *albida* As *C. siliquastrum* but with white flowers. 10 × 10m/30 × 30ft

Cercis canadensis 'Forest Pansy'

Chaenomeles speciosa 'Cardinalis'

Chaenomeles speciosa 'Moerloosei'

Chaenomeles speciosa 'Nivalis'

Chaenomeles × superba 'Pink Lady'

CHAENOMELES (Flowering quince, Japonica)

A genus of deciduous spiny shrubs grown for their single, semi-double and double flowers in the early part of the year and for their edible, autumnal fruits. Tolerant of shade but flower and fruit best when placed in full sun. May be wall trained.

C. speciosa 'Cardinalis' A widely spreading shrub with spiny branches and shiny, dark green leaves. Single scarlet flowers in spring followed by yellow-green fruit in autumn. 2.5 × 5m/8 × 15ft

C. speciosa 'Moerloosei' A widely spreading shrub with spiny branches and shiny, dark green leaves. Large, single white flowers, flushed with pale pink, are carried in spring. Fruit in autumn. 2.5 × 5m/8 × 15ft

C. speciosa 'Nivalis' A widely spreading shrub with spiny branches and shiny, dark green leaves. Single, pure white flowers in spring. Yellow autumn fruit. 2.5 × 5m/8 × 15ft

C. × superba 'Pink Lady' A spreading shrub with shiny leaves of mid-green and deep pink-red flowers in early spring. Green fruits in autumn ripen to yellow. 1.5 × 2m/5 × 6ft

Cerinthe major 'Purpurascens'

CERINTHE

A genus of hardy to half hardy annuals and perennials cultivated in the main for their unusual flowers.

C. glabra A hardy perennial plant with tongue-like leaves and clusters of yellow, tubular flowers with a purple-brown band in summer. 30 × 30cm/1 × 1ft

C. major 'Purpurascens' A half hardy, self-seeding annual with grey-green leaves and navy, purple and grey flowers in summer. Position in sun. 45 × 30cm/1.5 × 1ft

CESTRUM

Genus of deciduous and evergreen, frost hardy to frost tender shrubs cultivated for their tubular flowers, often scented, and berries. Best given the protection of a warm wall or grown as a container plant overwintered in a frost-free glasshouse or conservatory.

C. elegans A frost tender, evergreen shrub with spreading branches of mid-green leaves and carrying crimson to pink flowers from summer to autumn. Flowers are followed by deep red berries. 3 × 3m/10 × 10ft

Chaerophyllum hirsutum 'Roseum'

CHAEROPHYLLUM

A genus of annuals, biennials and perennials grown in the main for their ferny foliage and umbels of pink, white or yellow flowers.

C. hirsutum 'Roseum' An upright, hairy perennial with aromatic leaves of mid-green and flowers of lilac-pink in late spring and early summer. 60 × 30cm/2 × 1ft

Chamaecyparis lawsoniana 'Columnaris'

Chamaecyparis lawsoniana 'Ellwoodii'

Chamaecyparis lawsoniana 'Lemon Queen'

CHAMAECYPARIS (Cypress)

A genus of evergreen, coniferous trees grown either as specimens or for hedging. Cultivars of *Chamaecyparis* include those of dwarf habit suitable for the rock garden. Thriving in moist but well drained neutral to acid soil, most are tolerant of chalk. Best in sun.

C. lawsoniana 'Columnaris' A narrow, columnar coniferous tree of dense, pale blue-green foliage. 10 × 1m/30 × 3ft

C. lawsoniana 'Ellwoodii' A narrow, columnar coniferous tree of upright branches and young foliage of blue-grey. 3 × 1.5/10 × 5ft

C. lawsoniana 'Lemon Queen' A narrow conical tree of dense yellow-green foliage. 10 × 3m/30 × 10ft

C. lawsoniana 'Luteocompacta' A small conical tree with upright branches of dense yellow-green foliage. 2.5 × 1.5m/8 × 5ft

C. lawsoniana 'Minima Aurea' A dwarf, coniferous tree of dense habit with foliage of soft, golden-yellow held upright in vertical sprays. 1.5 × 1m/5 × 3ft

C. lawsoniana 'Triomf van Boskoop' A large, coniferous tree with loose sprays of glaucous-blue foliage requiring trimming to retain density and shape. 20 × 3m/70 × 10ft

C. lawsoniana 'Winston Churchill' A narrow, coniferous tree of conical shape with foliage of a rich golden-yellow throughout the year. 15 × 3m/50 × 10ft

Chamaecyparis lawsoniana 'Triomf van Boskoop'

Chamaecyparis lawsoniana 'Luteocompacta'

Chamaecyparis lawsoniana 'Minima Aurea'

Chamaecyparis lawsoniana 'Winston Churchill'

Chamaemelum nobile

Chelidonium majus 'Flore Pleno'

CHAMAEMELUM (Chamomile)

A genus of annuals and perennials cultivated for their aromatic foliage, feathery in appearance, and daisy like flowers. Best in light soil in full sun.

C. nobile An aromatic perennial with leaves of fresh green and white daisy-like flowers with yellow discs in summer. 30 × 45cm/1 × 1.5ft

C. nobile 'Treneague' A non-flowering cultivar of carpeting habit grown as an alternative to grass for small lawns. 10 × 45cm/4in × 1.5ft

CHELIDONIUM (Greater celandine)

A genus of a single species of biennial or short-lived perennial best suited to a wildflower garden where it will self-seed.

C. majus 'Flore Pleno' A clump forming perennial with leaves of blue-green and double yellow flowers in summer. 60 × 20cm/2ft × 8in

CHELONE (Turtlehead)

A genus of perennials cultivated for their colourful white, pink or purple flowers which appear from late summer. Tolerant of heavy clay and moist soil.

C. obliqua An upright perennial with deep pink-purple flowers from late summer to autumn. 60 × 30cm/2 × 1ft

Chiastophyllum oppositifolium

Chimonanthus praecox

CHIASTOPHYLLUM

A genus of a single species of succulent, evergreen perennial cultivated for its foliage and tiny hanging flowers of butter-yellow. Best in part shade.

C. oppositifolium A spreading, evergreen perennial with fleshy leaves of pale green and flowers of deep yellow in late spring and early summer. 20 × 15cm/8 × 6in

CHIMONANTHUS (Wintersweet)

A genus of deciduous and evergreen shrubs grown for their sweetly scented, waxy flowers which open in wintertime before young leaves emerge. Suitable for training against a wall. Protect unripened wood from extremes of cold.

C. praecox An upright, deciduous shrub with shiny leaves of mid-green and hanging bowl-shaped flowers in winter. 4 × 3m/12 × 10ft

Chionodoxa forbesii 'Pink Giant'

CHIONODOXA (Glory of the snow)

A genus of hardy to frost hardy bulbous perennials closely related to *Scilla*. Starry flowers emerge over narrow, basal leaves of mid-green in early spring.

C. forbesii 'Pink Giant' A hardy, bulbous perennial producing starry flowers of palest pink with white centres in early spring. 10cm/4in

C. luciliae A hardy, bulbous perennial producing starry flowers of blue with white centres in early spring. 10cm/4in

Chionodoxa luciliae

Choisya ternata

Choisya ternata 'Sundance'

Chusquea culeou

Choisya 'Aztec Pearl'

CHOISYA (Mexican orange blossom)

A genus of hardy to frost hardy evergreen shrubs cultivated for their attractive foliage and star-shaped, scented flowers. Best positioned in full sun. Frost hardy species, such as *C. arizonica*, should be afforded wall protection.

C. 'Aztec Pearl' A hardy shrub with finely cut leaves and small, white flowers flushed pink in spring and again in late summer into autumn. 2.5 × 2.5m/8 × 8ft

C. ternata A hardy shrub with dark green leaves and starry, scented flowers in late spring repeated in late summer and autumn. 2.5 × 2.5m/8 × 8ft

C. ternata ''Sundance' A hardy shrub with leaves of brilliant yellow, darkening to yellow-green in part shade. Seldom flowers. 2.5 × 2.5m/8 × 8ft

CHUSQUEA

A genus of hardy to frost tender, evergreen clump-forming bamboos cultivated mainly as specimen plants. For moist, humus-rich soil in sun or partial shade.

C. culeou A hardy, upright bamboo forming clumps of cylindrical yellow-green and olive canes. Papery-white leaf sheaths enclose young canes. 6 × 2.5m/20 × 8ft

69

Cimicifuga simplex

Cirsium rivulare 'Atropurpureum'

Cistus × aguilari 'Maculatus'

Cistus creticus

Cistus × cyprius

CIMICIFUGA (Bugbane)

A genus of upright perennials grown for their distinctive bottlebrush-type flowers. Most suited to humus-rich soil which remains moist in a partially shaded situation.

C. simplex A perennial forming clumps of basal leaves, some tinged purple, carrying racemes of white flowers in late summer and autumn. 1m × 60cm/3 × 2ft

C. simplex 'Brunette' As for *C. simplex* but with deep purple foliage and flowers of off-white tinged purple. 1m × 60cm/3 × 2ft

CIRSIUM

Genus of biennials and perennials with thistle-like leaves and flowerheads of purple, red, yellow and occasionally white. Some species are invasive, spreading by rhizomes or self-seeding. Best in sun in moist soil.

C. rivulare 'Atropurpureum' A perennial composed of dark green, spiny leaves and flowerheads of deep crimson in summer. 1.2m × 60cm/4 × 2ft

CISTUS (Rock rose, Sun rose)

A genus of frost hardy, evergreen shrubs cultivated for their profusion of flowers in shades of pink and white, many of which carry blotches. Cistus thrive in fertile but well drained soil in a position in full sun. Tolerant of lime, they become chlorotic on heavy chalk. Young shoots should be pinched out to encourage bushiness. Replace old plants as they become leggy.

C. × aguilari 'Maculatus' A frost hardy shrub with sticky leaves of bright green and white flowers, blotched dark red at the base of each petal, in early summer. 1.2 × 1.2m/4 × 4ft

C. creticus A frost hardy shrub with veined leaves of mid-green and light mauve-pink flowers with yellow stamens in early summer. 1 × 1m/3 × 3ft

C. × cyprius A frost hardy shrub with narrow, sticky leaves of deep green and white flowers, blotched yellow and dark crimson at the base of each petal, in early summer. 1.5 × 1.5/5 × 5ft

C. 'Elma' A frost hardy, spreading shrub with shiny dark green leaves and white flowers with yellow stamens in early summer. 2 × 2m/6 × 6ft

C. × hybridus A frost hardy, bushy shrub with dark green leaves and pure white flowers with yellow centres from late spring to summer. 1 × 1.5m/3 × 5ft

C. 'Paladin' A frost hardy shrub with leaves of mid-green, grey-green on the undersides, and white flowers, blotched dark red at the base of each petal, in early summer. 1.5 × 1.5m/5 × 5ft

C. 'Peggy Sammons' A frost hardy, upright shrub of compact habit with leaves of grey-green and flowers of rosy-pink in early summer. 1 × 1m/3 × 3ft

C. × pulverulentus A frost hardy shrub with leaves of grey-green and pink flowers in early summer. 60cm × 1m/2 × 3ft

C. × purpureus A frost hardy shrub of compact habit with deep green leaves and flowers of dark pink, blotched with maroon, in early summer. 1 × 1m/3 × 3ft

Cistus 'Elma'

Cistus × *hybridus*

Cistus 'Peggy Sammons'

Cistus × *pulverulentus*

Cistus 'Paladin'

Cistus purpureus

Clarkia amoena

CLARKIA (Syn. Godetia)
Genus of annuals flowering in a wide range of pastel colours and grown as summer bedding or for cutting. Clarkia thrive in moist but well drained neutral to acidic soil.

C. amoena (Satin flower) An upright annual with fluted flowers, both single and double, in shades of pink in summer. 75 × 30cm/2.5 × 1ft

71

Clematis 'Abundance'

Clematis alpina 'Frances Rivis'

Clematis alpina 'Willy'

Clematis armandii

Clematis 'Barbara Dibley'

Clematis 'Barbara Jackman'

Clematis alpina 'Ruby'

CLEMATIS (Old man's beard)

Genus of hardy to half hardy, evergreen and deciduous climbers and perennials of which there are numerous cultivars. Because of the diversity of the species, habit and leaf form vary greatly, as does the ultimate height of climbers which is, in any case, affected by position and soil condition. Climbers, in the main, will attach themselves to hosts by means of leaf stalks. Clematis are cultivated for their decorative flowers and, in some instances, seedheads. They thrive in humus-rich, well drained soil in sun or part shade. Herbaceous species are best in full sun. Pruning is according to type based on three main groups. Pruning Group 1: Early flowering species – these include *alpina*, *macropetala*, *montana* and their cultivars. Little pruning beyond the removal of weak and dead stems once flowering is over. Pruning Group 2: Early and mid-season large flowered cultivars. A light prune back to strong buds with the removal of weak and dead stems before flowering commences. Pruning Group 3: Late flowering species and small flowered cultivars. These include *texensis* and *viticella* and their cultivars as well as herbaceous types. Cut back to ground level over winter.

C. 'Abundance' A hardy, late flowering climber with single flowers of purple-red from midsummer to late autumn. (Pr. 3) 3m/10ft

C. alpina 'Frances Rivis' A hardy, early flowering climber with semi-double flowers of mid-blue from spring to early summer. (Pr. 1) 3m/10ft

C. alpina 'Willy' A hardy, early flowering climber with pale pink flowers, deeper on the reverse, from spring to early summer. (Pr. 1) 3m/10ft

C. armandii A frost hardy, evergreen climber of vigorous habit with open saucer-shaped, scented white flowers in early spring. (Pr. 1) 5m/15ft

C. 'Barbara Dibley' A hardy, early flowering climber with deep red flowers, with darker central bar, fading, in early summer. (Pr. 2) 2.5m/8ft

C. 'Barbara Jackman' A hardy, early flowering climber with flowers of mauve with magenta central band in summer. (Pr. 2) 3m/10ft

Clematis chrysocoma

Clematis cirrhosa

Clematis 'Comtesse de Bouchaud'

Clematis 'Doctor Ruppel'

Clematis × durandii

Clematis 'Elsa Späth'

Clematis × eriostemon 'Hendersonii'

Clematis 'Ernest Markham'

C. chrysocoma A hardy, early flowering climber with flowers, similar to a montana, of soft pink. (Pr. 1) 5m/15ft

C. cirrhosa A frost hardy, evergreen, early flowering climber with cream flowers, spotted red on the insides, in late winter and early spring (Pr. 1) 2m/6ft

C. 'Comtesse de Bouchaud' A hardy, late flowering climber with pearly mauve-pink flowers in late summer (Pr. 3) 3m/10ft

C. 'Doctor Ruppel' A hardy, early flowering climber with flowers of dark rose-pink, with deeper central bands, in summer. (Pr. 2) 2.5m/8ft

C. × durandii A frost hardy, non-clinging, late flowering climber with flowers of dark indigo-blue in midsummer. (Pr. 3) 2m/6ft

C. 'Elsa Späth' A hardy, early flowering climber with flowers of mauve-blue in early summer. (Pr. 2) 3m/10ft

C. × erisotemon 'Hendersonii' A hardy, late flowering climber, of trailing habit, with flowers of violet-blue in late summer and early autumn. (Pr. 3) 3m/10ft

C. 'Ernest Markham' A hardy, late flowering climber with flowers of bright magenta in summer. Position in full sun. (Pr. 3) 3m/10ft

C. 'Etoile de Malicorne' A hardy, early flowering climber with flowers of deep violet-pink, with deeper central bar, in early summer. (Pr. 2) 3m/10ft

Clematis 'Etoile de Malicorne'

Clematis 'Etoile Rose'

Clematis 'Etoile Violette'

C. 'Etoile Rose' A hardy, late flowering climber with bell-shaped flowers of rose-pink in mid to late summer. (Pr. 3) 2.5m/8ft

C. 'Etoile Violette' A hardy, late flowering climber with violet-blue flowers and contrasting yellow anthers from midsummer to autumn. (Pr. 3) 3m/10ft

C. florida 'Flore Pleno' A frost hardy, semi-evergreen, late flowering climber with double flowers of green–white in summer. (Pr. 2) 4m/12ft

C. florida 'Sieboldii' A frost hardy, late flowering climber with flowers of creamy-white with large domes of deep purple stamens in summer. (Pr. 2) 2m/6ft

C. forsteri A frost hardy, semi-evergreen, early flowering climber with fragrant flowers of creamy-white. (Pr. 1) 3m/10ft

C. 'Général Sikorski' A hardy, mid-season flowering climber with flowers of overlapping blue sepals and cream anthers in early summer. (Pr. 2) 3m/10ft

C. 'Gipsy Queen' A hardy, late flowering climber with flowers of deep velvet-purple in summer. (Pr. 3) 3m/10ft

C. heracleifolia A hardy, late flowering perennial with flowers of mid-blue in summer and early autumn. (Pr. 3) 75cm × 1m/2.5 × 3ft

C. integrifolia A hardy, mid-season flowering perennial with bell-shaped, mid-blue flowers, followed with brown seedheads, in summer. (Pr. 3) 60 × 60cm/2 × 2ft

Clematis florida 'Flore Pleno'

Clematis forsteri

Clematis 'Général Sikorski'

Clematis florida 'Sieboldii'

Clematis 'Gipsy Queen'

Clematis heracleifolia

Clematis integrifolia

Clematis 'Jackmanii Superba'

Clematis × jouiniana 'Praecox'

Clematis 'Lady Northcliffe'

Clematis 'Lasurstern'

Clematis 'Lincoln Star'

C. 'Jackmanii Superba' A hardy, late flowering climber with flowers of violet-purple in mid and late summer. (Pr. 3) 3m/10ft

C. × *jouiniana* 'Praecox' A hardy, late flowering, non-clinging climber with small white flowers in late summer. (Pr. 3) 2m/6ft

C. 'Lady Northcliffe' A hardy, mid-season flowering climber with flowers of mauve-plum in midsummer. (Pr. 3) 3m/10ft

C. 'Lasurstern' A hardy, early flowering climber with large blue flowers in early summer. (Pr. 2) 2.5m/8ft

C. 'Lincoln Star' A hardy, early flowering climber with flowers of pale pink with deeper pink band in early summer. (Pr. 2) 2.5m/8ft

C. 'Lord Nevill' A hardy, early flowering climber with flowers of intense blue in early summer. (Pr. 2) 3m/10ft

C. *macropetala* 'Maidwell Hall' A hardy, early flowering climber with flowers of violet-blue in spring. (Pr. 1) 3m/10ft

C. *macropetala* 'Markham's Pink' A hardy, early flowering climber with flowers of deep sugar-pink in spring. (Pr. 1) 3m/10ft

C. 'Madame Julia Correvon' A hardy, late flowering climber with flowers of wine-red in late summer and early autumn. (Pr. 3) 3m/10ft

C. 'Margot Koster' A hardy, late flowering climber with flowers of rosy-pink in late summer. (Pr. 3) 3m/10ft

Clematis 'Lord Nevill'

Clematis 'Madame Julia Correvon'

Clematis macropetala 'Maidwell Hall'

Clematis macropetala 'Markham's Pink'

Clematis 'Margot Koster'

Clematis 'Marie Boisselot'

Clematis montana

Clematis montana 'Elizabeth'

Clematis montana var. *rubens*

Clematis montana 'Tetrarose'

C. 'Marie Boisselot' (syn. 'Madame le Coultre') A hardy, mid-season flowering climber with flowers of sheer white in midsummer. (Pr. 2) 3m/10ft

C. *montana* A hardy, vigorous, early flowering climber with white flowers in late spring and early summer. (Pr. 1) 5–14m/15–46ft

C. *montana* 'Elizabeth' A hardy, early flowering climber with fragrant, pale pink flowers in late spring and early summer. (Pr. 1) 7m/22ft

C. *montana* var. *rubens* A hardy, early flowering climber with pink flowers in late spring and early summer. (Pr. 1) 10m/30ft

C. *montana* 'Tetrarose' A hardy, early flowering climber with satin pink flowers in late spring and early summer. (Pr. 1) 5m/15ft

C. 'Mrs Cholmondeley' A hardy, early flowering climber with large flowers of pale lavender-blue in early summer. (Pr. 2) 3m/10ft

C. 'Nelly Moser' A hardy, early flowering climber with pink–mauve flowers, with darker central band, in early summer. Fades in sun. (Pr. 2) 3m/10ft

Clematis 'Mrs Cholmondeley'

Clematis 'Nelly Moser'

Clematis 'Niobe'

Clematis 'Perle d'Azur'

Clematis 'Princess of Wales'

C. 'Niobe' A hardy, early flowering climber with deep wine-red flowers in summer (Pr. 2) 3m/10ft

C. 'Perle d'Azur' A hardy, late flowering climber with flowers of azure-blue from midsummer to autumn. (Pr. 3) 3m/10ft

C. 'Princess of Wales' A hardy, late flowering climber with trumpet-shaped flowers of deep rose-pink in summer. (Pr. 3) 2m/6ft

C. 'Proteus' A hardy, early flowering climber with large, double mauve-pink flowers in early summer. Some single flowers in midsummer. (Pr. 2) 3m/10ft

C. *rehderiana* A hardy, late flowering climber with scented, bell-shaped flowers of pale lemon-yellow from midsummer to autumn. (Pr. 3) 3m/10ft

C. *tangutica* A hardy, late flowering climber with butter-yellow, bell-shaped flowers, followed with fluffy seedheads, in late summer and autumn. (Pr. 3) 6m/20ft

C. 'Ville de Lyon' A hardy, late flowering climber with carmine-red flowers in midsummer. (Pr. 3) 3m/10ft

C. *viticella* 'Purpurea Plena Elegans' A hardy, late flowering climber with double flowers of purple-mauve from midsummer to autumn. (Pr. 3) 3m/10ft

Clematis 'Proteus'

Clematis rehderiana

Clematis tangutica

Clematis viticella 'Ville de Lyon'

Clematis viticella 'Purpurea Plena Elegans'

Cleome hassleriana

Clerodendrum bungei

Clerodendrum trichotomum

CLEOME (Spider flower)

A genus of half-hardy to frost tender annuals and evergreen shrubs of which only the annuals are widely cultivated as summer bedding. For light, sandy soil in full sun.

C. hassleriana An upright frost tender annual with fragrant flowers in shades of white, pink and purple in summer.
1.2m × 45cm/4 × 1.5ft

CLERODENDRUM

A genus of hardy to frost tender deciduous and evergreen trees, shrubs and climbers grown for their flowers which are often scented. Position hardy and frost hardy species in full sun in humus-rich soil which does not dry out.

C. bungei (Glory flower) A frost hardy, deciduous shrub of suckering habit with erect shoots carrying rounded flowerheads of scented, deep rose-pink flowers in late summer and autumn. 2 × 2m/6 × 6ft

C. trichotomum A hardy, deciduous shrub or small tree of suckering habit with scented white flowers in late summer and early autumn and jewel-like, turquoise berries. 5 × 5m/15 × 5ft

CLETHRA (Sweet pepper bush)

Genus of hardy to half hardy deciduous and evergreen trees and shrubs grown in the main for their scented flowers of white or yellowish white. For rich, acidic soil in partial shade.

C. alnifolia A hardy, upright shrub of suckering habit carrying bell-shaped, scented white flowers in late summer and early autumn. 2.5 × 2.5m/8 × 8ft

Clianthus puniceus 'Roseus'

Clivia miniata

Cobaea scandens

COBAEA

A genus of frost tender, evergreen and herbaceous climbers cultivated either as conservatory plants or as annuals. Plant in a sheltered situation in full sun.

C. scandens (Cathedral bell) A fast growing, frost tender, evergreen climber grown as an annual. Scented, bell-shaped flowers, creamy-green maturing purple, are carried from summer to autumn. *C. f. alba* has white flowers. 10m/30ft

CLIANTHUS

A genus of frost hardy to frost tender, evergreen shrubs of trailing or climbing habit. For a sheltered situation in full sun or for a frost free conservatory or glasshouse.

C. puniceus 'Roseus' (Lobster claw) A frost hardy, evergreen shrub with deep, rose-pink flowers in early summer. Suitable for wall training. 4 × 3m/ 12 × 10ft

CLIVIA

A genus of frost tender, evergreen perennials most suited to a warm conservatory or as houseplants. In the open, clivias prefer humus-rich, free draining soil in part shade.

C. miniata A frost tender, evergreen perennial with long, strap-like leaves and tubular flowers in shades of orange, red and yellow in spring and summer. 45 × 30cm/1.5 × 1ft

CODONOPSIS

A genus of hardy to frost hardy, mainly perennials of twining habit grown for their unusual flowers. Best in well drained soil in sun or part shade.

C. clematidea A hardy perennial of twining habit with leaves of grey-green and slate-blue, bell flowers, marked on the inside with black, purple and yellow, in mid to late summer. 1.5m/5ft

Colchicum autumnale

Colchicum speciosum 'Album'

COLCHICUM (Autumn crocus)

A genus of hardy to half hardy, cormous perennials with goblet-shaped flowers, mainly blooming from autumn to spring, before the emergence of leaves which remain until midsummer. Most require a sunny position and are suitable for naturalizing in grass.

C. autumnale (Meadow saffron) A hardy, cormous perennial with lance-shaped leaves and lavender-pink goblet flowers in autumn. 10 × 8cm/6 × 3in

C. speciosum 'Album' A hardy, cormous perennial with lance-shaped leaves and goblet flowers of white in autumn. 10 × 8cm/6 × 3in

C. 'Waterlily' A hardy, cormous perennial with narrow leaves and double flowers in autumn of lilac-pink. 12 × 10cm/5 × 4in

COLUTEA (Bladder senna)

Genus of hardy to frost hardy deciduous shrubs and some trees cultivated for their yellow and orange-red flowers and bladder-like fruits. Best in full sun.

C. arborescens A hardy shrub of somewhat lax habit with fresh green leaves and racemes of yellow flowers in summer. These are followed with green, opaque seed-pods. 3 × 3m/10 × 10ft

COMMELINA (Widow's tears)

A genus of frost hardy to frost tender annuals and perennials. Frost hardy species require a sheltered situation in sun or part shade in well-drained soil. Apply a thick mulch in winter.

C. coelestis A frost hardy, clump forming perennial with bright blue flowers from late summer to mid-autumn. *C. coelestis* var. *alba* has white flowers. 1m × 45cm/3 × 1.5ft

Convolvulous althaeoides

Convallaria majalis

Convolvulus cneorum

Convolvulus sabatius

CONVALLARIA (Lily-of-the-valley)

A genus of rhizomatous perennials producing mainly white, fragrant, hanging bell-shaped flowers in spring. Suitable as ground cover in shady areas.

C. majalis A perennial of spreading rhizomes with scented, white bells produced in late spring on leafless stems. *C. majalis* var. *rosea* has mauve-pink flowers. 25 × 30cm/10in × 1ft

CONVOLVULUS (Bindweed)

A genus of hardy to frost tender scrambling perennials and evergreen shrubs and sub-shrubs, some species of which are troublesome weeds. Most will tolerate poor soil in full sun. Frost tender species may be overwintered in a cold glasshouse.

C. althaeoides A frost tender perennial with long trailing stems and pink flowers in summer over heart-shaped leaves. 5cm/2in × indefinite spread

C. cneorum A small, neat, frost tender shrub with silvery green leaves carrying white flowers, pink in bud, from late spring to summer. 60cm × 1m/2 × 3ft

C. sabatius A frost tender perennial of trailing habit with royal-blue flowers carried over mid-green leaves for a prolonged period in summer. 15 × 60cm/6in × 2ft

Cornus alba 'Aurea'

Cornus alba 'Elegantissima'

Cordyline australis 'Purpurea'

Coreopsis verticillata

CORDYLINE (Cabbage palm)

A genus of half hardy to frost tender evergreen shrubs and woody perennials grown mainly as houseplants or as specimens to be overwintererd in frost free conditions. Position in sun or part shade in soil which enjoys good drainage.
C. australis 'Purpurea' A half hardy, evergreen shrub of palm-like habit with strap-like leaves tinged with pale plum-purple. 3 × 1m/10 × 3ft

COREOPSIS (Tickseed)

A genus of hardy to frost tender annuals and perennials with daisy-like flowerheads in shades of bright yellow. Several species, such as *C. grandiflora*, are mainly grown as annuals.
C. verticillata A hardy, spreading perennial with narrow, mid green leaves and open, golden-yellow flowers in early summer. *C. verticillata* 'Moonbeam' produces flowers of palest lemon. 60 × 45cm/2 × 1.5ft

CORNUS (Dogwood)

A genus of hardy to frost hardy, deciduous shrubs and trees, and some woody perennials, cultivated in the main for their attractive bracts, foliage, colourful in autumn, fruits and, in some instances, brightly coloured stems, most conspicuous in wintertime. Some species prefer acidic soil, others are tolerant of a range of conditions.
C. alba 'Aurea' A hardy, deciduous shrub of upright habit with white flowers in spring to early summer and ornamental yellow leaves. 3 × 3m/10 × 10ft
C. alba 'Elegantissima' A hardy, deciduous shrub with broadly white-margined leaves of grey-green and young stems of brilliant red. Prune to ground level in early spring for best stem colour. 3 × 3m/10 × 10ft
C. alba 'Sibirica' A hardy, deciduous shrub with dark green leaves, colouring red in autumn, and young stems of bright red, most apparent in winter. Prune to ground level in early spring for best stem colour. 3 × 3m/10 × 10ft
C. alternifolia 'Argentea' (Pagoda dogwood) A hardy, deciduous shrub or small tree of spreading, tiered habit with mid-green leaves margined with white. Well suited to growing as a specimen. 3 × 2.5m/10 × 8ft

Cornus alba 'Sibirica'

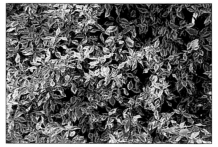

Cornus alternifolia 'Argentea'

Cornus canadensis

Cornus florida f. rubra

Cornus kousa var. chinensis

C. canadensis (Creeping dogwood) A ground hugging, hardy, deciduous perennial with mid-green leaves and white-green flowers, occasionally tinted pink, in late spring and early summer. These are followed by red fruits. Prefers acidic soil. 15cm/6in × indefinite spread.

C. florida f. rubra A hardy, deciduous shrub or tree with mid-green leaves colouring red-purple in autumn. Pink bracts in spring. 6 × 8m/20 × 25ft

C. kousa var. chinensis A hardy, deciduous tree with leaves of dark green colouring crimson in autumn and flower bracts of creamy-white maturing to red-pink in early summer. Red, strawberry-like fruits. 7 × 5m/22 × 15ft

C. mas (Cornelian cherry) A hardy, deciduous shrub of spreading habit. Dark green leaves colour wine-red and purple in autumn. Small yellow flowers appear on bare stems in late winter and early spring. Red berries in late summer. 5 × 5m/ 15 × 15ft

C. stolonifera 'Flaviramea' A hardy, deciduous shrub of suckering habit with leaves of dark green turning flame-coloured in autumn. White flowers in spring are followed by white fruits. Stems of yellow-green, most pronounced in winter. Hard prune in early spring for best stem colour. Tolerant of wet soil. 2 × 4m/6 × 12ft

Cornus mas

Cornus stolonifera 'Flaviramea'

Coronilla valentina

COROKIA

Genus of frost hardy, evergreen shrubs grown for their starry flowers and fruits in autumn. Position in full sun and afford some wall protection in cold areas.

C. cotoneaster (Wire netting bush) A frost hardy shrub of closely meshed branches carrying scented yellow flowers in late spring and red or yellow fruit in autumn. 2.5 × 2.5m/8 × 8ft

CORONILLA

A genus of hardy to frost hardy annuals, perennials, evergreen and deciduous shrubs grown for foliage and pea-like flowers, often scented. Place in full sun out of the reach of cold winds.

C. valentina A hardy, rounded evergreen shrub with fresh green leaves and scented, warm yellow flowers in late winter, early spring and again in summer. Seed-pods in autumn. 1.5 × 1.5m/5 × 5ft

Cortaderia selloana

Corydalis cheilanthifolia

Corydalis flexuosa

CORTADERIA (Pampas grass)

A genus of hardy to frost hardy, evergreen or semi-evergreen perennials forming clumps of narrow leaves, often grey-green, over which soar plume-like flower panicles in white, silver, gold or rose-pink in late summer and autumn. Cortaderia should be positioned in full sun and cut to ground level each spring to maintain healthy, vigorous plants.
C. selloana A hardy, evergreen perennial with leaves of mid-green and silvery-white or rose-pink flower panicles from late summer. 3 × 1.5m/10 × 5ft

CORTUSA

Genus of perennials with rounded leaves of deep green and bell-like flowers for moisture-retentive, humus-rich, neutral to acidic soil in partial shade. Cortusa will not tolerate hot, dry conditions.
C. matthioli A low growing perennial with rounded, hairy leaves over which are produced hanging flowers of deep purple-pink and magenta in late spring and early summer. Flowers may, on occasion, be white. 30 × 15cm/ 1ft × 6in

Corydalis lutea

Corydalis solida 'Beth Evans'

CORYDALIS

A genus of hardy to frost hardy annuals, biennials and perennials, a few of which are evergreen. Small, tubular flowers are carried over ferny leaves. Some species require full sun, others partial shade.
C. cheilanthifolia A hardy, evergreen perennial with light green leaves and deep yellow flowers in spring and summer. For sun or part shade. 30 × 25cm/1ft × 10in
C. flexuosa A hardy perennial with light green leaves and brilliant sky-blue flowers in spring and summer. Dies down after flowering. For part shade. 30 × 25cm/ 1ft × 10in
C. lutea A hardy, evergreen perennial with pale green leaves, grey-green on the undersides, and butter-yellow flowers from late spring to autumn. Unfussy as to conditions. Increase rapidly through self-seeding. 30 × 30cm/1 × 1ft
C. solida 'Beth Evans' A hardy perennial with grey-green leaves and pale pink flowers in spring. For full sun. 25 × 20cm/10 × 8in

Corylopsis pauciflora

Corylus 'Contorta'

Corylopsis sinensis var. *sinensis*

CORYLOPSIS

A genus of deciduous shrubs and small growing trees grown principally for their scented yellow flowers which appear on bare stems before the emergence of new leaves. For well drained, moist acidic soil. Prune, if required, immediately after flowering.

C. pauciflora A shrub of spreading habit with dark green leaves, blue-green on the undersides, and flowers of pale lemon in spring. 1.5 × 2.5m/5 × 8ft

C. sinensis var. *sinensis* An upright shrub of spreading habit with foliage of dark green, blue-green on the underside, and lemon-yellow flowers in spring. 4 × 4m/12 × 12ft

CORYLUS (Hazel)

A genus of deciduous trees and shrubs cultivated for their catkins and foliage. *C. avellana*, *C. maxima* and their cultivars are grown for their edible nuts. All species are tolerant of chalk.

C. 'Contorta' (Corkscrew hazel, Harry Lauder's walking stick) An upright tree bearing yellow catkins in spring on peculiarly twisted branches from which its common name is taken. 5 × 5m/15 × 15ft

Cosmos atrosanguineus

Cosmos 'Sensation'

Cotinus coggygria

Cotinus rubrifolius

COSMOS

A genus of frost hardy to frost tender annuals and perennials most widely grown either in containers or as summer bedding. Best in full sun.

C. atrosanguineus A frost hardy perennial with leaves of dark green and open, cup-shaped flowers of velvet-maroon from midsummer to autumn. Flowers are strongly scented of hot chocolate. Apply a heavy mulch in winter. 75 × 45cm/2.5 × 1.5ft

C. 'Sensation' A frost tender annual bearing flowers of pink, white or carmine-red in summer. 1m × 45cm/3 × 1.5ft

COTINUS (Smoke bush)

A genus of deciduous trees and shrubs valued for their foliage, colouring well in autumn, and for their panicles of small flowers which give the appearance of smoke clouds in summer.

C. coggygria (Venetian sumach) A spreading shrub or small tree with oval-shaped, mid-green leaves becoming flame-coloured in autumn. 5 × 5m/15 × 15ft

C. rubrifolius A spreading shrub or small tree with leaves of deep purple-red colouring vibrantly in autumn. 5 × 5m/15 × 15ft

Cotoneaster dammeri

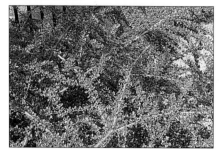

Cotoneaster horizontalis

Cotoneaster lacteus

Cotoneaster microphyllus

Cotoneaster salicifolius 'Exburyensis'

Cotoneaster salicifolius 'Rothschildianus'

Cotoneaster frigidus 'Cornubia'

COTONEASTER

A genus of deciduous, semi-evergreen shrubs and trees tolerant of a wide range of soil types and situations. Small flowers, usually white or in shades of pink, appear from spring to summer and are followed with ornamental fruits in autumn. Many species are well suited to wall training, others form good ground cover. The majority of species will not, if required, suffer from hard pruning.

C. dammeri A spreading, ground hugging evergreen shrub with dark green leaves, white flowers in early summer and red fruits in autumn. Best in sun. 1 × 2m/ 3 × 6ft

C. frigidus 'Cornubia' A semi-evergreen shrub of arching habit with dark green leaves, colouring in autumn, and white flowers in summer followed by an abudance of red fruits. 6 × 6m/20 × 20ft

C. horizontalis A deciduous shrub whose branches extend outward to form a herring-bone pattern. Shiny, dark green leaves, reddening in autumn, with pinky-white flowers in late spring followed by red fruits. 1 × 1.5m/3 × 5ft or more

C. lacteus An evergreen shrub with heavily veined, dark green leaves, the undersides of which are felted off-white. White summer flowers are followed by red fruits, lasting well into winter. 4 × 4m/12 × 12ft

C. microphyllus An evergreen shrub of somewhat stiff habit. Shiny, dark green leaves, grey-green on the undersides, and white flowers in early summer followed by magenta-red fruits. 1 × 1m/3 × 3ft

C. salicifolius 'Exburyensis' An evergreen, spreading shrub with heavily veined leaves of mid-green and white flowers in early summer. Pale yellow fruits, flushed pink in winter, follow the flowers. 5 × 5m/15 × 15ft

C. salicifolius 'Rothschildianus' An evergreen, spreading shrub with heavily veined leaves of pale green, white flowers in summer and deep, butter-yellow fruits from autumn into winter. 5 × 5m/15 × 15ft

Crambe cordifolia

Crambe maritima

CRAMBE

A genus of annuals and perennials grown mainly for their imposing foliage and attractive flowers. Best in full sun but tolerant of some shade.
C. cordifolia A woody based perennial with large, dark green basal leaves, dying down in late summer, and tall stems carrying many-branched panicles of small, scented flowers from late spring to midsummer. 2.5 × 1.5m/8 × 5ft
C. maritima (Seakale) A clump forming perennial with handsome, twisted leaves of blue-green and thick stems carrying racemes of white flowers in early summer. Leaf stems may be blanched and eaten as a vegetable. 75 × 60cm/2.5 × 2ft

Crassula sarcocaulis

Crataegus laevigata 'Paul's Scarlet'

CRASSULA

A genus of half hardy to frost tender annual and perennial succulents and evergreen succulent shrubs and sub-shrubs cultivated in the main for their leaves as well as for flowers.
C. sarcocaulis A frost hardy, perennial succulent with red flushed leaves of mid-green. Starry pink or white flowers in summer. For full sun.
30 × 30cm/1 × 1ft

CRATAEGUS (Hawthorn)

Genus of most often prickly, deciduous shrubs and trees, some of which may be semi-evergreen, grown as specimens or as hedging. *Crataegus* has a long period of interest, is extremely hardy and is tolerant of all conditions except that of waterlogged soil.
C. laevigata 'Paul's Scarlet' A deciduous tree of thorny stems and leaves of mid-green. Double-flowers of deep pink are borne in profusion in late spring. These are followed with red fruits. 8 × 8m/25 × 25ft
C. monogyna (May) A fast growing, deciduous tree with scented white flowers in late spring. Shiny, dark red fruits in autumn. Suitable for hedging.
10 × 8m/30 × 25ft

Crepis incana

Crinodendron hookerianum

Crinum powellii

CREPIS (Hawk's beard)

A genus of annuals and perennials of which some species are persistent weeds. Those in cultivation are suitable for the rock garden in full sun.
C. incana (Pink dandelion) A perennial forming a rosette of basal leaves above which are carried pink to magenta flowers in summer. 30 × 30cm/1 × 1ft

CRINODENDRON

A genus of evergreen shrubs and trees, hardy to −7°C (19°F), suitable for a sheltered, sunny situation. Requires acidic soil enriched with humus.
C. hookerianum (Lantern tree) A frost hardy, upright tree with leaves of dark green and lantern-shaped flowers of scarlet to carmine-pink from late spring to late summer. 6 × 5m/20 × 15ft

CRINUM

A genus of hardy to frost tender bulbous perennials. For well drained, humus-rich soil in full sun.
C. powellii A hardy, deciduous perennial with long, strappy leaves of lightish green and scented mid-pink flowers from late summer to autumn.
1.5m × 30cm/5 × 1ft

Crocosmia 'Lucifer'

Crocosmia 'Mount Usher'

Crocus chrysanthus 'Cream Beauty'

CROCOSMIA (Montbretia)

A genus of hardy to frost hardy cormous perennials with mainly ribbed, lance-shaped leaves and cultivated for their funnel-shaped flowers in a range of bright colours to include shades of gold, orange, red and yellow. Frost hardy species should be heavily mulched in winter.
C. 'Lucifer' A frost hardy, spreading perennial with arching stems carrying orange-red flowers in midsummer. 1.2m × 8cm/4ft × 3in
C. 'Mount Usher' A frost hardy perennial with flowers of golden-yellow borne on arching stems in midsummer. 60 × 8cm/2ft × 3in

Crocus chrysanthus 'Prins Claus'

Crocus tommasinianus

CROCUS

A genus of hardy to frost hardy, small cormous perennials grown in the main for their goblet-shaped flowers appearing, often before the narrow, lance-shaped leaves, from autumn to spring. Crocus species are suitable for naturalizing in short grass.
C. chrysanthus 'Cream Beauty' A hardy, cormous perennial with flowers of deep cream, golden-yellow at the throat, in spring. For full sun. 7 × 5cm/3 × 2in
C. chrysanthus 'Prins Claus' A hardy, cormous perennial with flowers of vivid purple and white in spring. For full sun. 7 × 5cm/3 × 2in
C. tommasinianus A hardy, cormous perennial with flowers of pale lilac from late winter to spring. Suitable for naturalizing. For full sun. 10 × 5cm/4 × 2in

Cucurbita

Cunninghamia lanceolata

× Cupressocyparis leylandii

CUCURBITA (Gourd)

A genus of frost tender annual and perennial climbers cultivated for their ornamental fruits (gourds) often used for decorative purposes indoors. Cucurbita requires fertile, well drained soil in full sun.
C. cucumerina A frost tender annual with white flowers in summer followed by gourd fruits. 3m/10ft

CUNNINGHAMIA (China fir)

A genus of evergreen, coniferous trees noteable for their fibrous bark of dark red-brown and pointed, narrow lance-shaped leaves. Suitable as a specimen in moist soil in sun or part shade. Tolerant of chalk.
C. lanceolata An upright, coniferous tree with shiny, green leaves, banded white on the undersides, and green-brown cones. 20 × 6m/70 × 20ft

× CUPRESSOCYPARIS

A hybrid genus of rapidly growing, evergreen, coniferous trees cultivated in the main either as specimen trees or as hedging.
× C. leylandii (Leyland cypress) A narrowing, coniferous tree with leaves of dark green, tinted blue-green. Dark brown cones. Frequently employed as a fast growing hedge. To 35 × 5m/ 120 × 15ft

Cupressus torulosa 'Cashmeriana'

Cyclamen coum

Cyclamen hederifolium

CUPRESSUS (Cypress)

A genus of hardy to half hardy, evergreen coniferous trees cultivated mainly as specimens. Suitable for any well drained soil in full sun.
C. torulosa 'Cashmeriana' (Kashmir cypress) A frost tender, coniferous tree with red-brown bark and long, hanging sprays of bright, blue-green leaves. Green-brown cones. To 30 × 10m/ 100 × 30ft

CYCLAMEN (Sowbread)

A genus of hardy to frost tender, tuberous perennials flowering, according to the species, all through the year. Frost hardy to frost tender species are suitable for cultivation in a cool glasshouse. Grow cultivars of *C. persicum* as houseplants.
C. coum A hardy, tuberous perennial with shiny leaves, often marked with silver, and flowers in shades of carmine, pink and white in late winter and early spring. 8 × 10cm/3 × 4in
C. hederifolium A hardy, tuberous perennial with triangular-shaped leaves, tinged purple on the undersides, and flowers in shades of pink with maroon markings in autumn before the emergence of the leaves. 10 × 15cm/4 × 6in

Cydonia oblonga

CYDONIA (Quince)

A genus of a single species of deciduous shrub or tree cultivated for its open cup-shaped flowers and ornamental fruits, edible when cooked. Not to be confused with *Chaenomeles*.
C. oblonga (Common quince) A rounded shrub or tree with leaves of dark green and pale pink or white flowers in late spring. Fruits ripening in autumn. For full sun. 5 × 5m/15 × 15ft

Cytisus battandieri

Cynara 'Scolymus'

CYNARA

Genus of hardy to frost hardy perennials cultivated as much for foliage as for flower. Some species possess edible leaves and flowerheads. Thistle-like flowers may be dried. Best in full sun.
C. 'Scolymus' (Globe artichoke) A hardy perennial with leaves of grey-green, woolly-white on the undersides, and purple flowerheads in late summer. Buds of these may be cooked as a vegetable. 2 × 1.2m/6 × 4ft

CYTISUS (Broom)

A genus of hardy to frost tender, deciduous and evergreen shrubs, very occasionally small trees, grown for their profusion of pea-like flowers, sometimes scented. Suitable for most well-drained soils in full sun but best in acidic conditions.
C. battandieri (Pineapple broom) A frost hardy, deciduous shrub of upright habit with silvery-grey leaves and racemes of scented, yellow flowers in summer. Suitable for wall training.
5 × 5m/15 × 15ft
C. × kewensis A hardy, low growing deciduous shrub with arching stems carrying flowers of pale cream in late spring. 30cm × 1.5m/1 × 5ft
C. × praecox 'Allgold' A hardy, deciduous shrub with flowers of deep yellow in spring. 1.2 × 1.5m/4 × 5ft

Cytisus × kewensis

Cytisus × praecox 'Allgold'

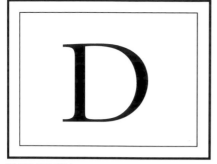

Dactylorhiza hybrid

DABOECIA

A genus of hardy to half hardy, evergreen shrubs for acidic soil in full sun. Grown for racemes of urn-shaped flowers and dark green foliage. Useful as ground cover in the rock garden.
D. cantabrica (St. Dabeoc's heath) A hardy, prostrate shrub carrying pink-purple flowers in summer over leaves of dark green, silvery beneath. 25 × 60cm/10in × 2ft

DACTYLORHIZA (Spotted orchid)

A genus of tuberous, perennial orchids grown for their mid-green leaves, occasionally spotted, and flowers in shades of pink, purple, red and white. For moist, humus-rich soil in part shade.
D. foliosa A perennial orchid with leaves of mid-green, sometimes spotted with brown or purple markings, and flowers in late spring and early summer of pink and mid-purple. 60 × 15cm/2ft × 6in

Dahlia – Decorative

Dahlia – 'Gerrie Hoek'

Dahlia merckii

Dahlia 'Moonfire'

Dahlia – Cactus

Dahlia – Pompon

DAHLIA

A genus of mainly tuberous, frost hardy to frost tender perennials of which there are numerous cultivars. Dahlias are grown for their flowerheads, in variety, and which divide into the following groups: single, waterlily, collerette, anemone, pompon, ball, semi-cactus, cactus, decorative, orchid and peony. Colours fall into the range of orange, pink, purple, red, yellow and white. Dahlias are suitable as border plants, as bedding or for exhibition purposes. Best in humus-rich, well drained soil in full sun. Overwinter tubers, after the first frosts, by lifting, drying off and storing in dry peat or sand in a frost free place.
D. Decorative Tuberous, half hardy perennials distinguished by fully double flowerheads without central disc and with broad, slightly incurved ray-florets in the full colour range from miniature to giant size.
D. Cactus Tuberous, half hardy perennials distinguished by fully double flowerheads with narrow, outwardly curved ray-florets in the full colour range from miniature to giant size.
D. Pompon Tuberous, half hardy perennials distinguished by fully double, spherical flowerheads with inwardly curved ray-florets in the full colour range in miniature size.
D. 'Gerrie Hoek' A tuberous, half hardy perennial with waterlily flowerheads of silver-pink. Flowers freely. 1.2m × 60cm/4 × 2ft
D. merckii A tuberous, hardy perennial with many slender stems carrying saucer-shaped flowers in shades of pink, purple or white from summer to autumn. Mulch heavily in winter. 1 × 1m/3 × 3ft
D. 'Moonfire' A tuberous, half hardy perennial with dark leafed foliage and flowers of soft apricot and vermilion. 60 × 60cm/2 × 2ft

Danae racemosa

DANAE

A genus of a single species of frost hardy, shrub-like, evergreen perennial cultivated for its foliage and fruit. Reduce old stems to ground level in spring.

D. racemosa (Alexandrian laurel) A frost hardy perennial with lance-shaped, shiny green leaves and small green-yellow flowers in early summer. These are followed with orange red-berries.
1 × 1m/3 × 3ft

Daphne bholua

DAPHNE

Genus of hardy to frost hardy, deciduous, semi-evergreen or evergreen shrubs valued for their most often scented flowers, foliage and fruit as well as for their neat growth habit. Daphnes require well drained, humus-rich soil which does not dry out. Mulch to keep roots cool in summer. Best in neutral to alkaline soil, rather than acidic. Daphnes resent disturbance and may prove to be short-lived for no apparent reason.

D. bholua A hardy, deciduous or evergreen shrub of upright habit with slender, shiny, dark green leaves and clusters of heavily scented, white flowers, tinged pink, in late winter followed by purple-black fruit. 2 × 1m/6 × 3ft

D. burkwoodii 'Carol Mackie' A hardy, semi-evergreen shrub of upright habit with leaves of mid-green narrowly edged golden-yellow, later cream, and clusters of scented white flowers, tinged pink, in late spring and occasionally for a second time in autumn. 1.2 × 1.2m/4 × 4ft

D. cneorum 'Exima' (Garland flower) A hardy, evergreen shrub of low habit. Dark green leaves, grey-green beneath, bear flowers of rose-pink, crimson in bud, in late spring. 20cm × 2m/8in × 6ft

D. mezereum A hardy, deciduous shrub with lance-shaped leaves of light green and clusters of scented pink and lilac-pink flowers in late winter and early spring. Flowers are followed with red fruits. 1.2 × 1m/4 × 3ft

D. odora A frost hardy, evergreen shrub of upright habit with shiny, dark green leaves and clusters of scented lilac-pink and white flowers from late winter to early spring followed by red fruits. 1.5 × 1.5m/5 × 5ft

D. pontica A hardy, evergreen shrub of spreading habit with shiny, dark green leaves and clusters of scented yellow flowers, tinged green, in spring followed by black fruit. 1 × 1.5m/3 × 5ft

D. tangutica A hardy, evergreen shrub of upright habit with lance-shaped leaves of dull green and clusters of purple or white-flushed pink flowers in late spring and early summer followed by red fruit. 1 × 1m/3 × 3ft

Daphne burkwoodii 'Carol Mackie'

Daphne cneorum 'Exima'

Daphne mezereum

Daphne pontica

Daphne tangutica

Daphne odora

Darmera peltata (flower)

Darmera peltata (foliage)

Davidia involucrata

DARMERA (syn. Peltiphyllum)

A genus of a single species of rhizomatous perennials of large leaves appearing after the starry flowers. Best in moisture retentive soil in sun or part shade.

D. peltata A spreading perennial with large, veined leaves of dark green and flowers of white and bright pink in late spring. 1 × 1m/3 × 3ft

DECAISNEA

A genus of deciduous shrubs mainly grown for their pinnate leaves and bean-like hanging fruits. Afford some shelter from strong winds and protect young foliage from late frosts.

D. fargesii A deciduous shrub of upright habit with dark green leaves, petalless yellow-green flowers in summer and dull blue-grey fruits in autumn.
6 × 6m/20 × 20ft

DAVIDIA (Handkerchief tree)

A genus of a single species of deciduous tree cultivated for its remarkable flowerheads surrounded by drooping white bracts. Best afforded some shelter from strong winds.

D. involucrata A deciduous tree of conical habit with red-stalked, heart-shaped leaves of mid-green and white flowerheads in late spring.
15 × 10m/50 × 30ft

Delphinium 'Emily Hawkins'

DELPHINIUM

A genus of annuals, biennials and perennials with basal leaves and spires of cup-shaped flowers in a wide range of colours for a situation in full sun out of the reach of strong winds. Cultivars may be divided into three main groups: Belladonna, Elatum and Pacific Hybrids.

D. 'Alice Artindale' An Elatum group perennial with spikes of fully double violet-blue flowers in early and midsummer. Slow to establish. 1.5m × 60cm/5 × 2ft

D. 'Emily Hawkins' An Elatum group perennial with semi-double, pale violet-mauve flowers in early and midsummer. 1.7m × 60cm/5.5 × 2ft

Delphinium 'Alice Artindale'

Dendranthema 'Corngold'

Dendranthema 'Golden Lady'

Dendranthema 'Nathalie'

Dendranthema 'Matthew Woolman'

Dendranthema 'Ruby Mound'

Dendranthema 'Julia'

DENDRANTHEMA

A genus of hardy to frost tender annuals and perennials, commonly known as Chrysanthemum, grown in the main for their colourful flowerheads and used for border display, for bedding and for exhibition purposes. Grow in a sunny situation and give protection to frost tender species. Most often dendranthema are grouped according to flowerhead form. These are single, incurved, intermediate, reflexed, fully reflexed, anemone-centred, pompon, spoon-shaped, quill-shaped and spider.
D. 'Corngold' A hardy perennial of intermediate flowerhead. Flowers, in late summer and early autumn, are of deep golden-yellow. 1.2m/4ft
D. 'Golden Lady' A hardy perennial of incurved flowerhead. Flowers, in late summer and early autumn, are of rich gold. 1.2/4ft
D. 'Julia' A hardy perennial of single flowerhead. Flowers, in late summer and early autumn, are of pale to deep rose-pink with central yellow disc. 1.2m/4ft
D. 'Nathalie' A hardy perennial of reflexed flowerhead. Flowers, in late summer and early autumn, are of deep crimson-red. 1m/3ft
D. 'Matthew Woolman' A hardy perennial of reflexed flowerhead. Flowers, in late summer and early autumn, are of mid to deep pink. 1.2m/4ft
D. 'Ruby Mound' A hardy perennial of reflexed flowerhead. Flowers, in late summer and early autumn, are of deep ruby-red. 1.2m/4ft

DESFONTAINIA

A genus of a single species of frost hardy, evergreen shrub for moist, acidic soil in a cool, partially shaded situation out of the reach of cold winds.

D. spinosa A frost hardy, evergreen shrub of dense, bushy habit bearing thin, tubular red flowers, tipped yellow, from midsummer to early autumn. 2 × 2m/ 6 × 6ft

Deutzia × elegantissima 'Rosealind'

Deutzia × hybrida 'Mont Rose'

Deutzia monbeigii

DEUTZIA

A genus of hardy to frost hardy, largely deciduous shrubs grown for their small, starry flowers, often scented, carried, according to species, from late spring to midsummer. Unfussy as to soil condition, deutzias prefer a position in full sun although will tolerate partial shade.

D. × elegantissima 'Rosealind' A hardy, deciduous shrub of upright habit. Flowers, of white flushed with pink, are carried over dull, mid-green leaves in late spring and early summer. 1.2 × 1.5m/4 × 5ft

D. × hybrida 'Mont Rose' A hardy, deciduous shrub with leaves of dark green and flowers, of white flushed pale mauve, in late spring and early summer. 1.2 × 1.2m/ 4 × 4ft

D. monbeigii A hardy, deciduous shrub of arching habit. White flowers are carried over dark green leaves in early and midsummer. 1.2 × 1.5m/4 × 5ft

D. setchuenensis var. *corymbiflora* A frost hardy, deciduous shrub with peeling bark, grey-green leaves and white flowers in midsummer. 2 × 1.5m/6 × 5ft

Deutzia setchuenensis var. *corymbiflora*

Dianthus barbatus

Dianthus deltoides

Dianthus 'Doris'

Dianthus gratianopolitanus

Dianthus 'Gravetye Gem'

DIANTHUS (Carnation, Pink)

A genus of mainly hardy, with the exception of perpetual flowering and Malmaison carnations, annuals, biennials, perennials and evergreen sub-shrubs usually with lance-shaped leaves, often grey-green, grown principally for their long-lasting flowers in summer. The majority will thrive in neutral to alkaline soil, although some alpine and biennial species prefer acid soil, in full sun.

Carnations are divided into perpetual-flowering, or florists' carnations and border carnations. Perpetual-flowering are frost tender to frost hardy with crinkly-edged flowers in various colours and are grown mainly in glasshouses: up to 1.2m × 30cm/4 × 1ft. Border carnations vary from half-hardy to hardy with flowers in a large range of colours and bicolours, which they bear once in midsummer: 30cm–1m × 30–45cm/1–3ft × 1–1.5ft. Old-fashioned pinks are very hardy, not as large as carnations, generally making a low, spreading mat up to 45cm/1.5ft across. They bear masses of scented flowers once in midsummer. Modern pinks usually make taller plants, are hardy and will flower two or three times during the summer.

D. barbatus (Sweet William) A hardy, short-lived perennial, often grown as a biennial, with flat clusters of flowers, in shades of pink, red and white, often bicoloured, in late spring and early summer. 45 × 30cm/1.5 × 1ft

D. deltoides (Maiden pink) A hardy, carpeting perennial with leaves of dark green and flowers of deep pink, red or white, usually with a darker eye, in summer. 20 × 30cm/8in × 1ft

D. 'Doris' A hardy perennial with bicoloured, scented, double flowers of pale pink with deeper pink centre in summer. 30 × 30cm/1 × 1ft

D. gratianopolitanus A hardy, carpeting perennial with highly scented, deep pink flowers in summer. 15 × 30cm/6in × 1ft

D. 'Gravetye Gem' A hardy perennial with scented flowers of deep crimson with lighter pink markings in summer. 15 × 30cm/6in × 1ft

D. 'La Bourboule' A hardy perennial with scented flowers of clear pink, the petals of which are fringed, in summer. 10 × 20cm/4 × 8 in

D. 'Mrs. Sinkins' A hardy perennial with sweetly fragrant, double flowers of pure white with fringed petals in summer. 30 × 30/1 × 1ft

D. 'Rose de Mai' A hardy perennial with double flowers of pale and deeper pink in summer. 30 × 30cm/8in × 1ft

Dianthus 'La Bourboule'

Dianthus 'Mrs Sinkins'

Dianthus 'Rose de Mai'

Diascia barberae 'Ruby Field'

DIASCIA

A genus of annuals and semi-evergreen, occasionally evergreen perennials, the majority of which are hardy to around −8°C (18°F), grown for their flowers produced over a prolonged period in summer. Best in full sun.

D. barberae 'Ruby Field' A low growing perennial with heart-shaped leaves and flowers of salmon-pink produced in profusion from summer to autumn. 25 × 60cm/10in × 2ft

D. vigilis A perennial of suckering habit with racemes of clear pink flowers from early summer to autumn. Amongst the hardiest of all species. 30 × 60cm/1 × 2ft

Diascia vigilis

DICENTRA

A genus of annuals and perennials cultivated for their much divided, fern-like leaves, sometimes grey-green, and arching stems of heart-shaped flowers in shades of pink, purple, red, yellow or white. Most require humus-rich soil, neutral to alkaline, in a partially shaded situation. Small species are well suited to the rock garden or alpine house.

D. 'Bacchanal' A perennial wth finely cut leaves of mid-green producing racemes of deep blood-red flowers in spring. 45 × 30cm/1.5 × 1ft

D. cucullaria (Dutchman's breeches) A low growing perennial with leaves of grey-green and racemes of tiny white, tinged pink, flowers in early spring. Requires good drainage. Keep dry during summer dormancy. 20 × 25cm/8 × 10in

D. 'Langtrees' A vigorous perennial with leaves of silver-grey and racemes of white flowers, flushed pink, from mid-spring to midsummer. 30 × 45/1 × 1.5ft

D. spectabilis (Bleeding heart) A perennial with leaves of fresh green and racemes of rose-pink and white flowers in late spring and early summer. 1m × 45cm/3 × 1.5ft

D. 'Spring Morning' A perennial with leaves of mid-green and racemes of pale, pearly-pink flowers in late summer and early autumn. 30 × 45cm/1 × 1.5ft

D. 'Stuart Boothman' A perennial with leaves of grey-green and deep pink flowers from mid-spring to midsummer. 30 × 45cm/1 × 1.5ft

Dicentra 'Bacchanal'

Dicentra cucullaria

Dicentra 'Langtrees'

Dicentra 'Spring Morning'

Dicentra spectabilis

Dicentra 'Stuart Boothman'

DICKSONIA

A genus of frost hardy to frost tender, evergreen or semi–evergreen ferns for cultivation as specimen plants in a cool conservatory, glasshouse or outside in favoured situations. Best in humus-rich, acidic soil in part or full shade.

D. antarctica (Soft tree fern) A frost hardy, often evergreen tree fern with stout trunk from which open pale green fronds, darkening in maturity. 6 × 4m/ 20 × 12ft but usually considerably less

DICTAMNUS (Burning bush)

A genus of a single species of woody perennial. Aromatic oil, contained in the flower stamens and unripened seeds, is volatile and may be set light in hot weather.

D. albus var. *purpureus* A perennial of lemony-scented leaves and flowers of lilac-mauve with darker veining in early summer. 60 × 60cm/2 × 2ft

Dictamnus albus var. *purpureus*

Dierama pulcherrimum

DIERAMA (Angel's fishing rod)

A genus of frost hardy to half hardy, evergreen, cormous perennials with grass-like leaves and bell flowers carried along the length of arching stems in summer. For full sun in humus-rich soil. Taller growing species are effective beside water.

D. pulcherrimum A frost hardy perennial with hanging flowers in shades of pink, purple-red or white in summer. 1–1.5m × 60cm/3–5 × 1ft

DIERVILLA (Bush honeysuckle)

A genus of suckering, deciduous shrubs cultivated for their yellow flowers. Well suited to the shrub or woodland garden. *D. sessilifolia* A suckering shrub with leaves of mid-green and flowers of sulphur-yellow in summer. 1 × 1.5m/ 3 × 5ft

Digitalis grandiflora

Digitalis × mertonensis

Digitalis parviflora

Digitalis ferruginea

DIGITALIS (Foxglove)

A genus of hardy to frost hardy, tall growing biennials and short-lived perennials with distinctive tubular flowers, often spotted on the inside. Best in partial shade although tolerant of most conditions and situations. Avoid extremes of wet and dry soils. Some species will self-seed freely and are, therefore, suitable for naturalizing.

D. ferruginea (Rusty foxglove) A hardy biennial or perennial with rosettes of dark green leaves and racemes of brown flowers, veined brown-red on the inside, in mid-summer. 1.2m × 45cm/4 × 1.5ft

D. grandiflora A hardy biennial or perennial with veined leaves of mid-green and racemes of pale lemon flowers, veined brown on the inside, in early and midsummer. 1m × 45cm/3 × 1.5ft

D. × mertonensis A hardy perennial with veined leaves of shiny, dark green and racemes of crushed strawberry-pink flowers in late spring and early summer. 1m × 30cm/3 × 1ft

D. parviflora A hardy perennial with leaves of deep green and racemes of orange-brown flowers, with dark purple lip, in early summer. 60 × 30cm/2 × 1ft

D. purpurea (Common foxglove) A hardy biennial or short-lived perennial with rosettes of dark green leaves and spikes of purple, pink or white flowers, spotted inside, in early summer. Easily grown from self-sown seed. 1.2m × 30cm/4 × 1ft

D. purpurea 'Sutton's Apricot' A hardy, perennial hybrid with apricot-like flowers in early summer. 1.2m × 30cm/4 × 1ft

Digitalis purpurea

Digitalis purpurea 'Sutton's Apricot'

Dionysia aretioides

Disanthus cercidifolius (autumn foliage)

DIONYSIA

A genus of sub-shrubby, evergreen perennials for cultivation in an alpine house or the rock garden where they should be protected from excessive wet. Best in full sun.

D. aretioides A low growing, hummock forming perennial with thin, grey-green leaves and fragrant, deep yellow flowers in spring. 7 × 30cm/3in × 1ft

DIPELTA

A genus of deciduous shrubs cultivated for their ornamental, peeling bark, scented tubular flowers and paper-like bracts surrounding fruits. For alkaline soil in sun or partial shade.

D. floribunda An upright, deciduous shrub with lance-shaped, pointed leaves of fresh green and pale pink flowers in late spring and early summer. 4 × 4m/ 12 × 12ft

DISANTHUS

A genus of a single species of deciduous shrub cultivated in the main for its vividly coloured autumnal foliage. For humus-rich, acidic soil in sun or part shade. Protect young shoots from damage by late frosts.

D. cercidifolius A deciduous shrub with blue-green leaves colouring flame in autumn. Lightly scented spider-like flowers of rose-red in autumn. 3 × 3m/ 10 × 10ft

DISPORUM (Fairy bells)

A genus of hardy to frost tender perennials with arching stems of mid-green leaves, carried alternately, and hanging tubular flowers followed by small berries. For partial shade in humus-rich soil.

D. sessile A hardy perennial of lance-shaped leaves and creamy-white, green-tipped flowers in late spring and early summer. Black berries in autumn. 60 × 60cm/2 × 2ft

Dodecatheon meadia

Dodecatheon meadia f. album

Doronicum columnae

DODECATHEON (Shooting stars)

A genus of principally hardy perennials grown for their hanging, cyclamen-like flowers and well suited to the rock or woodland garden. Keep moist in the growing season.

D. meadia A hardy perennial forming clumps of mid-green leaves over which are carried umbels of rich-rose flowers in mid and late spring. 25 × 15cm/10 × 6in

D. meadia f. *album* A hardy perennial similar to *D. meadia* but with flowers of creamy-white with darker centres. 25 × 15cm/10 × 6in

DORONICUM (Leopard's bane)

A genus of perennials grown for their bright, daisy-type flowers of yellow and gold. Generally unfussy but best in moisture retentive soil in part shade.

D. columnae A perennial forming clumps of mid-green, basal leaves over which are carried thin stems of butter yellow, daisy flowers in spring and early summer. 60 × 30cm/2 × 1ft

Dorycnium hirsutum

DORYCNIUM (Lotus)

A genus of hardy to frost tender annuals, short-lived perennials and deciduous, semi-evergreen and evergreen sub-shrubs for full sun. Suitable for a wide range of positions. Trailing species may be included in summer hanging baskets.

D. hirsutum A hardy to frost hardy, evergreen or semi-evergreen sub-shrub with leaves of grey-green and umbels of pea-like, off-white flowers in summer and early autumn. 60cm × 1m/2 × 3ft

DRABA (Whitlow grass)

A genus of annuals and evergreen or semi-evergreen perennials forming rosettes of linear, oblong or spoon-shaped leaves carrying racemes of cross-shaped flowers. Well suited to the alpine house, rock garden or scree bed. Protect from excessive wet.

D. mollissima A mound-forming, evergreen perennial with hairy, oblong leaves and racemes of tiny, brilliant yellow flowers in late spring. 8 × 20cm/3 × 8in

Dracunculus vulgaris

DRACUNCULUS (Dragon's arum)

A genus of frost hardy, tuberous perennials cultivated for their large spathes, smelling unpleasantly, and dark green leaves, sometimes white mottled. Generally hardy if planted in a sheltered spot in full sun. In cold areas protect over winter with a mulch.

D. vulgaris A frost hardy, tuberous perennial forming clumps of dark purple, mottled leaves and producing deep maroon spathes with upright spadices in late spring or early autumn. 1m × 60cm/3 × 2ft

Dorotheanthus bellidiformis

DOROTHEANTHUS (Livingstone daisy)

A genus of half hardy, succulent annuals producing daisy-like flowers in many shades of orange, pink, red, yellow and white throughout the summer. Position in poorish soil in full sun.

D. bellidiformis (syn. *Mesembryanthemum*) A half hardy annual of low growing habit. Many flowers of various colours, but mainly pinks, reds, yellows and white, in summer. 15 × 30cm/6in × 1ft

Dregea sinensis

Drimys lanceolata

DREGEA (syn. Wattakaka)

A genus of frost hardy, evergreen climbers grown for their bowl-shaped, scented yellow or white flowers. For a sheltered situation in well drained soil in sun or part shade.

D. sinensis A frost hardy climber with heart-shaped leaves of mid-green, the undersides of which are downy-grey, producing scented, cream flowers, pink with red markings inside, in summer. 3m/10ft

DRIMYS

A genus of frost hardy, evergreen shrubs and trees with handsome, aromatic leaves and small, starry flowers. Likely to prove hardy when positioned in a sheltered spot surrounded with protective trees and shrubs.

D. lanceolata A frost hardy, upright shrub or small tree. Shiny, dark green leaves and clusters of white flowers in spring. 4 × 2.5m/12 × 8ft

D. winteri (Winter's bark) A frost hardy, upright small tree with aromatic bark, leaves of dark green, blue-white on the undersides, and scented, light cream flowers in spring and early summer. 15 × 10m/50 × 30ft

Dryas octopetala

Dryopteris filix-mas

Dunalia australis

DRYAS (Mountain avens)

A genus of spreading, evergreen sub-shrubs with oak-like, dark green leaves and open flowers followed with seedheads. Well suited to the rock garden or to clothe a low retaining wall. Thrives with good drainage.

D. octopetala A carpeting sub-shrub with scalloped leaves and small pale cream flowers with yellow stamens in late spring and early summer. 10cm × 1m/4in × 3ft

DRYOPTERIS (Buckler fern)

A genus of mainly hardy, frost hardy and frost tender perennial ferns. Most are deciduous although some will retain their fronds during mild winters. Prefer humus-rich soil in part shade.

D. filix-mas (Male fern) A hardy, deciduous fern with fronds of mid-green rising from a central rhizome. 1.2 × 1.2m/3 × 3ft

DUNALIA (syn. Acnistus)

A genus of half hardy, fast growing, deciduous shrubs producing hanging, trumpet-like flowers held on short stems over dull, mid green leaves. Cultivated principally as a half hardy annual when it will flower from seed within a season. Best in sun.

D. australis A half hardy, deciduous shrub producing Brugmansia-like flowers in violet-purple and white in midsummer. 1.2 × 1.2m/4 × 4ft

Eccremocarpus scaber

Echeveria elegans

Eccremocarpus scaber f. *carmineus*

ECCREMOCARPUS (Chilean glory flower)

A genus of frost hardy to frost tender evergreen or herbaceous climbing perennials grown for their brilliantly coloured, tubular flowers. Suitable for cultivation in a cool conservatory or glasshouse or outdoors in full sun where best treated as an annual.

E. scaber A rapidly growing, frost hardy evergreen climber producing bright, orange-red flowers from late spring to autumn. *E.s.* f. *carmineus* is a red form. 3m/10ft

ECHEVERIA

A genus of frost tender, evergreen succulents and sub-shrubs, some of which are occasionally deciduous. Grown principally as houseplants, in cool glasshouses or as container plants. Some species are suitable for summer bedding schemes or as edging.

E. elegans A frost tender, evergreen succulent with rounded leaves of silver-blue producing single stems of pink flowers with yellow tips, orange shaded inside, from late winter to early summer. 5 × 45cm/2in × 1.5ft

Echinacea purpurea

ECHINACEA (Coneflower)

Genus of perennials carrying solitary, daisy-type flowers on stiff stems, in shades of pink, purple, red and white, with dark green leaves. Best in full sun although tolerant of part shade.

E. purpurea An upright perennial producing flowerheads of purple-red with cone-shaped disc of golden-brown from midsummer to early autumn. 1.2m × 45cm/ 4 × 1.5ft

E. purpurea 'Robert Bloom' An upright perennial producing flowerheads of mauve-red with cone-shaped disc of orange brown from midsummer to early autumn. 1.2m × 45cm/4 × 1.5ft

E. purpurea 'White Swan' An upright perennial producing white flowerheads with orange-brown disc from midsummer to early autumn. 60 × 45cm/2 × 1.5ft

Echinacea purpurea 'White Swan'

Echinops bannaticus

Echinops bannaticus 'Taplow Blue'

Echium vulgare 'Blue Bedder'

ECHINOPS (Globe thistle)
A genus of hardy to frost hardy annuals, biennials and perennials distinguished by spiny leaves, most often grey-green, and spherical flowerheads in shades of blue, grey and white. Tolerant of most soils and situations.
E. bannaticus A hardy perennial forming clumps of grey-green leaves above which rise tall stems of metallic-blue flowerheads in mid to late summer. *E.b.* 'Taplow Blue' has bright blue flowerheads. 1m × 60cm/3 × 2ft

ECHIUM
A genus of hardy to frost tender annuals and evergreen biennials and perennials. For full sun.
E. vulgare 'Blue Bedder' (Viper's bugloss) A hardy biennial with lance-shaped, bristly leaves and short spikes of light blue flowers, becoming pinkish, in early summer. 45 × 30cm/1.5 × 1ft

EDGEWORTHIA (Paper bush)
A genus of frost hardy to frost tender, deciduous or evergreen shrubs with distinctive papery bark and tubular flowers. For a cool glasshouse, against a warm wall or in a favourably sheltered situation in full sun or slight shade.
E. chrysantha A frost hardy, deciduous shrub of open habit with dark green leaves and scented, rounded flowerheads of butter-yellow in late winter and early spring. 1.5 × 1.5m/5 × 5ft

Edgeworthia chrysantha

Eichhornia crassipes

EICHHORNIA (Water hyacinth)
A genus of hardy, to 1°C/34°F, marginal to deep water aquatic perennials cultivated for the tropical aquarium or for outdoor ornamental pools and ponds in full sun.
E. crassipes A half hardy to hardy aquatic perennial to float on the surface of water. Pale blue to violet flower spikes are carried over rosettes of rounded leaves in summer. 45 × 45cm/1.5 × 1.5ft

Elaeagnus angustifolia

ELAEAGNUS
A genus of deciduous and evergreen shrubs and trees grown mainly for their attractive foliage, often silvery or variegated, bell-shaped flowers, sometimes scented, and brightly coloured berries. Best in full sun but tolerant of some shade.
E. angustifolia A deciduous shrub or small tree of spreading habit with willow-like leaves of silver and creamy-white scented flowers in summer followed by yellow fruit in autumn. 6 × 6m/20 × 20ft
E. pungens 'Dicksonii' An evergreen shrub whose young branches are clothed in brown scales. Over oblong leaves, variegated dark green with wide, golden margins, are produced silver-white flowers in autumn followed by fruit ripening red. 3 × 3m/10 × 10ft

Elaeagnus pungens 'Dicksonii'

ELYMUS (Wild rye grass)

A genus of perennial grasses of which the invasive couch grass, *E. repens*, is a species. Those in cultivation include species suitable for the rock garden or for the mixed border. Best in full sun.
E. canadensis A spreading, perennial grass with long, narrow leaves of blue-green. Green flower spikes are produced in late summer and early autumn.
1.2m × 60cm/4 × 2ft

Enkianthus perulatus

ENKIANTHUS

A genus of deciduous shrubs, and some trees, cultivated for their bell-shaped flowers and autumn coloured foliage. For humus-rich, acid to neutral soil in sun or part shade.
E. perulatus A deciduous shrub with leaves of mid-green colouring bright red in autumn. White flowers in mid-spring. 2 × 2m/6 × 6ft

Epimedium × perralchicum

Epimedium × youngianum 'Niveum'

Embothrium coccineum

EMBOTHRIUM (Chilean fire bush)

A genus of hardy to frost hardy evergreen trees and shrubs cultivated as specimens in soil which is neutral to acid. Afford shelter from cold winds.
E. coccineum An upright, hardy to frost hardy tree of suckering habit with lance-shaped leaves of dark green. Dense racemes of brilliant scarlet flowers in late spring and early summer. Semi-evergreen in extreme cold.
10 × 5m/30 × 15ft

EOMECON (Snow poppy)

A genus of a single species of rhizomatous perennial cultivated as a form of ground cover. Best in moist soil in partial shade.
E. chionantha A spreading perennial with dull green leaves of arrow-shape and white poppy-like flowers from late spring to midsummer. 45cm/1.5ft × indefinite spread.

Epilobium angustifolium album

EPILOBIUM (Willow herb)

A genus of annuals, biennials, semi-evergreen perennials and semi-evergreen sub-shrubs grown for their flowers, usually pink or white.
E. angustifolium f. *album* A spreading perennial of willow-like, pale green leaves with racemes of open white flowers from midsummer to autumn.
1.5 × 1m/5 × 3ft

Epimedium × youngianum 'Roseum'

EPIMEDIUM (Barrenwort)

A genus of evergreen and deciduous perennials grown in the main for their foliage, often bronze when young and colouring well in autumn, and dainty spring flowers of many colours. Best in partial shade.
E. × *perralchicum* A clump forming, evergreen perennial with shiny green leaves, bronze when young, and hanging flowers of bright yellow in spring. 30 × 30cm/ 1 × 1ft
E. × *youngianum* 'Niveum' A clump forming deciduous perennial with leaves of mid-green, colourfully tinted when young, and pure white flowers in spring. 25 × 30cm/10in × 1ft
E. × *youngianum* 'Roseum' Similar to *E.* x *youngianum* 'Niveum' but with flowers of dusky pink to mauve-purple. 25 × 30cm/10in × 1ft

EPIPACTIS (Helleborine)

A genus of herbaceous orchids for cultivation in damp, humus-rich soil, well drained, in a position of partial or full shade. Will increase readily given ideal conditions.

E. gigantea A rhizomatous orchid with upright, lance-shaped leaves and yellow-green flowers veined purple and maroon in spring and early summer.
30cm × 1.5m/1 × 5ft

Erica carnea 'Myretoun Ruby'

Eranthis hyemalis

Eremurus stenophyllus subs. *stenophyllus*

ERANTHIS (Winter aconite)

A genus of hardy to frost hardy, tuberous perennials cultivated for their open, cup-shaped flowers from late winter. Best as carpeting plants around deciduous trees and shrubs in sun or light shade.

E. hyemalis A hardy, tuberous perennial with glossy yellow flowers above a ruff of mid-green leaves in late winter and early spring. Naturalizes well in alkaline soil.
8 × 5cm/3 × 2in

EREMURUS (Foxtail lily)

A genus of clump forming perennials for free draining, sandy soil in full sun. Racemes of starry flowers, most often pink, white or yellow, are produced on tall stems in summer at which time basal leaves die down.

E. stenophyllus subs. *stenophyllus* A perennial forming rosettes of grey-green leaves over which rise flower spikes of deep, golden-yellow, fading to orange, in early and midsummer. 1.5m × 75cm/5 × 2.5ft

ERICA (Heath)

A genus of hardy to frost tender, prostrate to tree-like evergreen shrubs. In the main hardy ericas are grown as ground cover and for year-round interest and colour achieved through foliage and flower. For cultivation in acidic soil in full sun although some species will tolerate some alkalinity.

E. carnea 'Myretoun Ruby' A hardy, spreading, shrub with leaves of dark green and urn-shaped flowers of deep pink, darkening to crimson, in late winter and early spring. Tolerant of alkaline soil and some shade. 15 × 45cm/6in × 1.5ft

E. carnea 'Winter Beauty' A hardy, spreading shrub with leaves of mid-green and urn-shaped flowers of lilac-pink in late winter and early spring. Tolerant of alkaline soil and some shade. 15 × 45cm/6in × 1.5ft

E. darleyensis A hardy shrub of bushy growth with leaves of mid-green and urn-shaped flowers of white to rose-pink in late winter and early spring. Tolerant of most soils. 60 × 75cm/2 × 2.5ft

E. darleyensis 'Arthur Johnson' A hardy shrub similar to *E. darleyensis* but with flowers of white to deep pink. 60 × 75cm/2 × 2.5ft

E. darleyensis 'Silberschmelze' A hardy shrub with leaves of mid-green, cream tipped in spring becoming flushed red in autumn, and urn-shaped white flowers in late winter and early spring. 30 × 75cm/1 × 2.5ft

Erica carnea 'Springwood White'

Erica carnea 'Winter Beauty'

Erica darleyensis

Erica darleyensis 'Arthur Johnson'

Erica darleyensis 'Silberschmelze'

Erigeron hybrid

Erigeron karvinskianus

Erinus alpinus

Erodium guttatum

Erodium Merstham Pink'

ERIGERON (Fleabane)

A genus of annuals, biennials and perennials cultivated mainly for their yellow-centred, daisy-like flowers for full sun but with some shade during the hottest party of the day. Alpine species should be afforded protection from excessive wet.

E. hybrid A perennial hybrid with single and semi-double flowers in a wide range of colours carried over a prolonged period in summer.
60 × 45cm/2 × 1.5ft

E. karvinskianus A low growing, spreading perennial producing in summer a profusion of daisy flowers opening white and fading to pink and purple. Self-seeds freely. 15cm × 1m/6in × 3ft

ERINUS (Fairy foxglove)

A genus of semi-evergreen perennials forming rosettes of lance or wedge-shaped leaves and producing tiny, tubular flowers. Well suited to the rock garden in sun or part shade.

E. alpinus A short lived perennial with racemes of pink, purple or white flowers from late spring to summer.
8 × 10cm/3 × 4in

ERODIUM (Heron's bill)

A genus of hardy to frost hardy annuals, perennials and evergreen and deciduous sub-shrubs cultivated for their attractive foliage and their geranium-like flowers which are borne over a long period. Best in full sun in neutral to alkaline soil. Alpine species should be protected from excessive wet.

E. guttatum A hardy perennial or sub-shrub with small silver leaves and blush white flowers with two darkly blotched upper petals in summer. For well drained soil in full sun. 10 × 20cm/4 × 8in

E. 'Merstham Pink' A hardy perennial with small flowers of clear pink with darker veining. For well drained soil in full sun. 15 × 25cm/6 × 10in

Eryngium agavifolium

Eryngium giganteum

Eryngium bourgatii

ERYNGIUM (Sea holly)

A genus of hardy to frost hardy annuals, biennials and deciduous and evergreen perennials, the majority of which form basal rosettes of spiny leaves and carry thistle-like stalkless flowers on many branched stems. Best in full sun.

E. agavifolium A hardy, evergreen perennial forming rosettes of sharply pointed, shiny, leaves of mid-green over which are carried green-white flowers surrounded by spiny bracts in late summer. 1m × 60cm/3 × 2ft

E. bourgatii A hardy perennial forming a basal clump of silver-veined, dark green leaves over which in summer are carried grey-green flowers on bluish stems. 60 × 30cm/2 × 1ft

E. giganteum (Miss Willmott's ghost) A hardy, short lived perennial with basal leaves of mid-green and pale green flowers, turning silver-blue and surrounded by silvery-green bracts, in summer. 1m × 30cm/3 × 1ft

Milk
Cereal.
Bananas
Handwash.
Food. - meat.
Papers

Chopped ham
Yogurt.

Biscuits - cake.

Indian Tonic

ERYSIMUM (Wallflower)

A genus, now inclusive of *Cheiranthus*, of hardy to frost hardy annuals, biennials and largely evergreen perennials. Cultivated in the main for their scent and brightly coloured flowers and often included in spring bedding schemes. Perennial species flower over a long period.

E. 'Bowles' Mauve' A hardy, woody based, evergreen perennial with narrow, grey-green leaves. Racemes of variable mauve flowers are produced from late winter to midsummer, and longer. 75 × 60cm/2.5 × 2ft

E. cheiri 'Harpur Crewe' A hardy, woody based, evergreen perennial with narrow, grey-green leaves and racemes of double, golden-yellow flowers from late winter to early summer. 30 × 60cm/1 × 2ft

Erysimum 'Bowles' Mauve'

Erysimum cheiri 'Harpur Crewe'

ERYTHRONIUM (Dog's tooth violet)

A genus of bulbous perennials for humus-rich, well drained soil in part shade. Basal leaves, marbled in some species, form clumps over which are carried nodding flowers from spring to early summer.

E. californicum 'White Beauty' A bulbous perennial with leaves of dark green, mottled brown, and white with cream flowers in spring. 25 × 10cm/10 × 4in

E. 'Citronella' A bulbous perennial with leaves of mid-green, inclined to be shiny and mottled bronze, and pale creamy-yellow flowers with darker centres in spring. 25 × 10cm/10 × 4in

E. dens-canis A bulbous perennial with leaves of mid-green, marbled purple, and flowers of lilac, pink or white in spring. 15 × 10cm/6 × 4in

Erythronium californicum 'White Beauty'

Erythronium dens-canis

ESCALLONIA

A genus of hardy to frost hardy, evergreen shrubs and, very occasionally, small trees grown for their small, oval, shiny leaves and their mass of pink, red or white flowers in summer. Best in full sun.

E. 'Apple Blossom' A frost hardy, evergreen shrub of compact habit with shiny, dark green leaves and goblet-shaped, light to dark pink flowers with white centres in early and midsummer. Should prove fully hardy in a sheltered spot. 2.5 × 2.5m/ 8 × 8ft

E. 'Iveyi' A frost hardy, evergreen shrub of upright habit with dark green, shiny leaves and goblet-shaped, pure white flowers from mid to late summer. Should prove fully hardy in a sheltered spot. 3 × 3m/10 × 10ft

Escallonia 'Apple Blossom'

Escallonia 'Iveyi'

Eschscholzia californicum hybrid

Eucalyptus gunnii

Eucalyptus pauciflora subsp. *niphophila*

ESCHSCHOLZIA (California poppy)

A genus of annuals cultivated for their poppy-like flowers. Used for summer bedding or for cutting. Easily raised from seed, *Eschscholzia* thrive in poorish soil in full sun.

E. californicum hybrid An annual with finely cut foliage producing flowers in shades mainly of orange, red, yellow or white in summer. 15–30 × 15cm/ 6in–1ft × 6in

EUCALYPTUS (Gum)

A genus of hardy to frost tender, evergreen trees and shrubs cultivated for their attractive foliage, often aromatic, and interesting bark. Hardy species are best sited in full sun in soil which is neutral to acid out of the reach of drying winds.

E. gunnii (Cider gum) A generally hardy, evergreen tree of upright habit with green-white bark and rounded young leaves of mid-green, later becoming elongated and glaucous. Cream flowers in summer to autumn. 10 × 6m/30 × 20ft

E. pauciflora subsp. *niphophila* (Snow gum) A hardy, evergreen tree of spreading habit with grey-white bark and twigs covered in waxy bloom. Young leaves of grey-green maturing to blue-green. White flowers from late spring to summer. 6 × 6m/20 × 20ft

Eucomis bicolor

Eucryphia × *intermedia*

EUCOMIS (Pineapple flower)

A genus of hardy to frost tender bulbous perennials grown for their striking racemes of starry flowers, each stalk topped with a tuft of foliage. Bulbs should be planted deeply in full sun or cultivated in containers which may be overwintered in a frost free glasshouse.

E. bicolor A hardy (borderline) bulbous perennial forming basal rosettes of light green leaves and carrying pale green and purple flowers in late summer. 30–60 × 20cm/1–2ft × 8in

EUCRYPHIA

A genus of hardy to frost hardy, mainly evergreen trees and shrubs grown for their dark, leathery leaves and cup-shaped, scented white flowers. Position in a sheltered spot in soil which is neutral to acid. Provide roots with shade and allow the crown to enjoy full sun.

E. × *intermedia* A hardy, evergreen tree of upright habit with shiny leaves of dark green and bearing fragrant flowers from late summer to autumn. 10 × 6m/ 30 × 20ft

Euonymus alatus 'Compactus'

Euonymus europaeus 'Red Cascade'

Euonymus fortunei 'Sunshine'

Euonymus fortunei 'Silver Queen'

Euonymus japonicus 'Président Gauthier'

Euonymus planipes

EUONYMUS (Spindle tree)

A genus of hardy to frost hardy deciduous, semi-evergreen and evergreen shrubs, trees and climbers grown in the main for their foliage, often variegated, autumn colour and autumnal fruits. Cultivars with variegated foliage are best in full sun.

E. alatus 'Compactus' A hardy, deciduous shrub of dwarf, bushy habit. Dark green leaves colour fiery-red in autumn when purple-red fruits appear. 1 × 3m/3 × 10ft

E. europaeus 'Red Cascade' A hardy, deciduous shrub or small tree with leaves of dark green turning brilliant red for a brief period in autumn when red fruits appear. 3 × 2.5m/10 × 8ft

E. fortunei 'Silver Queen' A hardy, evergreen shrub with dark green leaves broadly margined white, later tinged pink. White fruits in autumn. Suitable for wall training. 2.5 × 1.5m/8 × 5ft

E. fortunei 'Sunshine' A hardy, evergreen shrub with bright green leaves broadly margined golden-yellow, later tinged pink. White fruits in autumn. Suitable for wall training. 2.5 × 1m/8 × 3ft

E. japonicus 'Président Gauthier' A frost hardy, evergreen shrub or small tree with dark green leaves broadly margined white and white fruits flushed pink in autumn. 4 × 2m/12 × 6ft

E. planipes A hardy, deciduous shrub of upright habit with mid-green leaves colouring flame-red in autumn. Red fruits follow. 3 × 3m/10 × 10ft

Eupatorium purpureum

EUPATORIUM (Hemp agrimony)

A genus of hardy to frost hardy annuals, perennials, sub-shrubs and evergreen shrubs.

E. purpureum (Joe Pye weed) A hardy perennial forming a clump of pointed, somewhat coarse, mid-green leaves over which are carried domed flowerheads of pink, purple-pink or off-white in midsummer and early autumn.
1.5 × 1m/5 × 3ft

Euphorbia amygdaloides var. *robbiae*

Euphorbia characias subsp. *wulfenii* 'Lambrook Gold'

Euphorbia dulcis 'Chameleon'

Euphorbia griffithii 'Fireglow'

Euphorbia × *martinii*

EUPHORBIA (Spurge)

A varied genus of hardy to frost tender annuals, biennials, semi-evergreen or evergreen perennials, deciduous or evergreen sub-shrubs, shrubs and trees suitable for a wide range of situations. Euphorbias contain a milky sap which may cause irritation to the skin.

E. amygdaloides var. *robbiae* A hardy, evergreen rhizomatous perennial of spreading habit. Leathery leaves of dark green carry acid-yellow flowerheads from mid-spring to early summer. For sun or part shade. 60 × 30cm/2 × 1ft

E. characias subsp. *wulfenii* 'Lambrook Gold' A frost hardy, evergreen shrub with grey-green leaves with bright, golden-green flowerheads from early spring to early summer. For full sun. 1.2 × 1.2m/4 × 4ft

E. dulcis 'Chameleon' A hardy, rhizomatous perennial with young leaves of deep, burgundy red, lightening with age, and purplish, yellow-green flowerheads in early summer. Sets seed freely. For a light shade. 30 × 30cm/1 × 1ft

E. griffithii 'Fireglow' A hardy, rhizomatous perennial of spreading habit and leaves of reddish-green colouring in autumn. Orange-red bracts are produced on coloured stems in early summer. For light shade. 1 × 1m/3 × 3ft

E. × *martinii* A hardy, evergreen sub-shrub of upright habit with narrow, mid-green leaves, flushed purple when young, and yellow-green flowerheads from spring to mid-summer. For full sun. 1 × 1m/3 × 3ft

E. mellifera (Honey spurge) A frost hardy, evergreen shrub with narrow, lance-shaped leaves of dark green and orange-brown flowerheads, smelling of honey, in late spring. For full sun. 1 × 1.2m/3 × 4ft

Euphorbia mellifera

E. myrsinites A hardy, evergreen perennial of prostrate habit with spirals of grey-blue leaves ending in acid-yellow flowerheads in spring. For full sun. 10 × 30cm/ 4in × 1ft

E. nicaeensis A hardy evergreen or semi-evergreen perennial with lance-shaped leaves of grey-blue and yellow-green flowerheads from late spring to midsummer. For full sun. 60 × 45cm/2 × 1.5ft

E. polychroma A hardy perennial of clump forming habit with dark green leaves, occasionally flushed purple, and bright yellow-green flowerheads from mid spring to midsummer. For sun or light shade. 45 × 60cm/1.5 × 2ft

Euphorbia myrsinites

Euphorbia polychroma

Euryops acreus

EURYOPS
A genus of hardy to half hardy annuals, perennials, evergreen shrubs and sub-shrubs grown for their showy, daisy-like flowers and attractive foliage. Position in full sun.

E. acreus A hardy, low-growing, evergreen shrub with silver-grey leaves and dark yellow flowers in late spring and early summer. Requires good drainage. Suitable for the rock garden. 30 × 30cm/1 × 1ft

E. pectinatus A half hardy, evergreen shrub with hairy, grey leaves and bright yellow flowers in summer. 1 × 1m/ 3 × 3ft

Euphorbia nicaeensis

Exochorda × macrantha 'The Bride'

EXOCHORDA
A genus of deciduous shrubs cultivated for their attractive habit and for their profusion of open cup-shaped flowers in spring and summer. Excellent as specimens or for inclusion in the mixed border or shrub garden. Tolerant of chalk. *E. racemosa* prefers lime free soil. For sun or part shade.

E. × macrantha 'The Bride' A shrub of arching habit with leaves of fresh green and carrying and abundance of pure white flowers in late spring and early summer. 2 × 3m/6 × 10ft

FABIANA

A genus of frost hardy, evergreen shrubs of heath-like appearance. Cultivated for their thin, needle-like leaves and bell-shaped flowers. For neutral to acid soil in full sun out of the reach of cold winds.

F. imbricata f. *violacea* A frost hardy, evergreen shrub of upright habit with lavender-blue flowers in early summer. 2 × 2m/6 × 6ft

Fabiana imbricata f. violacea

Fagus sylvatica

FAGUS (Beech)

A genus of large, deciduous trees grown for their foliage and attractive autumn colour. Best planted as specimen trees in a situation where they have room to develop *F. sylvatica* may be used for hedging or pleaching when it will retain its leaves over winter. Tolerant of most soil conditions including chalk.

F. sylvatica A spreading tree with young leaves of pale green, darkening with age, colouring yellow and orange-brown in autumn. 25 × 15m/80 × 50ft

F. sylvatica 'Pendula' (Weeping beech) A spreading tree whose branches fall towards the ground in a 'weeping' habit. 10 × 5m/30 × 15ft

FARGESIA (Bamboo)

A genus of hardy to half hardy bamboos of clump forming habit. Vigorous in growth, they are suitable as specimen plants or to provide a screen.

F. nitida (Fountain bamboo) A hardy bamboo slowly forming clumps of purple-green canes lined purple-brown. Upper part of the canes bear cascades of narrow, lance-shaped, dark green leaves. 5 × 1.5m/15 × 5ft

FASCICULARIA

A genus of frost tender (although may be half hardy or frost hardy if spared winter wet) evergreen bromeliads cultivated for the desert or rock garden or for containers. For poor soil with good drainage in full sun.

F. bicolor A frost tender, perennial bromeliad with spiny, rigid narrow leaves of dark green and carrying corymbs of pale blue flowers, surrounded by red bracts, in summer. 45 × 60cm/1.5 × 2ft

Fagus sylvatica 'Pendula'

Fargesia nitida

Fascicularia bicolor

× FATSHEDERA

A single hybrid genus of a frost hardy to half hardy spreading, evergreen shrub resulting from a cross between *Fatsia* and *Hedera*. Cultivated for its handsome foliage.

× *F. lizei* (Tree ivy) A frost hardy, evergreen shrub with divided, shiny leaves of dark green. Sterile white flowers in autumn. Well suited to the shrub border, a cool conservatory or glasshouse or as a houseplant. 2 × 3m/6 × 10ft

FATSIA

A genus of frost hardy to half hardy, evergreen shrubs or small trees cultivated for foliage and architectural habit.

F. japonica (Japanese aralia) A frost hardy, evergreen shrub of suckering habit. In autumn cream flowers are carried over the large, divided leaves, to be followed with black fruits. For a partially shaded situation. 1.5 × 4m/5 × 12ft

FELICIA

A genus of frost hardy to frost tender annuals, perennials and sub-shrubs cultivated for their daisy-like flowers borne in profusion for long periods in summer. For full sun in well drained soil.

F. amelloides (Blue daisy) A frost tender, bushy sub-shrub most often treated as an annual. Daisy flowers of mid-blue are produced in a mass from summer to autumn. 60 × 60cm/2 × 2ft

FERULA (Giant fennel)

A genus of essentially hardy perennials forming a mound of divided leaves over which are carried tall stems of purple, yellow or white flowers. Best grown as foliage plants in full sun.

F. communis A robust perennial producing clusters of small, yellow flowers in summer after a period of years. Likely to set seed and die. 2m × 60cm/6 × 2ft

FESTUCA (Fescue)

A genus of deciduous and evergreen grasses cultivated mainly for their attractive foliage of grey and blue-green. Best in poor, well drained soil in full sun.

F. glauca (Blue fescue) An evergreen, perennial grass with slender leaves of blue-green. Flower spikes in summer of similar colour, flushed violet. 30 × 25cm/1ft × 10in

FICUS (Fig)

A genus of hardy to frost tender largely evergreen shrubs, trees and climbers grown for their foliage and for their edible fruits. Suitable for cultivation under glass or outdoors in humus-rich, well drained soil in a sheltered situation.

F. carica 'Brown Turkey' A hardy, deciduous shrub or tree with rounded, lobed leaves and producing green, ripening to brown, fruits (figs). 3 × 4m/10 × 12ft

× *Fatshedera lizei*

Fatsia japonica

Felicia amelloides

Ferula communis

Festuca glauca

Ficus carica 'Brown Turkey'

Filipendula ulmaria

Filipendula rubra 'Venusta'

Foeniculum vulgare

Foeniculum vulgare 'Purpureum'

Forsythia suspensa

Forsythia × intermedia 'Lynwood'

FILIPENDULA (Meadowsweet)

A genus of perennials of divided leaves and plume-like flowers in shades of pink, red or white from late spring to late summer. *F. vulgaris* will thrive on chalk.

F. rubra 'Venusta' A spreading perennial with flowers of rose-pink, paler with age, in summer. 1.5m × 60cm/5 × 2ft

F. ulmaria A spreading perennial with flowers of creamy-white in summer

F. ulmaria 'Flore Pleno' has double flowers. 90 × 60cm/3 × 2ft

FOENICULUM (Fennel)

A genus of a single species of biennial or perennial cultivated as foliage plants or for culinary purposes. Best in full sun.

F. vulgare A perennial with flat umbels of tiny acid-yellow flowers in midsummer. Aromatic leaves and seeds have culinary and medicinal use. *F. v.* 'Purpureum' is the bronze form. 1.8m × 45cm/ 6 × 1.5ft

FORSYTHIA

A genus of deciduous and occasionally semi-evergreen shrubs cultivated in the main for their yellow flowers appearing on bare stems before the emergence of new leaves. Suitable for wall training. For sun or light shade.

F. × intermedia 'Lynwood' A deciduous shrub producing flowers of deep yellow in early and mid-spring. 3 × 3m/10 × 10ft

F. suspensa A deciduous shrub of arching habit producing flowers of a mid-yellow in early and mid-spring. 3 × 3m/10 × 10ft

FOTHERGILLA

A genus of deciduous shrubs valued for their bottlebrush-type flowers and their autumn colour. For humus-rich, acidic soil although tolerant of some alkalinity.
F. major A slow growing, deciduous shrub with shiny, dark green leaves colouring flame in autumn and scented white flowers in late spring and early summer. 2.5 × 2m/8 × 6ft

FRAGARIA (Strawberry)

A genus of stoloniferous perennials cultivated for their edible fruits as well as for their leaves of fresh green and small flowers, most often white but sometimes pink. Best in alkaline soil in sun.
F. vesca 'Variegata' A perennial grown for its foliage variegated grey-green and creamy-white. 30cm/1ft × indefinite spread

FRANCOA (Bridal wreath)

A genus of hardy to frost hardy perennials with softly hairy leaves and racemes of white or pink flowers carried on tall stems. Protect from an excess of winter wet.
F. sonchifolia A hardy/frost hardy perennial with rosettes of fresh green leaves and pale pink flowers in midsummer. 60 × 45cm/2 × 1.5ft

FRAXINUS (Ash)

A genus of hardy to frost hardy, deciduous trees, very occasionally evergreen, grown in the main as specimens or for inclusion in woodland. Best in neutral to alkaline soil.
F. excelsior A deciduous tree of spreading habit whose leaf buds are strikingly coloured black. Dark green leaves colouring yellow in autumn.
30 × 20m/100 × 70ft

FREESIA

A genus of half hardy, cormous perennials of which a large number of cultivars have been developed as cut flowers. Cultivated outdoors in sun as summer bedding.
F. lactea A half hardy, cormous perennial with fragrant white flowers, sometimes tinged purple, in summer. 30cm/1ft

FREMONTODENDRON (Flannel bush)

A genus of frost hardy, evergreen or semi-evergreen shrubs or trees with leaves of dark green against which are displayed flowers of brilliant yellow. Suitable either as specimen shrubs or for training against a warm, sheltered wall.
F. 'California Glory' A frost hardy, evergreen shrub of spreading habit. Open, cup-shaped flowers of butter-yellow are produced from late spring to autumn. 6 × 4m/20 × 12ft
F. mexicanum An upright, frost hardy evergreen or semi-evergreen shrub with flowers of golden-yellow from late spring to autumn. 6 × 4m/20 × 12ft

Fothergilla major

Fothergilla major (autumn foliage)

Fragaria vesca 'Variegata'

Freesia lactea

Fraxinus excelsior

Fremontodendron 'California Glory'

Fremontodendron mexicanum

Fritillaria imperialis 'Prolifera'

Fritillaria meleagris

Fritillaria pyrenaica

Fritillaria persica

FRITILLARIA (Fritillary)

A genus of hardy to frost hardy, bulbous perennials with most often lance-shaped leaves and bell-shaped, tubular or saucer-shaped flowers in a wide range of colours and shades in spring or early summer. Requirements for cultivation vary considerably according to the species, many of which thrive where winters and summers are dry but with adequate wet during the growing season. Others will benefit from moist soil and cool, damp summers.

F. imperialis 'Prolifera' (Crown imperial) A hardy, bulbous perennial producing whorls of orange-red flowers carried in tiers one above the other in early summer. For well drained soil in full sun. 1m × 30cm/3 × 1ft

F. meleagris (Snake's head fritillary) A hardy, bulbous perennial with drooping bell-shaped flowers in deep pink, maroon or white with distinctive mottling of a deeper shade in spring. Suitable for naturalizing in grass in sun or light shade. 30 × 8cm/1ft × 3in

F. persica A hardy, bulbous perennial with leaves of grey-green and bell-shaped flowers of green-brown to purple in spring. For well drained soil in full sun. 1m × 10cm/3ft × 4in

F. pyrenaica A hardy, bulbous perennial with leaves of grey-green and producing bell-shaped flowers of dark brown-purple, sometimes yellow, in late spring. 45 × 8cm/1.5ft × 3in

Fuchsia 'Annabel'

Fuchsia 'Beacon Rosa'

Fuchsia 'Border Queen'

FUCHSIA

A genus of hardy to frost tender deciduous or evergreen shrubs, trees and some perennials from which have been developed a vast number of hybrids and cultivars valued for their distinctive and varied flowers which may be single, semi-double or double. Much used for summer bedding, for containers and hanging baskets, hardier fuchsias may be planted outdoors in well drained soil in sun or part shade.

F. 'Annabel' A half hardy, deciduous shrub with double flowers of pure white in summer. Very free flowering. 45 × 45cm/1.5 × 1.5ft

F. 'Beacon Rosa' A half hardy to hardy, deciduous shrub with single flowers of bright pink in summer. 30 × 30cm/1 × 1ft

F. 'Border Queen' A half hardy, deciduous shrub with single flowers of pale pink sepals and violet corolla in summer. 45 × 45cm/1.5 × 1.5ft

F. 'Brutus' A half hardy, deciduous shrub of arching habit with single flowers of deep pink sepals and dark purple corolla in early summer. 45 × 45cm/1.5 × 1.5ft

F. 'Checkerboard' A half hardy to hardy, deciduous shrub with single flowers of white sepals and deep red corolla in summer and autumn. 75 × 45cm/2.5 × 1.5ft

F. 'Coachman' A half hardy, deciduous shrub of arching habit with single flowers of salmon sepals and glowing orange corolla in summer. 45 × 45cm/1.5 × 1.5ft

F. 'Display' A frost hardy, deciduous shrub with single flowers of pink sepals and deep rose-red corolla in summer. 60 × 45cm/2 × 1.5ft

F. 'Dollar Princess' A frost hardy, deciduous shrub of upright habit with double flowers of cerise sepals and rich purple corolla in early summer. 30 × 45cm/1 × 1.5ft

Fuchsia 'Brutus'

Fuchsia 'Coachman'

Fuchsia 'Display'

Fuchsia 'Checkerboard'

Fuchsia 'Dollar Princess'

Fuchsia 'Garden News'

Fuchsia 'Gartenmeister Bonstedt'

F. 'Garden News' A frost hardy, deciduous shrub of upright habit with semi-double flowers of pink sepals and magenta-rose corolla in summer. 45 × 45cm/1.5 × 1.5ft

F. 'Gartenmeister Bonstedt' A frost tender, deciduous shrub with dark, bronze foliage and long, tubular flowers of brick-red in summer. 60 × 45cm/2 × 1.5ft

F. 'Leonora' A half hardy, deciduous shrub of upright, arching habit with single flowers of salmon-pink sepals and rose-pink corolla in summer. 60 × 30cm/2 × 1ft

F. 'Lye's Unique' A half hardy deciduous shrub of upright habit and vigorous growth producing medium sized, slender tubular flowers of white sepals and red corolla. 1.5 × 1m/5 × 3ft

F. magellanica var. *molinae* A frost hardy to hardy, deciduous shrub of upright, arching habit with small single flowers with pale lilac sepals and deeper lilac corolla in summer. 1m × 75cm/3 × 2.5ft

F. 'Margaret' A frost hardy, deciduous shrub of upright habit with double flowers of scarlet sepals and violet-purple corolla in late summer. 1.2 × 1.2m/4 × 4ft

F. 'Marin Glow' A half hardy, deciduous shrub of upright habit with single flowers of pure white sepals and deep purple, tubular corolla in summer. 45 × 45cm/1.5 × 1.5ft

F. 'Marinka' A half hardy, deciduous, free flowering shrub of cascading habit with single flowers of shiny red sepals and darker red corolla in summer. 30 × 60cm/1 × 2ft

F. 'Mieke Meursing' A half hardy deciduous shrub of upright habit with medium sized single flowers of red sepals and pink veined corolla. 1m × 75cm/3 × 2.5ft

Fuchsia 'Leonora'

Fuchsia 'Lye's Unique'

Fuchsia 'Mieke Meursing'

Fuchsia magellanica var. *molinae*

Fuchsia 'Margaret'

Fuchsia 'Marin Glow'

Fuchsia 'Marinka'

Fuchsia 'Mrs Popple'

Fuchsia 'Snowcap'

Fuchsia 'Royal Velvet'

Fuchsia 'Swingtime'

Fuchsia 'Red Spider'

Fuchsia 'Rufus'

Fuchsia 'Tennessee Waltz'

Fuchsia 'Thalia'

F. 'Mrs Popple' A hardy, deciduous shrub of upright habit with single flowers of scarlet sepals and purple-violet corolla in summer and early autumn.
1 × 1m/3 × 3ft
F. 'Red Spider' A half hardy deciduous shrub of pendulous habit with single flowers of crimson sepals and rose-pink veined corolla. 1.5 × 2m/5 × 6ft
F. 'Royal Velvet' A half hardy, deciduous shrub of upright habit with double flowers of deep pink sepals and dark purple corolla in summer. 45 × 30cm/1.5 × 1ft
F. 'Rufus' Vigorous half hardy deciduous shrub of upright habit with small, single red flowers. 1.5m × 75cm/5 × 2.5ft
F. 'Snowcap' A frost hardy, deciduous shrub of upright habit with semi-double flowers of bright, shiny red sepals and white corolla in summer. 60 × 60cm/2 × 2ft
F. 'Swingtime' A half hardy, deciduous, free flowering shrub with double flowers of shiny, deep pink sepals and white, pink veined corolla in summer.
45 × 45cm/1.5 × 1.5ft
F. 'Tennessee Waltz' A frost hardy, deciduous shrub of arching habit with double flowers of pink sepals and lavender rose-streaked corolla in summer.
60 × 60cm/2 × 2ft
F. 'Thalia' A frost tender, deciduous shrub of upright habit with dark foliage and tubular flowers of orange-scarlet in late summer. 60 × 60cm/2 × 2ft
F. 'Tom Thumb' A frost hardy, deciduous, free flowering shrub of dwarf habit with single flowers of carmine-red sepals and mauve corolla from early summer.
30 × 30cm/1 × 1ft

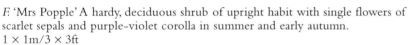

Fuchsia 'Tom Thumb'

GAILLARDIA (Blanket flower)
A genus of hardy to frost hardy annuals, biennials and perennials of which numerous cultivars are grown as summer bedding. Daisy-like flowerheads are produced in many bright colours over a long period. Best in full sun.
G. 'Kobold' A hardy, short lived perennial with flowers of rich red and yellow ray-florets with dark red disc-floret from early summer to autumn.
30 × 45cm/1 × 1.5ft

Galanthus nivalis 'Flore Pleno'

GALANTHUS (Snowdrop)
Genus of hardy to frost hardy, bulbous perennials in flower mainly from late winter to early spring. Many are suitable for naturalizing and most prefer humus-rich soil which remains moist in part shade. Species of galanthus are prone to hybridize in gardens so may not come true from seed.
G. 'Magnet' A hardy, bulbous perennial with slender leaves of grey-green and bearing large white flowers, marked with a distinctive green V on the inner petals, in late winter and early spring. 20 × 8cm/8 × 3in
G. *nivalis* 'Flore Pleno' A hardy, bulbous perennial with narrow green-grey leaves and irregular double, green tipped, white flowers in late winter and early spring.
10 × 10cm/4 × 4in

Galanthus 'Magnet'

Galega orientalis

Galium odoratum

Galtonia candicans

GALEGA (Goat's rue)
A genus of perennials with leaves of light green, sometimes tinted blue, and pea-like flowers in blue, mauve or white, or bicoloured. Generally unfussy as to soil and situation.
G. *orientalis* A perennial of somewhat loose habit with leaves of light green and racemes of violet-blue flowers in late spring and early summer.
1.2m × 60cm/4 × 2ft

GALIUM (Woodruff)
A genus of hardy to frost hardy annuals and perennials of which some species may prove to be invasive. G. *odoratum* is useful as an attractive form of ground cover.
G. *odoratum* A hardy perennial of spreading habit with leaves of bright green and tiny, starry white flowers from late spring to midsummer. 30cm/1ft × indefinite spread

GALTONIA
A genus of hardy to frost hardy, bulbous perennials grown for their tubular or trumpet-shaped white and green flowers over upright, lance-shaped leaves. For full sun in soil which does not dry out.
G. *candicans* A hardy, bulbous perennial producing tubular flowers of white, flushed green at the base, over grey-green leaves in late summer.
60 × 10cm/2ft × 4in

Garrya elliptica

Gaultheria mucronata

Gaultheria procumbens

GARRYA

A genus of frost hardy to half hardy, evergreen shrubs and small trees grown for their broad, tapering leaves and striking, hanging catkins. Given the shelter of a wall, frost hardy species should prove relatively hardy.

G. elliptica A frost hardy, evergreen shrub with leaves of grey-green and producing blue-grey catkins from mid-winter to early spring. 4 × 4m/12 × 12ft

GAULTHERIA (syn. Pernettya)

A genus of hardy to half hardy, evergreen shrubs valued for their leathery leaves, urn-shaped flowers and rounded fruits. For acidic to neutral soil, which remains moist, in partial shade.

G. mucronata A hardy, evergreen shrub of suckering habit with white flowers, occasionally flushed pink, in late spring and early summer followed by fruit of purple, red or white. 1.2 × 1.2m/4 × 4ft

G. procumbens (Wintergreen) A hardy, low growing evergreen shrub of creeping habit. Shiny leaves set off flowers of white or pale pink in summer followed by bright red fruits which continue until spring. 15cm × 1m/6in × 3ft

GAURA

A genus of annuals, biennials, perennials and sub-shrubs producing starry, pink or white flowers of graceful appearance. Best positioned in full sun.

G. lindheimeri A clump forming perennial carrying star-shaped, white flowers on slender stems from early summer to early autumn. 1m × 60cm/3 × 2ft

Genista aetnensis

Gazania 'Dorothy'

Genista hispanica

Genista lydia

GAZANIA

A genus of half hardy to frost tender annuals or evergreen perennials cultivated mainly for their brightly coloured, daisy-like flowers as summer bedding. Best in free draining soil in full sun.

G. 'Dorothy' A half hardy, hybrid perennial grown as an annual. Deep yellow flowers, closing up when out of the sun, in summer. 20 × 20cm/8 × 8in

GENISTA (Broom)

Genus of hardy to half hardy, largely deciduous shrubs and sometimes trees noted for their pea-like yellow flowers. For poor soil in full sun.

G. aetnensis (Mount Etna broom) A frost hardy, deciduous shrub with cascading branches of bright green shoots and scented, golden-yellow flowers in summer. 8 × 8m/25 × 25ft

G. hispanica (Spanish gorse) A hardy, spiny, deciduous shrub forming a dense mound. Racemes of golden-yellow flowers are produced in late spring and early summer. 75cm × 1.5m/2.5 × 5ft

G. lydia A hardy, deciduous shrub with arching branches of grey-green shoots and flowers of bright yellow borne in profusion in early summer. 60cm × 1m/2 × 3ft

Gentiana asclepiadea

Gentiana acaulis

Gentiana lutea

Gentiana sino-ornata

GENTIANA (Gentian)

Genus of annuals, biennials, and deciduous, semi-evergreen and evergreen perennials grown for their usually trumpet-shaped flowers of mainly intense blue, but sometimes white, yellow or red, from spring to autumn. Smaller species are suitable for the rock garden. Cultivate in humus-rich, predominantly neutral to acid soil in partial shade.

G. acaulis (Trumpet gentian) An evergreen, ground hugging perennial with lance-shaped leaves of dark green and deep blue trumpet flowers in late spring and early summer. 8 × 30cm/3in × 1ft

G. asclepiadea (Willow gentian) An herbaceous perennial forming clumps of dull green, lance-shaped leaves and carrying trumpet flowers of light to dark blue in mid and late summer. 60 × 45cm/2 × 1.5ft

G. lutea (Yellow gentian) An herbaceous perennial forming clumps of blue-green, basal leaves over which rise stems carrying clusters of starry yellow flowers in mid-summer. 1.2m × 60cm/4 × 2ft

G. sino-ornata A semi-evergreen perennial forming rosettes of pointed, dark green leaves and carrying trumpet flowers mainly of bright blue, striped purple-blue and green-white, in autumn. 5 × 30cm/2in × 1ft

Geranium cinereum 'Ballerina'

Geranium clarkei 'Kashmir White'

Geranium endressii

Geranium himalayense 'Plenum'

Geranium 'Johnson's Blue'

Geranium himalayense 'Gravetye'

Geranium macrorrizhum 'Album'

Geranium macrorrizhum 'Bevan's Variety'

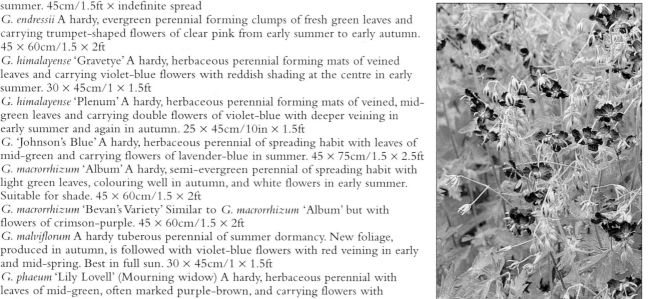

Geranium malviflorum

Geranium phaeum 'Lily Lovell'

GERANIUM (Cranesbill)

A genus of hardy to half hardy, annuals, biennials, deciduous, semi-evergreen and evergreen, sometimes tuberous, perennials not to be confused with the genus *Pelargonium* which is commonly called, incorrectly, geranium. Leaves are mainly divided, often aromatic, whilst flowers, in shades of blue, pink, purple and white, are largely saucer-shaped or starry, frequently veined and carried over a prolonged period. Generally geraniums are unfussy as to soil and situation although smaller species benefit from full sun.

G. cinereum 'Ballerina' A hardy, evergreen perennial forming rosettes of grey-green leaves and carrying light purple-red flowers with deeper red veining in late spring and early summer. Benefits from sharp drainage. 15 × 30cm/6in × 1ft

G. clarkei 'Kashmir White' A hardy, herbaceous perennial of spreading habit with finely cut leaves of mid-green and carrying white flowers with lilac-pink veining in summer. 45cm/1.5ft × indefinite spread

G. endressii A hardy, evergreen perennial forming clumps of fresh green leaves and carrying trumpet-shaped flowers of clear pink from early summer to early autumn. 45 × 60cm/1.5 × 2ft

G. himalayense 'Gravetye' A hardy, herbaceous perennial forming mats of veined leaves and carrying violet-blue flowers with reddish shading at the centre in early summer. 30 × 45cm/1 × 1.5ft

G. himalayense 'Plenum' A hardy, herbaceous perennial forming mats of veined, mid-green leaves and carrying double flowers of violet-blue with deeper veining in early summer and again in autumn. 25 × 45cm/10in × 1.5ft

G. 'Johnson's Blue' A hardy, herbaceous perennial of spreading habit with leaves of mid-green and carrying flowers of lavender-blue in summer. 45 × 75cm/1.5 × 2.5ft

G. macrorrhizum 'Album' A hardy, semi-evergreen perennial of spreading habit with light green leaves, colouring well in autumn, and white flowers in early summer. Suitable for shade. 45 × 60cm/1.5 × 2ft

G. macrorrhizum 'Bevan's Variety' Similar to *G. macrorrhizum* 'Album' but with flowers of crimson-purple. 45 × 60cm/1.5 × 2ft

G. malviflorum A hardy tuberous perennial of summer dormancy. New foliage, produced in autumn, is followed with violet-blue flowers with red veining in early and mid-spring. Best in full sun. 30 × 45cm/1 × 1.5ft

G. phaeum 'Lily Lovell' (Mourning widow) A hardy, herbaceous perennial with leaves of mid-green, often marked purple-brown, and carrying flowers with reflexed petals of purple-mauve in late spring and early summer. 75 × 45cm/2.5 × 1.5ft

Geranium pratense 'Mrs Kendall Clark'

Geranium psilostemon

Geranium pratense

Geranium renardii

Geranium × riversleaianum 'Mavis Simpson'

G. *pratense* A hardy, herbaceous perennial with deeply divided leaves and carrying veined flowers in blue, violet or white in summer. 60 × 60cm/2 × 2ft

G. *pratense* 'Mrs. Kendall Clark' A hardy, herbaceous perennial with deeply divided leaves and carrying flowers of pearl-grey tinged pink in summer. Most often offered with flowers of lilac-blue veined as here. 60 × 60cm/2 × 2ft

G. *psilostemon* A hardy, herbaceous perennial with leaves of mid-green, emerging crimson in spring and colouring red in autumn, and carrying veined flowers of deep magenta with black eye in summer. 1m × 60cm/3 × 2ft

G. *renardii* A hardy, herbaceous perennial with scalloped leaves of soft grey-green and carrying palest lavender flowers, often almost white, with violet veins in summer. 30 × 30cm/1 × 1ft

G. × *riversleaianum* 'Mavis Simpson' A hardy, herbaceous perennial of trailing habit with divided leaves of grey-green and carrying light pink flowers, paler at the centre, in summer. 30cm × 1m/1 × 3ft

G. *sanguineum* A hardy, herbaceous perennial with leaves of dark green and carrying veined, deep magenta flowers with white eyes in summer. 20 × 30cm/8in × 1ft

G. *sanguineum* var. *striatum* Similar to *G. sanguineum* but more compact and with flowers of flesh-pink with darker pink veining. 10 × 30cm/4in × 1ft

G. *sylvaticum* 'Mayflower' A hardy, herbaceous perennial with basal leaves of mid-green and carrying violet-blue flowers with white centres in late spring and early summer. Best in moist soil. 75 × 60cm/2.5 × 1ft

Geranium sanguineum

Geranium sanguineum var. *striatum*

Geranium sylvaticum 'Mayflower'

GERBERA

A genus of half hardy to frost tender perennials with daisy-like flowers, both single and double, most often grown as summer bedding in well drained soil in full sun.

G. jamesonii (Transvaal daisy) A frost tender perennial with leaves of dark green, paler on the undersides, and bearing orange-scarlet flowers from late spring to late summer.
60 × 30cm/2 × 1ft

Geum 'Red Wings'

Geum rivale

Geum rivale 'Album'

Geum 'Borisii'

GEUM (Avens)

A genus of perennials cultivated for their saucer- to bowl-shaped flowers in various shades of cream, orange, pink, red and yellow carried over a prolonged period in late spring and summer. For well drained soil in full sun although *G. rivale* and its cultivars prefer moisture retentive soil.

G. 'Borisii' A clump forming perennial with leaves of fresh green and carrying orange-red flowers with noticeable yellow stamens from late spring to late summer. 45 × 30cm/1.5 × 1ft

G. 'Red Wings' A clump forming perennial with leaves of light green and many semi-double, scarlet flowers in summer. 60 × 45cm/2 × 1.5ft

G. rivale A perennial of upright habit with leaves of mid-green and bell-shaped flowers in shades of dusky pink to deep orange-red from spring to midsummer. 30 × 30cm/1 × 1ft

G. rivale 'Album' Similar to *G. rivale* but with flowers of creamy-white from spring to midsummer. 30 × 30cm/1 × 1ft

Gillenia trifoliata

GILLENIA

A genus of perennials valued for their leaves of bronze-green and somewhat airy flowers of pale pink or white. Best in neutral to acid soil in partial shade.

G. trifoliata (Indian physic) An upright perennial carrying starry flowers on tall, red tinted stems in white or white-pink from late spring to late summer.
1m × 60cm/3 × 2ft

GINKGO (Maidenhair tree)

A genus of a single species of deciduous tree cultivated mainly as a specimen. Noted for its divided, fan-shaped leaves of mid to yellow-green colouring gold in autumn. Position in full sun.

G. biloba An upright, columnar tree, widening with age, with furrowed, grey bark. Fleshy fruits are produced in autumn. 30 × 8m/100 × 25ft

Ginkgo biloba

Gladiolus callianthus

Gladiolus × colvillei

Gladiolus communis subsp. byzantinus

Gladiolus large-flowered hybrid

GLADIOLUS

A genus of hardy to frost tender, cormous perennials cultivated in the main for their showy, many coloured spikes of usually funnel-shaped flowers. Hybrids and cultivars number more than 10,000. Most prefer well drained soil in full sun. Corms of those species which are not hardy may be lifted in autumn and overwintered in a frost free environment.

G. callianthus A half-hardy, cormous perennial with strap-like leaves and carrying fragrant, white flowers with purple-red markings in late summer and early autumn. 75 × 5cm/2.5ft × 2in

G. × colvillei A half hardy, cormous perennial with slender leaves and producing flowers of white, orange or peach-pink with contrasting light and dark throats from early spring to early summer. 45 × 5cm/1.5ft × 2in

G. communis subsp. byzantinus A hardy, cormous perennial with linear leaves of dark green and producing spikes of magenta flowers from late spring to early summer. 60 × 8cm/2ft × 3in

G. large-flowered hybrid. A half hardy, cormous perennial flowering from early to late summer in a wide range of colours. Useful for cutting 1.5m × 15cm/5ft × 6in or more

G. papilio A frost hardy, cormous perennial of spreading habit. Greenish flowers, flushed purple, are carried over sword-like leaves from midsummer to early autumn. 75 × 8cm/2.5ft × 3in

Glaucidium palmatum

Gleditsia triacanthos 'Sunburst'

GLAUCIDIUM

A genus of a single species of perennial grown for its peony or poppy-like flower and deeply lobed leaves. For humus-rich soil in part or total shade.
G. palmatum A clump forming perennial producing solitary flowers of lilac-pink in late spring and early summer. 45 × 45cm/1.5 × 1.5ft

GLEDITSIA

A genus of deciduous, mainly spiny, trees noted for their attractive form and fern-like leaves. For full sun. Young growth may be damaged by late frosts.
G. triacanthos 'Sunburst' (Honey locust) A deciduous, fast growing tree of spreading habit with golden-yellow foliage maturing to pale green. Colours yellow in autumn. 12 × 10m/40 × 30ft

Gladiolus papilio

GLOBULARIA (Globe daisy)

A genus of largely evergreen perennials or sub-shrubs with leathery leaves and spherical flowerheads. Well suited to the rock garden, containers or to cultivation in the alpine house. Best with sharp drainage in full sun.

G. cordifolia A dwarf, evergreen perennial of spreading habit with shiny, dark green leaves and lavender-blue flowers in summer. 5 × 20cm/2 × 8in

GLOXINIA

A genus of frost tender perennials or shrubs grown for their bell-shaped, pink or blue flowers produced from summer to autumn. Suitable for a conservatory or glasshouse.

G. perennis A frost tender perennial with shiny leaves of mid-green and carrying lavender-blue flowers, suffused violet at the bases, from early summer to autumn. 1.2 × 1m/4 × 3ft

Grevillea rosmarinifolia

GREVILLEA

A genus of frost hardy to frost tender, evergreen shrubs and trees cultivated for their varied foliage and unusual petalless flowers. For acidic soil in full sun or for cultivation under glass.

G. rosmarinifolia A frost hardy shrub of widely branching, spreading habit. Spider-like racemes of pink, light red or cream flowers are produced over lance-shaped leaves from late autumn to early summer. 0.5–3 × 1.5m/1.5–10 × 5ft

Griselinia littoralis

Griselinia littoralis 'Variegata'

GRISELINIA

A genus of frost hardy or half hardy, evergreen shrubs and trees valued for their leathery leaves and purple fruits which follow inconspicuous flowers borne in late spring. For full sun out of the reach of drying winds.

G. littoralis A frost hardy (will withstand temperatures as low as −12°C/10°F), upright shrub with shiny, bright green leaves well suited as hedging or windbreak in coastal areas.
To 8 × 5m/25 × 15ft

G. littoralis 'Variegata' Similar to *G. littoralis* but with leaves edged creamy-white and streaked grey-green.
To 8 × 5m/25 × 15ft

Gunnera manicata

GUNNERA

A genus of hardy to frost hardy, herbaceous or evergreen perennials mainly grown for their handsome foliage as well as for flower spikes and fruit. For moisture retentive, humus-rich soil in sun or part shade. Protect the crowns of large-leafed species with a dry mulch in winter.

G. manicata A hardy, herbaceous perennial of large, clump forming habit with handsome, dark green leaves up to 2m/6ft long and panicles of tiny green-red flowers in summer. 2.5 × 3m/8 × 10ft

Gypsophila 'Rosy Veil'

GYPSOPHILA

Genus of hardy to frost hardy annuals and herbaceous, semi-evergreen and evergreen perennials with lance-shaped, grey-green leaves and small, starry flowers in white or pink. For full sun in well drained soil. Intolerant of winter wet.

G. 'Rosy Veil' A hardy, herbaceous perennial producing tiny pink flowers in summer. 45 × 45cm/1.5 × 1.5ft

Hakea lissosperma

Hakonechloa macra 'Alboaurea'

HACQUETIA

A genus of a single species of small, clump forming perennial grown for its yellow flowers surrounded by bracts of light green. For neutral to acid soil in part shade.
H. epipactis A perennial of light green leaves and tiny yellow flowers over a long period in late winter and early spring. 5 × 15cm/2 × 6in

HAKEA

A genus of half hardy to frost tender, evergreen trees and shrubs with most often slender, needle-like leaves. For acidic soil in sun.
H. lissosperma (Mountain hakea) A half hardy shrub or small tree of bushy habit. Small white flowers in spring and summer are carried over spiny grey-green leaves and are followed by brown seed pods. 3–6 × 1–4m/10–20 × 3–12ft

HAKONECHLOA

A genus of a single species of perennial grass cultivated for its ornamental foliage. Suitable for containers. Variegated cultivars are best positioned in partial shade.
H. macra 'Alboaurea' A perennial grass with leaves of bright yellow decorated with a narrow, green stripe. Pale green spikelets are carried in summer and autumn. 30 × 45cm/1 × 1.5ft

Halesia monticola

× *Halimiocistus sahucii*

× *Halimiocistus wintonensis*

× *Halimiocistus wintonensis* 'Merrist Wood Cream'

HALESIA (Snowdrop tree)

A genus of deciduous trees grown mainly for their hanging, bell-like flowers, their winged fruits and bright autumn colour. For neutral to acid soil which remains moist.
H. monticola A tree of conical shape with leaves of mid-green. Clusters of white flowers appear with new leaves in late spring and are followed by green fruit. Yellow autumn colour. 12 × 8m/40 × 25ft

× HALIMIOCISTUS

A hybrid genus of hardy to frost hardy, evergreen shrubs resulting from a cross between *Halimium* and *Cistus*. Grown mainly for their flowers which are similar to those of *Cistus* and *Helianthemum*. Best in full sun and protect from cold winds.
× *H. sahucii* A hardy shrub forming a spreading mound. Open, saucer-shaped white flowers appear in summer over dark green leaves. 45cm × 1m/1.5 × 3ft
× *H. wintonensis* A hardy shrub of spreading habit with grey-green leaves and producing flowers of white with crimson bands in late spring and early summer. 60cm × 1m/2 × 3ft
× *H. wintonensis* 'Merrist Wood Cream' Similar to × *H. wintonensis* but with yellow centred, cream flowers banded maroon. 60cm × 1m/2 × 3ft

Hamamelis × intermedia 'Aphrodite'

Hamamelis × intermedia 'Pallida'

Hamamelis × intermedia 'Jelena'

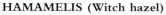

Hamamelis × intermedia 'Pallida'

Hamamelis mollis 'Goldcrest'

HAMAMELIS (Witch hazel)

Genus of deciduous shrubs cultivated mainly for their spider-like flowers, often scented, which are carried on bare wood in late winter and early spring. Good autumn colour. Best in acidic to neutral soil in an open but sheltered situation.

H. × intermedia 'Aphrodite' A deciduous shrub of upright habit producing flowers of burnt apricot in late winter and early spring. 4 × 4m/12 × 12ft

H. × intermedia 'Jelena' A deciduous shrub of upright habit producing flowers of burnished copper in late winter. Flame coloured autumn foliage. 4 × 4m/12 × 12ft

H. × intermedia 'Pallida' A deciduous shrub of upright habit producing flowers of pale sulphur-yellow in late winter. 4 × 4m/12 × 12ft

H. mollis 'Goldcrest' A deciduous shrub of upright habit producing flowers of golden-yellow, stained red towards the base of each petal, from midwinter to spring. 4 × 4m/12 × 12ft

Hebe cupressoides 'Boughton Dome'

Hebe macrantha

Hebe ochracea 'James Stirling'

Hebe pinguifolia 'Pagei'

Hebe rakaiensis

Hebe 'Simon Delaux'

Hebe 'Pewter Dome'

HEBE

A genus of hardy to half hardy, evergreen shrubs, seldom trees, cultivated for their foliage and flowers and suitable for a wide range of situations. Hebes will thrive in fairly poor, neutral to alkaline soil in sun or part shade out of the reach of cold, drying winds. Less hardy species may be grown under cover of glass.

H. cupressoides 'Boughton Dome' A hardy, slow growing shrub forming a dome of grey-green, slender leaves but seldom flowering. An ideal subject for a rock garden. 30 × 60cm/1 × 2ft

H. macrantha A frost hardy, spreading shrub with bright green leaves and producing clusters of large white flowers in early summer. 60cm × 1m/2 × 3ft

H. ochracea 'James Stirling' A hardy shrub of arching habit with slim, triangular leaves of yellow-ochre and carrying small white flowers in late spring and early summer. 45 × 60cm/1.5 × 2ft

H. 'Pewter Dome' A frost hardy, dome-shaped shrub with grey-green leaves and carrying racemes of small white flowers in late spring and early summer. 45 × 60cm/1.5 × 2ft

H. pinguifolia 'Pagei' A hardy shrub of prostrate habit with blue-green leaves and carrying a mass of white flowers in late spring and early summer. 30cm × 1m/1 × 3ft

H. rakaiensis A shrub of rounded habit with leaves of shiny, bright green and producing racemes of large white flowers in summer. 1 × 1.2m/3 × 4ft

H. 'Simon Delaux' A half hardy, rounded shrub with dark green leaves, tinged purple when young, and crimson-red flowers in summer. 1.2 × 1.2m/4 × 4ft

Hedera colchica 'Sulphur Heart'

Hedera canariensis 'Gloire de Marengo'

HEDERA (Ivy)

A genus of hardy to half hardy, evergreen climbers of trailing or self-clinging habit, varying greatly in leaf shape, leaf colour, size and vigour. Both species and cultivars are grown in the main for cover of walls and fences, for introducing colour into dark areas or as ground cover. Generally unfussy about soil and situation, variegated forms prefer more light whereas green leafed varieties will often tolerate partial or complete shade.

H. canariensis 'Gloire de Marengo' A frost hardy climber suitable for a sheltered site. Pale silver-green leaves are variegated creamy-white. Often grown as a houseplant. 4m/12ft

H. colchica 'Dentata Variegata' A hardy, vigorous climber with leaves of light green mottled grey-green and edged with creamy-white. Suitable as ground cover. 5m/15ft

H. colchica 'Sulphur Heart' Similar to *H. colchica* 'Dentata Variegata' but faster growing and with leaves of mid-green flushed creamy-yellow. 5m/15ft

H. helix 'Angularia Aurea' A hardy cultivar of the species. Shiny leaves of mid-green, slightly angular in appearance, are flushed and variegated with pale yellow in maturity. 5m/15ft

H. helix 'Buttercup' A hardy climber of moderate growth. Pale green leaves colour warm, buttery yellow when positioned in sun. 2m/6ft

H. helix 'Glacier' A hardy climber of moderate growth. Grey-green leaves contain silver-grey and cream variegation. Often grown as a houseplant. 2m/6ft

Hedera colchica 'Dentata Variegata'

Hedera helix 'Angularia Aurea'

Hedera helix 'Glacier'

Hedera helix 'Buttercup'

Hedera helix 'Marginata'

Hedychium coccineum 'Tara'

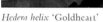

Hedera helix 'Goldheart'

Hedera helix 'Parsley Crested'

H. helix 'Goldheart' A hardy climber of vigorous growth once established. Dark green leaves are splashed golden-yellow. Variegation is less when used as ground cover. 8m/25ft

H. helix 'Marginata' A hardy climber of vigorous growth with leaves of mid-green containing creamy-yellow variegation, most pronounced at the margins. 5m/15ft

H. helix 'Parsley Crested' A frost hardy climber of moderate growth with mid to dark green leaves crested and waved at the edges. 2m/6ft

HEDYCHIUM (Ginger lily)

A genus of frost hardy to frost tender, rhizomatous perennials grown mainly for their distinctive foliage and often scented white, yellow or orange-red flowers. In cold areas apply a heavy mulch in winter to frost hardy species. *H. coccineum* 'Tara' A frost hardy, rhizome forming perennial with long, spear-shaped leaves and orange flowers with prominent red stamens in late summer. 1.2 × 1m/4 × 3ft

HEDYSARUM

A genus of perennials and sub-shrubs cultivated mainly for their pea-like flowers in pink, purple, red or violet, sometimes white or yellow, borne in spring and early summer. Attractive to bees. Best in free draining, poor soil in full sun.

H. coronarium (French honeysuckle) A perennial or occasionally biennial of upright habit with scented flowers of deep red in spring. 1m × 60cm/3 × 2ft

Helenium 'Golden Youth'

HELENIUM (Helen's flower)

A genus of hardy to frost hardy annuals, biennials and perennials of clump forming habit with daisy-like flowerheads. Best in moist but free draining soil in full sun.

H. 'Golden Youth' (syn. 'Goldene Jugend') A hardy perennial producing large flowers on tall stems of honey-yellow from early summer to early autumn. 1m × 60cm/3 × 2ft

H. 'Moerheim Beauty' A hardy perennial producing flowers on tall stems in various shades of bronze-red from midsummer to early autumn. 1m × 60cm/3 × 2ft

Helenium 'Moerheim Beauty'

Helianthemum 'Annabel'

Helianthemum 'Golden Queen'

HELIANTHEMUM (Rock rose)

Genus of hardy to frost hardy, evergreen or semi-evergreen shrubs grown for their open, saucer-shaped flowers in a wide range of colours and borne over a prolonged period. Well suited to the rock garden, front of border or containers. Best in free draining soil in full sun.

H. 'Annabel' A hardy, evergreen shrub of spreading habit producing semi-double pink flowers over grey-green leaves in midsummer. 20 × 45cm/8in × 1.5ft

H. 'Golden Queen' A hardy, evergreen shrub of spreading habit producing pale golden-yellow flowers from late spring to early autumn. 30cm × 1m/1 × 3ft

H. 'Henfield Brilliant' A hardy, evergreen shrub of spreading habit with leaves of silver-green over which are carried orange-red flowers in midsummer. 30 × 30cm/1 × 1ft

H. 'Wisley Primrose' A hardy, evergreen shrub of spreading habit with leaves of grey-green over which are carried pale lemon flowers in midsummer. 25 × 45cm/10in × 1.5ft

Helianthemum 'Henfield Brilliant'

Helianthemum 'Wisley Primrose'

Helianthus decapetalus 'Triomphe de Gand'

Helianthus 'Monarch'

HELIANTHUS (Sunflower)

A genus of hardy to frost hardy annuals and perennials of coarse foliage and tall stemmed, daisy-like flowerheads. Excellent as cut flowers and attractive to bees. Tolerant of dry soil and drought conditions.

H. decapetalus 'Triomphe de Gand' A hardy, rhizome forming perennial producing deep yellow flowers with brown centres carried on tall stems from late summer to mid autumn. 1.5 × 1m/5 × 3ft

H. 'Monarch' A hardy perennial producing flowers of clear yellow with a black eye on tall stems in late summer. 2.1 × 1m/7 × 3ft

Helichrysum italicum

Helichrysum petiolare

Helictotrichon sempervirens

Helichrysum bracteatum

HELICTOTRICHON

A genus of deciduous and evergreen perennial grasses generally preferring alkaline soil in full sun. Glaucous or light green foliage is mound forming and bears upright or hanging panicles of flower spikes.

H. sempervirens (Blue oat grass) An evergreen, perennial glaucous grass forming a dome-shaped tuft over which are produced straw-coloured, purple-marked flower spikes on tall stems in early summer. 45 × 30cm/1.5 × 1ft

HELIOPSIS (Ox eye)

A genus of perennials grown for their sunflower-like flowerheads principally in shades of yellow. Best in free draining, moist soil in full sun. Suitable as cut flowers.

H. helianthoides subsp. *scabra* 'Light of Lodden' A perennial forming mounds of dark green leaves with semi-double, golden-yellow flowerheads in summer. 1m × 60cm/3 × 2ft

HELICHRYSUM

A genus of hardy to frost tender annuals, herbaceous or evergreen perennials and evergreen shrubs and sub-shrubs grown for flower and foliage. Smaller species are well suited to the rock garden, scree bed or alpine house. Frost tender species are cultivated mainly as summer bedding. For neutral to alkaline soil in full sun and sheltered from cold, drying winds.

H. bracteatum (Golden everlasting strawflower) A half hardy, upright annual producing straw-like flowers in a wide range of colours in midsummer. Useful for drying. 30 × 30cm/1 × 1ft

H. italicum A frost hardy, evergreen sub-shrub producing sulphur-yellow flowers over silver foliage from summer into autumn. 60 × 60cm/2 × 2ft

H. petiolare A half hardy, small, mound forming evergreen shrub of soft, grey leaves. Insignificant white flowers are produced in late summer. 45 × 45cm/1.5 × 1.5ft

Heliotropium arborescens

Helipterum manglesii

HELIOTROPIUM (Heliotrope)

A genus of half hardy annuals, perennials, sub-shrubs and shrubs grown mainly for their perfumed flowers and most often employed as summer bedding. For free draining, moist soil in full sun.

H. arborescens (Cherry pie) A short lived, half hardy shrub most often cultivated as an annual. Mauve-purple flowers, over veined, dark green leaves in summer. 45 × 45cm/1.5 × 1.5ft

HELIPTERUM (Strawflower)

A genus of half hardy annuals, perennials and sub-shrubs of upright habit and grown for their single to double flowerheads in shades of pink, white or yellow produced mainly in summer.

H. manglesii A half hardy annual producing light pink flowers from midsummer to early autumn. Tolerant of infertile soil conditions but best in moist, fertile soil in full sun. 60 × 30cm/2 × 1ft

Helleborus argutifolius

Helleborus foetidus

Helleborus foetidus Wester Flisk

Helleborus orientalis hybrid

Helleborus lividus

Helleborus niger

Helleborus orientalis subsp. *abchasicus*

HELLEBORUS (Hellebore)

A genus of hardy to frost hardy rhizomatous and clump forming perennials with deciduous basal leaves, or almost shrub-like, with leafy, biennial stems grown for their wide range of flower colour to include white, cream, pink, yellow, purple or green, sometimes spotted, from late winter to mid-spring. Hellebores are tolerant of humus-rich soils in partial shade but each one has a preferred set of cultivation conditions.

H. argutifolius (Corsican hellebore) A hardy, vigorous perennial producing overwintering, leafy biennial flowering stems. Pale green flowers are held over dark, shiny green leaves in spring. Tolerant of dry shade. 60 × 60cm/2 × 2ft

H. foetidus (Stinking hellebore) A hardy perennial of upright habit with biennial leaf stems producing ice-green flowers in early spring. Dark green leaves when crushed give an unpleasant smell. For neutral to alkaline soil in light shade. 45 × 45cm/1.5 × 1.5ft

H. foetidus Wester Flisk Similar to *H. foetidus* but with brilliant red stems and leaves of grey-green. For sun or shade. 45 × 45cm/1.5 × 1.5ft

H. lividus A frost hardy perennial of spreading habit with long, biennial stems. Pink-green flowers are carried over deeply marked foliage from midwinter to early spring. In cold areas overwinter in a cold glasshouse. Best in neutral to alkaline soil in light shade. 45 × 45cm/1.5 × 1.5ft

H. niger (Christmas rose) A hardy, clump forming perennial with overwintering, shiny basal leaves. From early winter to early spring reddish stems carry snow-white flowers, sometimes flushed pink. Best in neutral to alkaline soil in light shade. 30 × 45cm/1 × 1.5ft

H. orientalis (Lenten rose) A hardy perennial of overwintering basal leaves and from which are produced strong stems of large, open flowers in a wide range of colours, often spotted, from midwinter to late spring. Colour range results from hybridization between the various orientalis cultivars. Best in humus-rich, neutral to alkaline soil in part shade. 45 × 60cm/1.5 × 2ft

H. orientalis subsp. *abchasicus* Similar to *H. orientalis* but with pale green flowers tinged purplish pink, sometimes with darker purple spots, from midwinter to early spring. 45 × 60cm/1.5 × 2ft

Hemerocallis 'Joan Senior'

Hemerocallis lilioasphodelus

Hemerocallis 'Pink Damask'

Hemerocallis 'Bonanza'

HEMEROCALLIS (Day lily)

A genus of hardy to frost hardy, evergreen, semi-evergreen and herbaceous perennials from which numerous named cultivars have been raised. Mound forming, sometimes rhizomatous, they are mainly grown for their flowers in a wide range of colours which bloom for one day only, hence the common name, and are immediately replaced. Best in well drained soil in sun but tolerant of partial shade.

H. 'Bonanza' A hardy perennial with flowers of deep yellow striped brown carried over sword-like leaves in summer. 1 × 1m/3 × 3ft

H. 'Joan Senior' A hardy, semi-evergreen perennial of vigorous habit carrying large white flowers from mid to late summer. 60 × 75cm/2 × 2.5ft

H. lilioasphodelus A hardy, rhizomatous, semi-evergreen perennial with scented flowers of clear yellow from late spring to early summer. 75 × 75cm/2.5 × 2.5ft

H. 'Pink Damask' A hardy perennial bearing rich pink flowers over a prolonged period in summer. 1m × 60cm/3 × 2ft

H. 'Stella de Oro' A hardy, evergreen perennial of vigorous habit. Butter-yellow flowers are borne in profusion in early summer. 30 × 45cm/1 × 1.5ft

H. 'Summer Wine' A hardy perennial of rush-like leaves over which are carried magenta-pink flowers with yellow stripes in summer. 60 × 60cm/2 × 2ft

Hemerocallis 'Stella de Oro'

Hemerocallis 'Summer Wine'

Hepatica nobilis

HEPATICA

A genus of spring flowering perennials cultivated for their starry flowers usually opening before the leaves are fully formed. Best in neutral to alkaline soil in a partially shaded situation. Hepaticas resent disturbance and do not transplant well.

H. nobilis A semi-evergreen perennial of three-lobed leaves and small flowers of blue, blue-purple, pink or white in early spring. 10 × 15cm/4 × 6in

Hermodactylus tuberosus

Hesperis matronalis

× *Heucherella alba* 'Bridget Bloom'

HERMODACTYLUS

A genus of a single species of tuberous perennial with strap-like leaves and iris-type flowers. For well drained soil with lime content in full sun. Afford protection from excess of summer wet.
H. tuberosus (Widow iris) A tuberous perennial with glaucous leaves bearing iris-type flowers of greenish-yellow rimmed with black in spring. In cold areas protect early flowers from frost. 30 × 5cm/1ft × 2in

HESPERIS

A genus of biennials and perennials grown for their sweetly scented flowers of lilac or white. Some cultivars possess double flowers. Best in neutral to alkaline soil.
H. matronalis (Sweet rocket) A rosette forming, short lived perennial with coarse leaves and scented flowers of lilac or white, the scent most noticeable in the evening. 75 × 60cm/2.5 × 2ft

× HEUCHERELLA

A hybrid genus of evergreen perennials resulting from crosses between *Heuchera* and *Tiarella*. Bell-shaped pink or white flowers are carried over heart-shaped, deeply veined leaves from spring to autumn. Suitable for naturalizing in woodland.
× *H. alba* 'Bridget Bloom' A perennial of clump forming habit with large leaves of mid-green and producing tall stems of white flowers from late spring to mid-autumn. Leaves colour reddish-brown in autumn. 30 × 45cm/1 × 1.5ft

Heuchera 'Persian Carpet'

Heuchera micrantha var. *diversifolia* 'Palace Purple'

HEUCHERA (Coral flower)

Genus of hardy to frost hardy, evergreen or semi-evergreen perennials grown mainly for their attractive, clump forming leaves, often tinted bronze or purple and sometimes with marbled markings, as well as for their small flowers with colourful calyces attractive to bees. Tolerant of full shade in moist soil.
H. micrantha var. *diversifolia* 'Palace Purple' A hardy, evergreen, mound forming perennial with variable deep red, jagged leaves and wands of cream flowers in early summer. 45 × 45cm/1.5 × 1.5ft
H. 'Persian Carpet' A hardy, evergreen, mound forming perennial with leaves of deep purple marbled silver and slender stems of pale pink flowers in summer. 45 × 45cm/1.5 × 1.5ft
H. 'Rachel' A hardy, semi-evergreen, mound forming perennial with ruby coloured leaves and pale pink flowers carried on slender stems in summer. 45 × 30cm/ 1.5 × 1ft

Heuchera 'Rachel'

Hibiscus syriacus 'Blue Bird'

Hibiscus syriacus 'Woodbridge'

Hippophae rhamnoides

Hippeastrum 'Picotee'

Hoheria lyallii

HIBISCUS

A genus of hardy to frost tender annuals, perennials, deciduous and evergreen shrubs and trees grown for their flowers which range in colour from blue, pink, purple, red, white or yellow and which are borne over a long period from spring to autumn. Best in full sun. Less hardy species and cultivars should be given the protection of a warm glasshouse over winter. Some perennials may be grown as annuals.
H. syriacus 'Blue Bird' A hardy, deciduous shrub of upright habit with leaves of deep green and producing violet-blue flowers in late summer. 2 × 2m/6 × 6ft
H. syriacus 'Woodbridge' Similar to *H. syriacus* 'Blue Bird' but with rich pink flowers with darker centres in summer. 2.5 × 2m/7 × 6ft

HIPPEASTRUM

A genus of mainly frost tender, bulbous perennials cultivated for their showy flowers carried on leafless stems most often from winter to spring. Grown as houseplants or in a warm conservatory or glasshouse.
H. 'Picotee' A frost tender, bulbous perennial with large, white amaryllis-type flowers edged in deep pink in winter and spring. 60 × 30cm/2 × 1ft

HIPPOPHAE

A genus of deciduous shrubs and trees grown mainly for their silvery leaves and round, usually orange, fruits. Best in neutral to alkaline, sandy soil in full sun.
H. rhamnoides (Sea buckthorn) A large, deciduous shrub of suckering habit with linear grey leaves. Green-yellow flowers borne in racemes in spring are followed by small golden berries where both male and female plants are present. 5 × 5m/16 × 16ft

HOHERIA

A genus of frost hardy, deciduous and evergreen shrubs and trees grown mainly for their elegant form and scented white flowers. Afford protection from cold, drying winds. Deciduous species are more reliably hardy than those which are evergreen.
H. lyallii A frost hardy, spreading, deciduous tree with glaucous leaves and large white flowers with purple anthers in midsummer. 7 × 7m/22 × 22ft

HOLBOELLIA

A genus of frost hardy, evergreen climbers grown mainly for their attractive foliage. For full sun or partial shade and afford protection from cold winds.
H. coriacea A frost hardy, vigorous climber with leaves of dark green. Clusters of small flowers, greenish white female, mauve male, are produced in spring. Occasionally purple fruits follow the flowers. 7m/22ft

Hosta 'Gold Standard'

Hosta 'Frances Williams'

Hosta 'Halcyon'

HOSTA (Plantain lily)

A genus of clump forming, occasionally rhizomatous or stoloniferous perennials grown mainly for their bold foliage, the leaf colour ranging from blue-green, grey-green through green to yellow, often with variegation. Generally for moisture retentive soil in partial or total shade although those with yellow leaves retain their colour more in full sun. Intolerant of drought. Apply a mulch annually in spring.
H. 'Frances Williams' A clump forming perennial with ribbed leaves of grey-green edged with yellow, fading with age. Lilac flowers in summer. 75 × 75cm/2.5 × 2.5ft
H. 'Gold Standard' A clump forming perennial with golden leaves edged finely with dark green. Retains its colour well. Lavender flowers in summer.
60 × 60cm/2 × 2ft
H. 'Halcyon' A clump forming perennial of compact habit with heart-shaped leaves of gunmetal blue. Lavender flowers in summer. Best in moist soil.
45 × 45cm/1.5 × 1.5ft
H. sieboldiana A clump forming perennial with heavily ribbed, glaucous leaves. Pale lilac flowers in early summer. 75 × 75cm/2.5 × 2.5ft
H. undulata var. *undulata* A clump forming perennial with twisted, deeply ribbed, lance-shaped leaves of white and green variegation. Rich lilac flowers in summer.
45 × 45cm/1.5 × 1.5ft

Hosta sieboldiana

Hosta undulata var. *undulata*

HOTTONIA

A genus of hardy to half hardy, aquatic perennials. Primula-like white to lilac flowers are produced over feathery, light green foliage in spring. Cultivated mainly as oxygen-producing plants and best planted in still, shallow water in full sun.
H. palustris (Water violet) A hardy, aquatic perennial with spreading and upright stems and producing pale lilac or white flowers with yellow throats in spring. 60cm/2ft × indefinite spread

HOUTTUYNIA

A genus of a single species of spreading, rhizomatous perennial grown mainly as a form of ground cover and for leaf colour. Best in humus-rich soil in full sun or light shade. May become invasive.
H. cordata 'Chameleon' A spreading perennial with variegated leaves in shades of green, red and yellow. Less vigorous than the species. 30cm/1ft × indefinite spread

Houttuynia cordata 'Chameleon'

Humulus lupulus 'Aureus'

HUMULUS (Hop)

A genus of hardy to half hardy herbaceous perennials with twining stems. The cultivars are grown for their brightly coloured foliage.
H. lupulus 'Aureus' A hardy, rhizomatous perennial with large leaves of golden-yellow. Scented green, then straw-coloured spikes of female flowers are produced in summer. Protect from excess of winter wet. 6m/20ft

Hyacinthoides italica

Hyacinthoides non-scripta

HYACINTHUS (Hyacinth)

Genus of bulbous perennials cultivated mainly for their dense clumps of strongly scented flowers in a wide colour range. Most often used as spring bedding or in containers. Pot grown plants need protection from excessive winter wet.
H. orientalis A bulbous perennial with sword-like leaves of bright green. Upright racemes of heavily scented, bell-shaped flowers in shades of blue, red, pink, purple, orange, yellow and white are produced in early spring.
30 × 8cm/1ft × 3in

Hyacinthoides hispanica

HYACINTHOIDES (Bluebell)

A genus of vigorous, bulbous perennials bearing racemes of bell-shaped blue, white or sometimes pink flowers in spring. Suitable for naturalizing in grass or woodland. Best in light shade.
H. hispanica (Spanish bluebell) A bulbous, clump forming perennial with strappy leaves of shiny, dark green and scented blue, white or pink flowers in spring.
45 × 10cm/1.5ft × 4in
H. italica A bulbous perennial with lance-shaped leaves of dull, dark green and upward facing flowers of mid-blue in spring. 20 × 5cm/8 × 2in
H. non-scripta (English bluebell) A bulbous, clump forming perennial with lance-shaped leaves of shiny, dark green and scented flowers of mid-blue, sometimes white, in spring. 45 × 30cm/1.5 × 1ft

Hyacinthus orientalis

Hydrangea arborescens

Hydrangea aspera Villosa

Hydrangea anomala subsp. *petiolaris*

HYDRANGEA

A genus of hardy to frost hardy, deciduous and evergreen shrubs and climbers, rarely trees, grown principally for their bold flowerheads and attractive foliage with good autumn colour. Best in humus-rich, moist soil which is not allowed to dry out. Some species are intolerant of shallow, limy conditions.

H. anomala subsp. *petiolaris* (Climbing hydrangea) A hardy, woody, deciduous climber supporting itself by means of aerial roots. Dark green, rounded leaves colour yellow in autumn. Pure white flowers are produced in lacy corymbs in summer. For moist, leafy soil. Tolerant of shade. 6m/20ft

H. arborescens (Sevenbark) A hardy, deciduous shrub of rounded habit with heart-shaped leaves, dark green above, paler on the undersides, and corymbs of dull white flowers in summer. 2.5 × 2.5m/8 × 8ft

H. aspera Villosa A hardy, deciduous shrub or small tree of upright habit carrying lace-cap flowerheads of faded lilac-blue in late summer. Best in part shade in acidic or neutral soil. 2.4 × 2m/8 × 6ft

H. macrophylla 'Ayesha' A hardy, deciduous shrub of rounded habit with shiny green leaves and flowers of lilac-pink in midsummer. 1 × 1.5m/3 × 5ft

H. macrophylla 'Madame Emile Mouillère' A hardy, deciduous shrub of rounded habit with white flowers becoming pink-tinged with age. 1 × 1.5m/3 × 5ft

H. macrophylla 'Mariesii' A hardy, deciduous shrub of rounded habit producing lace-cap flowerheads in profusion of pale pink to pale blue in summer. 1.5 × 1.5m/5 × 5ft

H. macrophylla 'Mariesii Perfecta' (syn. 'Blue Wave') A hardy, deciduous shrub with lace-cap-type flowerheads in summer. Lime free soil produces bluest flowerheads otherwise pink or red. 2 × 2.5m/6 × 7ft

Hydrangea macrophylla 'Madame Emile Mouillère'

Hydrangea macrophylla 'Mariesii'

Hydrangea macrophylla 'Mariesii Perfecta'

Hydrangea macrophylla 'Ayesha'

Hydrangea paniculata

Hydrangea macrophylla 'Veitchii'

Hydrangea 'Preziosa'

H. macrophylla 'Veitchii' A hardy, deciduous shrub of rounded habit with flowerheads of blue, the outer florets white fading to pink, in summer. Tolerant of lime. 2 × 2.7m/6 × 9ft

H. paniculata A hardy, deciduous shrub of upright habit carrying long panicles of white flowers from late summer to early autumn. For moist, humus-rich soil. 2.7 × 2.1m/9 × 7ft

H. 'Preziosa' A frost hardy, deciduous shrub of upright habit with shiny leaves of mid-green and carrying small corymbs of pink flowers, turning to rich red, blue or mauve on acid soil, in late summer. 1.5 × 1.5m/5 × 5ft

H. quercifolia (Oak-leafed hydrangea) A hardy, deciduous shrub of rounded habit with leaves of mid-green cut like an oak turning to grape-purple in autumn. Lacy panicles of cream flowers, becoming tinged pink with age, are produced from midsummer to autumn. 1.5 × 2.1m/5 × 7ft

H. serrata 'Grayswood' A frost hardy, deciduous shrub of upright habit with pointed leaves of mid-green and bearing lilac and white flowerheads in summer. 2 × 2m/6 × 6ft

Hydrangea quercifolia

Hydrangea serrata 'Grayswood'

Hypericum 'Hidcote'

Hypericum × inodorum 'Elstead'

Hypericum calycinum

HYPERICUM (St. John's wort)
Genus of hardy to frost tender annuals, herbaceous perennials, deciduous, evergreen and semi-evergreen shrubs and trees grown mainly for their bold yellow flowers with prominent stamens and ornamental fruits. Larger species will tolerate sun or part shade; dwarf species are best in full sun.

H. calycinum (Rose of Sharon) A hardy, evergreen or semi-evergreen dwarf shrub of low growing habit carrying open, saucer-shaped flowers of clear yellow in profusion from midsummer to autumn. 30cm/1ft × indefinite spread

H. 'Hidcote' A hardy, evergreen or semi-evergreen shrub of dense habit carrying golden-yellow flowers from midsummer to mid-autumn. 1.2 × 1.5m/4 × 5ft

H. × inodorum 'Elstead' A hardy, deciduous or semi-evergreen shrub of upright habit with small flowers of bright yellow from midsummer to early autumn. These are followed with decorative orange-red fruits. 1.2 × 1.2m/4 × 4ft

H. kouytchense A hardy, deciduous or semi-evergreen shrub of bushy habit with large, deep yellow flowers in summer followed by brick-red fruits. 1 × 1.5m/3 × 5ft

H. olympicum A hardy, deciduous dwarf shrub with glaucous leaves producing vivid yellow flowers in summer. 30 × 30cm/1 × 1ft

Hypericum olympicum

Hypericum kouytchense

Hyssopus officinalis

HYSSOPUS (Hyssop)
A genus of herbaceous perennials and evergreen or semi-evergreen shrubs grown for their aromatic foliage and flowers of violet-blue to pink and white. Leaves have culinary and medicinal value. Best in full sun.

H. officinalis A dwarf, semi-evergreen shrub with dark green aromatic leaves and tiny blue flowers from midsummer to autumn. 60cm × 1m/2 × 3ft

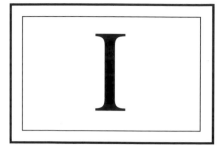

Iberis sempervirens

Iberis umbellata

Ilex × altaclarensis 'Lawsoniana'

Ilex × altaclarensis 'Golden King'

Ilex aquifolium 'Ferox Argentea'

Ilex aquifolium 'Golden Milkboy'

IBERIS (Candytuft)

A genus of hardy to frost hardy annuals, perennials and evergreen sub-shrubs. Annuals flower over a prolonged period and are most often grown as summer bedding. Best in full sun.

I. sempervirens A hardy, evergreen sub-shrub of spreading habit with narrow leaves of deep green and carrying spherical white flowers from spring to early summer. 30 × 60cm/1 × 2ft

I. umbellata (Common candytuft) A hardy annual producing a dense mat of deep green foliage and carrying scented white, lilac, pink, purple or red flowers from summer to early autumn. 15 × 30cm/6in × 1ft

ILEX (Holly)

A genus of hardy to frost tender, deciduous and evergreen shrubs, trees and climbers cultivated for their bold foliage and colourful fruits. Leaves, often spiny, may be green, yellow or variegated whilst flowers of blue, green, pink or, more usually, cream or white are borne from spring to early summer. Male and female flowers are normally carried on separate plants, both sexes being needed to produce fruits. Variegation is best in full sun. Frost tender species need the protection of a cool glasshouse over winter.

I. × altaclarensis 'Lawsoniana' A frost hardy, evergreen female shrub of dense habit with leaves of dark green irregularly splashed with gold. Brown fruits ripen to red with age. 6 × 5m/ 20 × 15ft

I. altaclarensis 'Golden King' A frost hardy, evergreen female shrub with purple flushed branches when young. Oblong, sometimes spiny leaves are marked light grey-green towards the centre with a vibrant yellow strip at the margin. Brown-red fruits are produced in small number. 6 × 5m/20 × 15ft

I. aquifolium 'Ferox Argentea' (Silver hedgehog holly) A hardy, evergreen male shrub with purple flushed branches when young. Mid-green leaves with surface spines are margined cream. Slow growing. 6 × 4m/20 × 12ft

I. aquifolium 'Golden Milkboy' A hardy, evergreen male shrub producing purple flushed branches when young. Oval leaves of vivid green are prominently splashed bright yellow in the centre. 6 × 4m/20 × 12ft

IMPATIENS (Busy Lizzie)

A genus of hardy to frost tender annuals and evergreen perennials and sub-shrubs with brittle stems and fleshy leaves. Grown mainly for their long lasting colour throughout the summer, often as bedding schemes or for containers. Best in part shade with protection from drying winds.

I. hybrid A frost tender perennial most often grown as an annual. Flowers in a wide range of colours from early summer to autumn. 30 × 15cm/1ft × 6in

IMPERATA

Genus of rhizomatous, perennial grasses grown principally for their vibrant foliage. All require long hot summers to flower well but are tolerant of light shade. *I. cylindrica* 'Rubra' (Japanese blood grass) A perennial grass of slow, spreading habit to form a clump of strap-like leaves with blood-red tips. Flower spikes of silver-white are produced in late summer. 45 × 30cm/1.5 × 1ft

INCARVILLEA

A genus of hardy to frost hardy annuals and perennials grown for their large, trumpet-shaped flowers in shades of pink, purple or white.

I. delavayi A hardy, tap-rooted perennial forming clumps of deeply cut leaves over which are carried mid-pink flowers in early summer. These are followed by attractive seed capsules. 60 × 30cm/ 2 × 1ft

INDIGOFERA

A genus of hardy to frost hardy annuals, herbaceous perennials, deciduous or evergreen shrubs and trees grown mainly for their attractive foliage and pea-like flowers. Best in full sun.

I. heterantha A hardy, deciduous shrub of freely branching habit with glaucous leaves and mid-pink, pea-like flowers from early summer to early autumn. For a hot, dry situation. 2 × 2m/6 × 6ft

Impatiens hybrid

Incarvillea delavayi

Indigofera heterantha

Inula hookeri

Ipheion uniflorum 'Froyle Mill'

INULA

A genus of hardy to frost hardy annuals, biennials, perennials and some sub-shrubs valued for their flat, daisy-like flowers. Low growing species are well suited to cultivation in the rock garden. Some taller growing species may prove to be invasive. Best in sun.

I. hookeri A hardy perennial of clump forming habit. Acid-yellow, daisy-like flowers are produced over hairy leaves in summer. 75 × 45cm/2.5 × 1.5ft

IPHEION

A genus of frost hardy to frost tender, bulbous perennials grown for their attractive, star-like flowers. For humus-rich, free draining soil in full sun. Apply a protective mulch in winter to the crowns.

I. uniflorum 'Froyle Mill' A frost hardy, bulbous perennial with strap-like leaves and starry violet-blue flowers in spring. Leaves when crushed give an onion-like smell. 15 × 8cm/6 × 3in

I. 'Rolf Fiedler' A frost hardy, bulbous perennial forming a clump of narrow, strap-like leaves with scented, starry flowers of mid-blue in spring. 15 × 8cm/6 × 3in

Ipheion 'Rolf Fiedler'

143

Ipomoea 'Early Call'

IPOMOEA (Morning glory)

A genus of frost tender annuals and perennials, a large number of which are climbers, and some evergreen shrubs and trees. Annuals require a sunny, sheltered spot whilst perennials are best cultivated under glass.

I. 'Early Call' A frost tender annual or short-lived perennial climber grown for its tubular flowers in various shades produced from summer to autumn. 5m/15ft

I. lobata A frost tender perennial climber treated as an annual. Crimson flushed stems carry scarlet, tubular flowers, later orange-yellow, from summer to autumn. 2–5m/6–15ft

Iris chrysographes

Iris danfordiae

Dutch iris (*I. xiphium* hybrid)

Ipomoea lobata

IRIS

A genus of hardy to frost tender, largely rhizomatous or bulbous perennials of upright habit, the majority of which are deciduous, flowering in the main from spring to summer. For convenience, irises may be divided as follows: rhizomatous, to include bearded, beardless, Pacific Coast, Siberian, laevigata, Louisiana, unguicularis, and crested, and bulbous to include reticulata, juno and xiphium. Most iris will succeed in well drained soil in a position in full sun or light shade. Rhizomes of bearded irises should be exposed in part to the sun.

I. chrysographes A hardy, rhizomatous, beardless perennial with strap-like leaves. Small flowers of near black with yellow markings on the falls are produced in early summer. 45 × 6cm/1.5ft × 2.5in

I. danfordiae A hardy, bulbous perennial producing large, clear yellow flowers in late winter and early spring. 15 × 5cm/6 × 2.5in

Dutch iris (*I. xiphium* hybrid) A hardy, bulbous perennial of vigorous habit with sword-shaped leaves producing deep blue or violet, sometimes yellow or white, flowers in late spring and early summer. 60 × 10cm/2ft × 4in

I. ensata A hardy, rhizomatous, beardless perennial with upright standards, smaller than the falls, of plum-purple produced in midsummer. 1m × 30cm/3 × 1ft

I. foetidissima (Stinking iris, Gladwin iris) A hardy, broad leafed perennial with lilac or yellow flowers in summer. Pods release vibrant, orange seeds in winter. 45 × 60cm/1.5 × 2ft

I. 'Florentina' (Orris root) A hardy, rhizomatous, bearded perennial with fan-like, sometimes evergreen, leaves. Strongly perfumed white flowers are produced in late spring. 60 × 30cm/2 × 1ft

I. forrestii A hardy, rhizomatous, beardless perennial with shiny green leaves and producing perfumed flowers of Chinese yellow with brown markings in early summer. 30 × 30cm/1 × 1ft

I. germanica 'Pam's Wedding' A hardy, rhizomatous, bearded perennial with fan-like, evergreen leaves. Blue-white flowers in late spring. 1m × 30cm/3 × 1ft

I. graminea (Plum tart iris) A hardy, rhizomatous perennial with flat, strap-like leaves and producing violet-purple flowers, smelling of cooked plums, set deep amongst the foliage in late spring and early summer. 30 × 30cm/1 × 1ft

I. 'Holden Clough' A hardy, rhizomatous, beardless perennial with arching, sometimes evergreen leaves. In late spring deep yellow flowers, heavily marked in purple, are produced. 1m × 60cm/3 × 2ft

I. innominata A hardy, beardless, Pacific Coast perennial with flowers in late spring to early summer. Flower colour ranges through blue, cream, gold, pink, purple and yellow. 25cm/10in × indefinite spread

Iris ensata

Iris foetidissima

Iris 'Florentina'

Iris germanica 'Pam's Wedding'

Iris forrestii

Iris graminea

Iris 'Holden Clough'

Iris innominata

Iris 'Joyce'

Iris 'Mandarin'

Iris 'Margot Holmes'

Iris pallida subsp. *pallida*

Iris pallida 'Variegata'

Iris pseudacorus var. *bastardii*

Iris missouriensis

I. 'Joyce' A hardy, bulbous perennial bearing deep blue flowers in the early spring well suited to cultivation in the rock garden or alpine trough. 12 × 5cm/5 × 2in

I. 'Mandarin' A hardy, rhizomatous perennial with thin, strap-like leaves producing rich purple flowers in early summer. 1m × 30cm/3 × 1ft

I. 'Margot Holmes' A hardy rhizomatous perennial with tapering, strap-like leaves producing light mauve flowers in early summer. 1m × 30cm/3 × 1ft

I. missouriensis A hardy, variable, rhizomatous, beardless perennial with thin, strap-like leaves rising above the short flowers of blue or lilac-purple with larger falls of dark purple markings carried on slender stems in summer. Best in damp soil. 60 × 60cm/2 × 2ft

I. pallida subsp. *pallida* A hardy, rhizomatous, bearded perennial with semi-evergreen leaves which are topped by flower stems carrying shiny, paper-like bracts. In late spring and early summer large, perfumed, light blue flowers with yellow beards are produced. 1.2m × 60cm/4 × 2ft

I. pallida 'Variegata' Similar to *I. pallida* subsp. *pallida* but with pale yellow striped clear green leaves. 1.2m × 60cm/4 × 2ft

I. pseudacorus var. *bastardii* (Yellow flag) A hardy, rhizomatous, beardless perennial of extremely vigorous habit with coarse leaves of mid-green. In early to mid-summer deep yellow flowers are produced. Best in moist to wet soil and suitable for shallow water. 1m/3ft × indefinite spread

I. pumila A hardy, variable, rhizomatous bearded perennial of dwarf habit. Flowers of blue, purple or yellow produced in mid-spring. 15 × 15cm/6 × 6in

I. setosa A hardy, variable, rhizomatous beardless perennial with strap-like leaves often tinged red at the base. Blue flowers produced in late spring and early summer. 60 × 30cm/2 × 1ft

I. sibirica 'Soft Blue' A hardy, rhizomatous beardless perennial with narrow rush-like leaves and producing flowers of palest blue, darker in bud, in early summer. 1m × 30cm/3 × 1ft

I. unguicularis (Algerian iris) A hardy, rhizomatous beardless perennial of vigorous habit. Large, scented, lavender-blue flowers are produced in late winter and early spring. For an open, sunny position with sharp drainage. 60 x 30cm/2 x 1ft

I. versicolor 'Kermesina' (Blue flag) A hardy, rhizomatous beardless perennial producing plum-purple flowers marked with gold in early and midsummer. For moist soil or shallow water. 75 × 30cm/2.5 × 1ft

Iris pumila

Iris setosa

Iris sibirica 'Soft Blue'

Iris unguicularis

Iris versicolor 'Kermesina'

Isoplexis canariensis

Itea ilicifolia

ISOPLEXIS

A genus of frost tender, evergreen sub-shrubs or shrubs grown for their showy flowers in summer. Afford protection from cold winds.

I. canariensis A frost tender, clump forming shrub of upright habit with serrated leaves of dark green. Long, tubular flowers of orange or yellow-brown are produced in summer.
1 × 1m/3 × 3ft

ITEA

A genus of hardy to frost hardy, deciduous and evergreen shrubs and trees grown for their attractive, holly-like foliage and showy catkin-like flowers. Best in well drained soil in full sun. *I. virginica* requires moist, acidic soil in partial shade.
I. ilicifolia A frost hardy, evergreen shrub with holly-like leaves producing long, ice-green, fragrant catkin inflorescences in summer. 3 × 3m/10 × 10ft

Jasione laevis 'Blue Light'

JASIONE (Sheep's bit)

A genus of annuals, biennials and perennials grown for their scabious-like flowers, generally blue, produced in summer. Best on light, sandy soil in full sun.

J. laevis 'Blue Light' A perennial of clump forming habit with rounded flowerheads of intense blue from midsummer to early autumn. 30 × 20cm/1ft × 8in

Jasminum nudiflorum

Jasminum officinale

Jasminum stephanense

Juglans regia

JASMINUM (Jasmine)

A genus of hardy to frost tender deciduous and evergreen shrubs and climbers grown for their elegant habit and often sweetly scented flowers.

J. nudiflorum (Winter jasmine) A hardy, deciduous shrub with arching, whippy stems of dark green. Clear yellow flowers are produced before new leaves emerge in winter and early spring. May be wall trained. 3 × 3m/10 × 10ft

J. officinale (Common jasmine) A frost hardy, deciduous, sometimes semi-deciduous, climber of vigorous habit with green or variegated leaves. Highly scented white flowers are produced from summer to early autumn. Best in sun but tolerant of most situations. 7m/23ft × indefinite spread

J. × stephanense A frost hardy, deciduous climber of vigorous habit with green or variegated leaves. Scented flowers of pale pink are produced in early and midsummer. 5m/15ft × indefinite spread

JEFFERSONIA

A genus of perennials with kidney-shaped leaves and small flowers on thin stems in late spring and early summer. For a woodland situation in partial or full shade.

J. dubia A low growing perennial with leaves of grey-green and flowers of lavender-blue, occasionally white, in late spring and early summer. 20 × 15cm/8 × 6in

JUGLANS (Walnut)

Genus of hardy to frost hardy, deciduous trees and occasionally shrubs. Male and female flowers produced separately on the same plant in late spring and early summer. Ideal as specimen trees on account of elegant habit, foliage and fruit.

J. regia (Common walnut) A hardy tree of spreading habit with aromatic leaves, bronze coloured when young, and producing rounded fruits containing edible nuts. 30 × 15m/100 × 50ft

Juniperus communis 'Compressa'

Juniperus communis 'Hibernica'

Juniperus sabina 'Tamariscifolia'

Juniperus × *pfitzeriana* 'Pfitzeriana Aurea'

JUNIPERUS (Juniper)

Genus of hardy to frost hardy, evergreen, coniferous shrubs and trees principally grown as specimens, the smallest species being suitable for the rock garden, those of spreading habit making useful ground cover. Tolerant of a wide range of soils and conditions, including chalk and sand, but best in sun.

J. communis 'Compressa' A hardy, evergreen tree of dwarf habit, small enough to be container grown. Position out of the reach of cold winds. 75 × 15cm/2.5ft × 6in

J. communis 'Hibernica' A hardy, evergreen tree of columnar habit with dense foliage of grey green. Slow growing. 4m × 45cm/13 × 1.5ft

J. × *pfitzeriana* 'Pfitzeriana Aurea' A hardy, evergreen shrub of spreading habit with strong ascending branches and gold-green foliage. Grown for its dramatic colour and use as ground cover. 1.8 × 4m/6 × 13ft

J. sabina 'Tamariscifolia' A hardy, evergreen shrub of spreading habit forming a flat top of rich green foliage, grey when young. 1 × 2m/3 × 6ft

J. squamata 'Blue Carpet' A hardy, evergreen shrub of spreading habit with silver-blue foliage and flaky, brown bark. Best in sun with good drainage. 45cm × 2m/1.5 × 6ft

Juniperus squamata 'Blue Carpet'

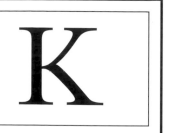

Kalmia latifolia 'Nimuck Red Bud'

Kalmia latifolia

Kerria japonica 'Pleniflora'

KALMIA

A genus of evergreen shrubs grown for their glossy, leathery leaves and attractive cup or saucer-shaped flowers produced from late spring to midsummer. For moist, humus-rich, acidic soil in sun or part shade.

K. latifolia (Calico bush) A slow growing, evergreen shrub producing pink, occasionally white, flowers from deeply coloured buds from late spring to midsummer. 3 × 3m/10 × 10ft

K. latifolia 'Nimuck Red Bud' A slow growing, evergreen shrub producing flowers of deep, sugar pink, lighter at the centre, from late spring to midsummer. 3 × 3m/10 × 10ft

K. polifolia (Eastern bog laurel) A small, thinly branched shrub producing flowers of purple-pink in mid and late spring. 60cm × 1m/2 × 3ft

KERRIA (Jew's mantle)

A genus of a single species of deciduous shrub grown for its attractive foliage and golden-yellow flowers in spring.

K. japonica A shrub of suckering habit with bright, light green leaves and golden-yellow, open flowers in mid and late spring. 2 × 2.5m/6 × 8ft

K. japonica 'Pleniflora' As *K. japonica* but with double, pompon-like flowers of golden-yellow in spring. 2 × 2.5m/6 × 8ft

Kirengeshoma palmata

Knautia arvensis

Knautia macedonica

KIRENGESHOMA

A genus of clump forming, rhizomatous perennials grown for their sycamore-like foliage and waxy, lemon flowers. Best in moisture retentive, humus-rich, lime free soil with protection from cold winds.

K. palmata A perennial with leaves of pale green and producing lemon flowers in late summer and early autumn. 1m × 75cm/3 × 2.5ft

KNAUTIA

A genus of annuals and perennials with scabious-like flowers of lilac to deep purple which are attractive to bees. Best in well drained, limey soil in a position in full sun.

K. arvensis (Field scabious) A tap-rooted perennial forming clumps of dull green leaves over which are carried flat headed, lilac-blue flowers in midsummer. 1m × 30cm/3 × 1ft

K. macedonica A clump forming perennial producing plum-purple, pincushion flowerheads in profusion in mid and late summer. Sets seed freely. 60 × 45cm/2 × 1.5ft

Kniphofia 'Atlanta'

Kniphofia 'Little Maid'

Kniphofia northiae

Kniphofia pumila

KNIPHOFIA (Red hot poker)

A genus of hardy to frost tender, deciduous or evergreen, rhizomatous perennials mainly of clump forming habit with grass-like or strap-shaped leaves. Poker-like flowers are produced in colours ranging from red, orange and yellow to white which are attractive to bees. Tolerant of a wide range of soil conditions and situations. Young plants should be afforded some form of protection over winter.

K. 'Atlanta' A hardy, evergreen perennial with glaucous leaves and producing flowers of deep orange, fading to pale yellow with age, in late spring and early summer. 1.2m × 75cm/4 × 2.5ft

K. 'Little Maid' A hardy, deciduous perennial with grassy leaves and flowers of creamy-yellow in late summer and early autumn. 60 × 45cm/2 × 1.5ft

K. northiae A hardy, evergreen perennial forming rosettes of broad leaves of grey-green and producing cream and red flower spikes in summer. 1 × 1m/3 × 3ft

K. pumila A hardy, evergreen perennial with long, tapering leaves and flowers of dull crimson and creamy yellow in late summer and early autumn. 1 × 1m/3 × 3ft

K. 'Torchbearer' A hardy, evergreen perennial with broad leaves and tall spikes of creamy flowers in midsummer. 1.5 × 1m/5 × 3ft

KOELREUTERIA

Genus of hardy to frost hardy, deciduous trees or shrubs grown for their elegant habit, foliage and flowers. Position in full sun.

K. paniculata (Pride of India) A hardy tree of domed habit with pinnate leaves of dark green, opening red in late spring and colouring yellow in autumn. Panicles of small, golden-yellow flowers are produced in late summer. 10 × 10m/33 × 33ft

KOLKWITZIA (Beauty bush)

A genus of a single species of deciduous shrub grown for its prolifically flowering habit. Best in well drained soil in full sun.

K. amabilis A deciduous shrub of suckering habit with long, arching stems and leaves of dark green colouring reddish in autumn. Pale pink, foxglove-like flowers, flushed yellow are produced in late spring and early summer. 3 × 3m/10 × 10ft

Koelreuteria paniculata

Kniphofia 'Torchbearer'

Kolkwitzia amabilis

151

LABURNUM (Golden rain tree)

Genus of deciduous trees grown mainly
for their prolific flowering habit.
Racemes of hanging, pea-like flowers
are produced in a mass in late spring
and early summer. Suitable as
specimens. All parts of the laburnum are
poisonous. Best in full sun.
L. × *watereri* 'Vossii' A spreading tree
with leaves of dark green and long
racemes of deep yellow flowers in late
spring and early summer.
10 × 10m/33 × 33ft

Laburnum × *watereri* 'Vossii'

Lamium galeobdolon 'Florentinum'

Lamium maculatum 'White Nancy'

LAMIUM (Dead nettle)

A genus of annuals and generally rhizomatous perennials grown largely for their
foliage and ability to provide excellent ground cover. Some species may become
invasive and are best confined to the wild or woodland garden. Smaller species are
well suited to the rock garden.
L. galeobdolon 'Florentinum' A rhizomatous perennial spreading rapidly by means of
creeping stems. Whorls of pale yellow flowers are carried in late spring and early
summer over leaves of silver and dark green. 30cm/1ft × indefinite spread
L. galeobdolon 'Hermann's Pride' A rhizomatous perennial forming a dense clump of
deep green leaves heavily streaked with silver. Pale yellow flowers in late spring and
early summer. 30 × 60cm/1 × 2ft
L. maculatum 'White Nancy' A rhizomatous perennial of spreading habit bearing
whorls of snow white flowers above silver leaves, narrowly edged green, in late
spring and early summer. 15cm × 1m/6in × 3ft
L. maculatum 'Wootton Pink' A rhizomatous perennial of creeping habit bearing
whorls of clear pink flowers above white striped leaves in late spring and early
summer. 15 × 30cm/6in × 1ft
L. orvala A perennial of clump forming habit. Rose-pink flowers are set off by
textured leaves of dark green from late spring to summer. 60 × 30cm/2 × 1ft

Lamium maculatum 'Wootton Pink'

Lamium orvala

Lantana camara hybrid

Lapageria rosea

Larix decidua (autumn foliage)

LANTANA

A genus of frost tender perennials and
evergreen shrubs grown for their
brightly coloured flowers borne in
clusters above the leaves. For moist, well
drained soil in full sun.
L. camara hybrid A frost tender, variable,
often prickly shrub with ridged, dark
green leaves. Flowers, in late spring to
late autumn, of pink to red, purple,
yellow or white. 1 × 1m/3 × 3ft

LAPAGERIA

A genus of a single species of frost hardy
to half hardy, woody, evergreen climbers
valued for their showy flowers. Grow in
humus-rich, moist but well drained
neutral to acid soil in part shade.
L. rosea (Chilean bell flower) A frost
hardy climber of suckering habit with
dark green leaves. Tubular bell-shaped,
waxy flowers of pink or red from
summer to late autumn. 5m/15ft

LARIX (Larch)

A genus of deciduous, coniferous trees
grown for their attractive foliage, fresh
green in spring and colouring well in
autumn. Cultivated mainly either as
specimens or within woodland. Tolerant
of a wide range of growing conditions.
L. decidua A deciduous, coniferous tree
of conical shape bearing female cones.
Light green leaves colour straw-yellow
in autumn. 30 × 6m/100 × 20ft

Lathraea clandestina

LATHRAEA

A genus of leafless, mainly underground, parasitic perennials grown for their ground-level white or lilac flowers in spring. For moist, well drained soil in partial shade at the base of a host tree.
L. clandestina (Purple toothwort) A rhizomatous, parasitic perennial most frequently to be found at the base of alder, poplar and willow. Lilac flowers in spring. 2cm/¾in × indefinite spread

Lathyrus latifolius

Lathyrus latifolius 'White Pearl'

Lathyrus odoratus hybrid

LATHYRUS (Everlasting pea)

A genus of hardy to frost hardy annuals and herbaceous or evergreen perennials grown principally for their numerous attractive, pea-like flowers in a wide colour range. Many are of climbing habit, others are clump forming.
L. latifolius (Perennial pea) A hardy, herbaceous perennial climber producing racemes of magenta-pink flowers from summer to early autumn. 2m/6ft
L. latifolius 'White Pearl' Similar to *L. latifolius* but with snow white flowers over fresh green leaves from summer to early autumn. 2m/6ft
L. ordoratus hybrids (Sweet pea) Hardy annuals of climbing habit producing flowers in an extensive colour range in summer. All are fragrant. Older varieties tend to have most scent but with smaller flowers and are less tidy in growth. 2m/6ft

Laurus nobilis

LAURUS

A genus of frost hardy, evergreen shrubs and trees grown for their aromatic foliage and their capacity to be shaped as topiary specimens. Afford protection from cold winds which may cause damage to young leaves.
L. nobilis (Bay laurel) A frost hardy, cone-shaped tree or large shrub with aromatic, shiny, dark green leaves which may be used for culinary purposes. Clusters of yellow-green flowers are produced in spring. 12 × 10m/40 × 30ft

Lavandula angustifolia 'Hidcote'

Lavandula × *intermedia* 'Grappenhall'

Lavandula stoechas

Lavandula stoechas f. *leucantha*

LAVANDULA (Lavender)

A genus of hardy to half hardy, aromatic, evergreen shrubs and sub-shrubs grown mainly for their highly scented flowers which are attractive to bees. Both leaves and flowerheads may be dried and used in arrangements or pot-pourri. Best in moderately fertile soil in full sun.
L. angustifolia 'Hidcote' A hardy shrub of compact habit with thin, glaucous leaves and flowers of intense violet-blue in mid to late summer. 60 × 45cm/2 × 1.5ft
L. × *intermedia* 'Grappenhall' A hardy, clump forming shrub with aromatic, hairy, glaucous leaves. Spikes of pale purple flowers are produced in summer.
1 × 1.5m/3 × 5ft
L. stoechas (French lavender) A hardy to frost hardy shrub of compact habit with grey-green leaves over which are carried deep purple flowerheads on short stems from late spring to summer. *L.s.* f. *leucantha* has white flowers. 60 × 60cm/2 × 2ft

Lavatera 'Barnsley'

Lavatera maritima

Lavatera olbia 'Rosea'

Leptospermum scoparium

Leucojum aestivum

Leucojum vernum var. *carpathicum*

LAVATERA (Mallow)

A genus of hardy to frost hardy annuals, biennials, herbaceous, semi-evergreen or evergreen perennials and deciduous shrubs and sub-shrubs grown for their showy flowers in a range of colours to include shades of pink, mauve and white. Best in full sun.

L. 'Barnsley' A hardy, semi-evergreen sub-shrub of vigorous habit with felted leaves of mid-green and pink centred, off white-cream flowers, becoming pink with age, in summer. 2 × 1m/6 × 3ft

L. maritima (syn. *bicolor*) A hardy, evergreen shrubby perennial of upright habit with grey-green leaves and blush-pink centred, rose flowers in summer. 2 × 1m/6 × 3ft

L. olbia 'Rosea' A hardy, semi-evergreen sub-shrub of vigorous habit with leaves of silver-green and deep pink, open flowers in summer. 2 × 2m/6 × 6ft

L. trimestris 'Silver Cup' A hardy annual with felty leaves of mid-green and carrying vivid rose-pink flowers in summer. 75 × 45cm/2.5 × 1.5ft

Lavatera trimestris 'Silver Cup'

Leucanthemum × *superbum*

LEPTOSPERMUM (Tea tree)

A genus of hardy to frost tender, evergreen shrubs and trees grown for their aromatic foliage and profusion of small, pink, red or white flowers. For full sun or a cool conservatory.

L. scoparium A frost tender, compact shrub of arching habit with mid and dark green, aromatic leaves and cup-shaped white flowers in late spring and early summer. 3 × 3m/10 × 10ft

LEUCANTHEMUM

A genus of hardy, sometimes frost hardy, perennials grown for their white or yellow daisy flowers. Best in full sun.

L. × *superbum* (Shasta daisy) A hardy perennial of robust habit forming clumps of shiny, lance-shaped leaves. Single, occasionally double, white, with central disc of yellow, flowers are carried on tall stems in late summer to early autumn. 1m × 60cm/3 × 2ft

LEUCOJUM (Snowflake)

A genus of hardy to frost hardy, bulbous perennials, closely related to *Galanthus* (snowdrop), cultivated for their hanging, bell-shaped flowers, most often white, sometimes pink, in spring, summer and autumn.

L. aestivum A hardy, bulbous perennial of robust habit with strap-like leaves of shiny, dark green and carrying snowdrop-like, scented white flowers with green tips in spring. 60 × 8cm/2ft × 3in

L. vernum var. *carpathicum* A hardy, bulbous perennial with upright, strap-like leaves of shiny green producing bell-shaped, white flowers with yellow tips in early spring. 30 × 8cm/1ft × 3in

Leucothoe walteri

Lewisia cotyledon hybrids

Leycesteria formosa

LEUCOTHOE (Switch ivy)
Genus of hardy to frost hardy, deciduous, semi-evergreen or evergreen shrubs valued for their decorative leaves and most often cylindrical or urn-shaped, white flowers. For humus-rich, acid soil in part or full shade.
L. walteri A hardy, evergreen shrub of upright habit with broad, shiny, lance-shaped leaves of dark green and producing white, cylindrical flowers in spring.
1 × 2m/3 × 6ft

LEWISIA
A genus of deciduous or evergreen perennials noted for their fleshy leaves and funnel-shaped flowers of many colours to include magenta, pink, purple, orange, yellow and white. Well suited to the rock garden or alpine house. Afford protection from excess of winter wet. Best in sharply drained, neutral to acidic soil.
L. cotyledon hybrids Hardy, evergreen perennial, forming flat rosettes of lance-shaped leaves over which rise mainly striped pink to purple, more rarely apricot, cream, yellow or white, flowers in spring and summer. Up to 30 × 25cm/1ft × 10in

Liatris spicata 'Kobold'

LEYCESTERIA (Pheasant bush)
A genus of hardy to half hardy, deciduous shrubs of suckering habit with hollow stems and producing racemes or spikes of tubular flowers. Well suited to the woodland garden.
L. formosa A hardy shrub of upright habit forming thickets of hollow, green stems. White flowers, surrounded by purple-red bracts and followed by similar coloured berries, are produced from summer to early autumn. 2 × 2m/6 × 6ft

LIATRIS (Gayfeather)
A genus of perennials grown principally for their spikes or racemes of tubular flowers opening, unusually, from the top downwards. Best in full sun.
L. spicata 'Kobold' A perennial forming basal clumps of lance-shaped leaves over which rise deep purple flower spikes from late summer to early autumn.
45 × 45cm/1.5 × 1.5ft

Libertia grandiflora

LIBERTIA
A genus of hardy to frost hardy, rhizomatous, evergreen perennials of clump forming habit with thin, tapering leaves and producing open, saucer-shaped white or blue flowers. Smaller species are well suited to the rock garden. Best in full sun.
L. grandiflora A hardy, rhizomatous perennial forming thick clumps of slender leaves and bearing clusters of white flowers from late spring to early summer.
1m × 60cm/3 × 2ft

LIGULARIA
A genus of perennials of vigorous habit noted for their large, shaped leaves and corymbs or racemes of daisy-like flowers in shades of orange or yellow. Best in moisture retentive soil in sun.
L. przewalskii A vigorous perennial of clump forming habit with deeply cut leaves and carrying racemes of yellow flowerheads on tall, dark stems in mid and late summer. 2 × 1m/6 × 3ft

Ligularia przewalskii

LIGUSTRUM (Privet)
A genus of hardy to frost hardy, deciduous, semi-evergreen and evergreen shrubs and trees grown for their foliage as specimens or for hedging. Variegated forms are best positioned in sun.
L. ovalifolium 'Aureum' (Golden privet) A hardy evergreen or semi-evergreen shrub of upright, vigorous habit with leaves of mid-green broadly edged in bright yellow. Insignificant, small white flowers in midsummer. 4 × 4m/12 × 12ft

Ligustrum ovalifolium 'Aureum'

Lilium candidum

Lilium 'King Pete'

LILIUM (Lily)

A genus of hardy to half hardy, bulbous perennials valued for their often tall growing stems of showy flowers, many of which are heavily scented. Some species are tolerant of a wide range of conditions, the majority preferring acidic to neutral soil in sun. Well suited to cultivation in pots. For classification purposes they fall into the following groups: Asiatic hybrids, Martagon hybrids, Candidum hybrids, American hybrids, Longiflorum hybrids, Trumpet and Aurelian hybrids, Oriental hybrids and species.

L. candidum (Madonna lily) A hardy, species perennial with lance-shaped leaves of mid-green and pure white, scented, trumpet flowers, yellowing at the base, from mid to late summer. 1–2m/3–6ft

L. 'Golden Splendor' A hardy, Trumpet hybrid perennial with outward facing, scented flowers of yellow with a dark burgundy band in midsummer. 1.2–2m/4–6ft

L. 'King Pete' A hardy, Asiatic hybrid perennial with outward facing, bowl-shaped flowers of deep cream spotted orange in midsummer. 1m/3ft

L. martagon (Turkscap) A hardy, species perennial of clump forming habit with small purple-pink, spotted flowers carried on bright green stems from early to midsummer. *L.m.* var. *album* has pure white flowers. 1m/3ft

L. 'Mont Blanc' A hardy, Asiatic hybrid perennial with upward facing, wide, cup-shaped flowers of white, freckled brown in the centre, from early to midsummer. 60–75cm/2–2.5ft

L. 'Olivia' A hardy, Trumpet hybrid perennial with outward facing, bowl-shaped flowers of pure white in midsummer. 1m/3ft

Lilium 'Golden Splendor'

Lilium martagon

Lilium martagon var. *album*

Lilium 'Mont Blanc'

Lilium 'Olivia'

Lilium pyrenaicum

Lilium pardalinum

Lilium 'Pink Perfection'

L. pardalinum A hardy, species perennial of clump forming habit with lance-shaped leaves of dull green and producing turkscap-type flowers of orange-red to crimson, with maroon and some yellow markings, in midsummer. 1.5–2.5m/5–8ft

L. 'Pink Perfection' A hardy, Trumpet hybrid perennial with scented flowers of purple-pink with orange anthers in midsummer. 1.5–2m/5–6ft

L. pyrenaicum A hardy species perennial of clump forming habit with lance-shaped leaves of bright green and producing turkscap-type flowers of yellow or green-yellow with maroon markings in early and midsummer. 30cm–1m/1–3ft

L. regale (Regal lily) A hardy, species perennial with upright stems of grey-green carrying highly scented, trumpet-shaped flowers of white, flushed purple on the outsides, in midsummer. 60cm–2m/2–6ft

L. speciosum var. *rubrum* A hardy, species perennial carrying fragrant, turkscap-type carmine-red flowers on dark stems in late summer and early autumn. Best in moist, acidic soil in part shade. 1–2m/2–6ft

L. speciosum 'Uchido' Similar to *L. speciosum* var. *rubrum* but with crimson-red flowers with deeper red markings. 1–2m/3–6ft

L. 'Star Gazer' A hardy, Oriental hybrid perennial with turkscap-type flowers of red with darker spots. Well suited to cultivation in containers. 1–1.5m/3–5ft

Lilium speciosum var. *rubrum*

Lilium speciosum 'Uchido'

Lilium regale

Lilium 'Star Gazer'

Limnanthes douglasii

Linaria maroccana 'Fairy Lights'

Linum narbonense 'Heavenly Blue'

Liriodendron tulipifera

Limonium platyphyllum

Linaria purpurea 'Canon Went'

Liquidamber styraciflua (autumn foliage)

LIRIODENDRON (Tulip tree)

A genus of deciduous trees cultivated usually as specimens on account of their elegant habit and attractively shaped leaves. Best in neutral to acidic soil.
L. tulipifera A deciduous, columnar tree with unusually shaped leaves of dark green colouring yellow in autumn. Pale green flowers, banded orange at the base, appear in midsummer.
30 × 15m/100 × 50ft

LIMNANTHES (Poached egg plant)

A genus of annuals of low growing habit of which only a single species, *L. douglasii*, is widely cultivated. Valued for bright green leaves and colourful flowers which are attractive to bees. Best positioned in full sun.
L. douglasii A self-seeding annual of spreading habit producing scented, open, white rimmed, yellow flowers from summer to autumn. 15 × 15cm/ 6 × 6in or more

LIMONIUM (Statice)

A genus of hardy to frost tender annuals, biennials and deciduous and evergreen perennials and sub-shrubs grown largely for their paper-like flowers extending over a long period. Tolerant of most sunny situations.
L. platyphyllum 'Violetta' A hardy perennial forming a rosette of deep green leaves over which are carried tubular flowers of dark violet in late summer. 60 × 45cm/2 × 1.5ft

LINARIA (Toadflax)

A genus of hardy to half hardy annuals, biennials, and perennials with mainly grey-green leaves and carrying spurred flowers in a range of colours to include orange, pink, purple, red, yellow and white. Best in full sun.
L. maroccana 'Fairy Lights' A hardy annual with narrow, linear leaves of mid-green and bearing a profusion of purple, yellow and white lipped flowers in summer. 30 × 15cm/1ft × 6in
L. purpurea 'Canon Went' A hardy perennial of grey-green, linear leaves producing spires of pale pink flowers from early summer to early autumn.
1m × 30cm/3 × 1ft

LINUM (Flax)

A genus of hardy to frost hardy annuals, biennials and deciduous, semi-evergreen and evergreen perennials, shrubs and sub-shrubs grown mainly for their funnel or saucer-shaped flowers in a wide range of colours and extending over a prolonged period. Best in full sun.
L. narbonense 'Heavenly Blue' A hardy to frost hardy perennial with lance-shaped leaves of grey-green and carrying saucer-shaped flowers of intense violet-blue in early and midsummer.
60 × 45cm/2 × 1.5ft

LIQUIDAMBER

A genus of hardy to frost hardy, deciduous trees of upright habit and cultivated mainly for their maple-like foliage which colours well in autumn. Suitable as specimens or for woodland gardens. Best in acidic to neutral soil but not totally intolerant of some lime.
L. styraciflua (Sweet gum) A hardy, deciduous tree of conical shape with cork-like young branches and leaves of mid-green colouring flame in autumn.
25 × 12m/80 × 40ft

Liriope muscari

LIRIOPE (Lily turf)

A genus of rhizomatous and tuberous, evergreen and semi-evergreen perennials noted for their grass-like leaves and spikes or racemes of flowers. Tolerant of most conditions but best in slightly acidic soil.

L. muscari An evergreen, tuberous perennial forming thick clumps of strap-shaped leaves of deep green and producing spikes of violet-mauve, muscari-like (grape hyacinth) flowers in autumn. 30 × 45cm/1 × 1.5ft

Lithodora diffusa 'Star'

LITHODORA

A genus of hardy to frost hardy, evergreen shrubs and sub-shrubs grown mainly for their tubular flowers of blue or white. Best in full sun on alkaline to neutral soil although *L. diffusa* requires acidic conditions.

L. diffusa 'Star' A hardy, evergreen shrub of low, spreading habit with narrow leaves of dark green and producing star-like, white and blue flowers in profusion in late spring and summer. 15 × 60cm/6in × 2ft

L. zahnii A frost hardy, evergreen shrub with narrow leaves of dark green, grey on the reverse, and producing blue or white flowers over a prolonged period in summer and occasionally in autumn. 30 × 45cm/1 × 1.5ft

Lithodora zahnii

Lobelia 'Dark Crusader'

Lobelia 'Queen Victoria'

Lobelia siphilitica

LOBELIA

A genus of hardy to frost tender annuals, perennials, some aquatics, and shrubs grown in the main for the brilliance of their flowers. Best in moisture retentive soil, aquatics require acidic conditions on the edges of pools and streams. Annual species frequently employed in summer bedding schemes.

L. 'Dark Crusader' A hardy perennial with deep, maroon coloured leaves and carrying flowers of velvet-red in mid and later summer. 75 × 30cm/2.5 × 1ft

L. erinus hybrids Half-hardy annuals with blue, white or rose flowers from summer to autumn. Bushy or trailing habit. 15 × 20cm/6 × 8in

L. 'Queen Victoria' A hardy perennial forming clumps of deep purple-red leaves and carrying scarlet flowers borne on dark stems from late summer to mid-autumn. 1m × 30cm/3 × 1ft

L. siphilitica (Blue cardinal flower) A hardy perennial forming clumps of pale green leaves over which are carried tubular flowers of bright blue from late summer to mid-autumn. 60 × 30cm/2 × 1ft

Lobelia erinus hybrid

LOBULARIA (Sweet alyssum)

A genus of annuals and perennials of low, clump forming or spreading habit grown mainly for their bright flowers and used as an edging or for summer bedding schemes.

L. maritima A low growing annual or short-lived perennial with grey-green leaves and producing tiny white, sometimes pale purple, flowers in summer. 5–30 × 20–30cm/ 2in–1ft × 8in–1ft

LOMATIA

A genus of frost hardy, evergreen shrubs and trees producing racemes of tubular, starry flowers. For acid to neutral soil in a sheltered situation with protection from cold winds.

L. myricoides A frost hardy, evergreen shrub of upright habit with leaves of dark green and producing creamy flowers in summer. 2 × 2m/6 × 6ft

Lobularia maritima

Lomatia myricoides

Lonicera × brownii 'Dropmore Scarlet'

Lonicera etrusca

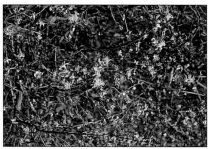

Lonicera fragrantissima

Lonicera japonica 'Halliana'

Lonicera nitida 'Baggesen's Gold'

LONICERA (Honeysuckle)

Genus of hardy to half hardy, deciduous and evergreen shrubs and climbers grown principally for their tubular or bell-like flowers, many of which are scented. All species are tolerant of full sun but are best sited in part sun and part shade. Half hardy species may be cultivated in a cool greenhouse.

L. × brownii 'Dropmore Scarlet' A hardy, deciduous or semi-evergreen climber with leaves of blue-green and scarlet with orange flowers, followed occasionally by red berries, in summer. 4m/12ft

L. etrusca A hardy to frost hardy, deciduous or semi-evergreen climber with leaves of mid-green, blue-green on the undersides, and scented yellow flowers, followed by red berries, from midsummer to autumn. 4m/12ft

L. fragrantissima A hardy, deciduous or semi-evergreen shrub of spreading habit with leaves of dull green and carrying scented, cream-white flowers in late winter and early spring. 2 × 3m/6 × 10ft

L. japonica 'Halliana' A hardy, evergreen or semi-evergreen climber of vigorous habit producing pure white flowers, becoming deep yellow with age, from spring to late summer. 10m/30ft

L. nitida 'Baggesen's Gold' A hardy, evergreen shrub of bushy habit with leaves of bright yellow, the colour most conspicuous in sun, and creamy flowers in spring. 1.5 × 1.5m/5 × 5ft

L. periclymenum 'Belgica' A hardy, deciduous climber with leaves of mid-green and producing white flowers, streaked with red, becoming yellow and followed with berries, in mid and late summer. 7m/22ft

L. periclymenum 'Graham Thomas' A vigorous deciduous climber with fragrant yellow and white flowers in clusters from summer to autumn. 7m/22ft

L. periclymenum 'Serotina' Similar to 'Belgica' but with flowers of creamy-white streaked dark purple. 7m/22ft

L. pileata A hardy, evergreen shrub of spreading habit with lance-shaped leaves of dark green and creamy flowers in late spring followed by purple berries. 60cm × 2.5m/2 × 8ft

L. tatarica A hardy, deciduous shrub of dark green leaves, grey-green on the undersides, with tubular pink or red flowers in late spring to summer followed by scarlet to orange berries. 4 × 2.5m/12 × 8ft

L. × tellmanniana A frost hardy, deciduous climber requiring part-shade with clusters of yellow-orange flowers in late spring and early summer. 5m/15ft

L. tragophylla A hardy, deciduous climber with leaves of mid-green, whitish on the undersides, and long, tubular flowers of orange-yellow in mid summer. 6m/20ft

Lonicera periclymenum 'Belgica'

Lonicera periclymenum 'Graham Thomas'

Lonicera periclymenum 'Serotina'

Lonicera pileata

Lonicera tatarica

Lotus berthelotii

Lonicera tellmanniana

Lonicera tragophylla

LOTUS

A genus of hardy to frost tender annuals, short-lived perennials and deciduous, semi-evergreen or evergreen sub-shrubs with pea-like flowers in a wide range of colours. Frost tender species are suitable for a cool glasshouse. Best in full sun.

L. berthelotii (Parrot's beak) A half hardy, evergreen sub-shrub of trailing habit with leaves of silver-grey and unusual orange to red, black-centred flowers in spring and early summer.

20cm/8in × indefinite spread

Lunaria annua

Lunaria annua 'Alba Variegata'

Lupinus arboreus

LUNARIA (Honesty)

A genus of annuals, biennials and perennials valued as much for their translucent seed-pods, used in dried arrangements, as for their self-seeding flowers.

L. annua An annual or biennial with heart-shaped leaves of lightish green producing white to pale purple flowers in late spring and summer. Later flat, silvery seedpods are formed. 1m × 30cm/3 × 1ft

L. annua 'Alba Variegata' Similar to *L. annua* with white, variegated leaves and creamy-white and white flowers. 1m × 30cm/3 × 1ft

LUPINUS (Lupin)

A genus of hardy to half hardy annuals, perennials and semi-evergreen and evergreen sub-shrubs or shrubs with mainly basal leaves of mid-green, sometimes silver-green, and racemes or spikes of pea-like flowers in a wide range of colours. Tolerant of most conditions and situations.

L. arboreus (Tree lupin) A frost hardy, evergreen or semi-evergreen shrub or sub-shrub with grey-green leaves and carrying scented yellow, occasionally blue, flowers in late spring and summer. 2 × 2m/6 × 6ft

L. 'The Chatelaine' A hardy perennial of clump forming habit producing racemes of bicoloured pink and white flowers in summer. 1m × 75cm/3 × 2.5ft

LUZULA (Woodrush)

A genus of principally hardy, mainly evergreen, grassy perennials, rarely annuals, grown for their ability to tolerate shade and to act as effective ground cover. For part or total shade with the exception of *L. nivea* which requires full sun.

L. sylvatica A hardy, evergreen perennial forming clumps of narrow, grass-like, dark green leaves and carrying small red-brown flowers in spring and early summer. 75 × 45cm/2.5 × 1.5ft

Lupinus 'The Chatelaine'

Lychnis coronaria

Lychnis chalcedonica

LYCHNIS (Campion)

A genus of biennials and perennials valued for their tubular or starry flowers in shades of pink, purple, red or white, some of which may be double. Unfussy generally as to conditions and situation.

L. chalcedonica (Maltese cross) A hardy perennial forming clumps of basal leaves of mid-green over which are carried bright orange-scarlet flowers on stiff stems in early and midsummer. 1m × 30cm/3 × 1ft

L. coronaria (Rose campion) A biennial or short-lived perennial forming basal clumps of grey-white leaves and producing purple-red flowers on long stems in late summer. *L.e.*'Alba' has white flowers. 75 × 45cm/2.5 × 1.5ft

Lychnis coronaria 'Alba'

Lysichiton americanus

LYSICHITON (Skunk cabbage)

A genus of large leafed, aquatic perennials grown mainly for their striking spathes of yellow or white in spring. For rich, moisture-retentive soil at the margins of a pool or stream.

L. americanus An aquatic perennial with large, shiny, paddle-shaped leaves of mid-green and producing butter-yellow, musk-smelling spathes in early spring. 1 × 1.2m/3 × 4ft

L. camtschatcensis Similar to *L. americanus* but with white spathes. 75 × 75cm/ 2.5 × 2.5ft

Lysichiton camtschatcensis

Lysimachia clethroides

LYSIMACHIA (Loosestrife)

A genus of hardy to frost tender, herbaceous and evergreen perennials with variably shaped flowers most usually in shades of yellow or white but sometimes pink or purple. Most species prefer humus-rich, moist soil.

L. clethroides A hardy, rhizomatous perennial with tapering leaves of mid-green, paler on the reverse, and carrying racemes of saucer-shaped, white flowers in summer. 1m × 60cm/3 × 2ft

L. nummularia (Creeping Jenny) A hardy, evergreen perennial spreading by means of stem-rooting shoots with rounded leaves of mid-green and producing upward-facing, open–cup flowers of bright yellow in summer.
5cm/2in × indefinite spread

L. punctata A hardy, rhizomatous perennial with lance-shaped leaves of dark green and producing whorls of cup-shaped, light golden flowers in summer. 1m × 60cm/3 × 2ft

Lysimachia punctata

Lysimachia nummularia

LYTHRUM

A genus of annuals and perennials with spikes of small, starry or funnel-shaped flowers in shades of pink and purple and occasionally white. For moist soil in sun.

L. salicaria 'Firecandle' A perennial of clump forming habit with lance-shaped leaves and spikes of star-shaped, rose-red flowers from midsummer to autumn.
1m × 45cm/3 × 1.5ft

Lythrum salicaria 'Firecandle'

Macleaya microcarpa

Magnolia campbellii

MAACKIA

A genus of deciduous trees and shrubs grown mainly for their attractive foliage and small, pea-like flowers. For neutral to acidic soil in full sun.

M. amurensis A deciduous tree of spreading habit with leaves of deep green, opening silver-white, and producing racemes of white flowers in mid and late summer.
15 × 10m/50 × 30ft

Magnolia campbellii subsp. *mollicomata*

Magnolia denudata

Magnolia grandiflora 'Exmouth'

Magnolia kobus

MACLEAYA (Plume poppy)

A genus of rhizomatous perennials cultivated for their attractive, heart-shaped foliage and light inflorescences of petalless, tubular flowers. Tolerant of most soils and situations but best in full sun.

M. microcarpa A rhizomatous perennial with leaves of grey to olive-green and carrying tall stems of coral-coloured flowers in early and midsummer.
2.2 × 1m/7 × 3ft

MAGNOLIA

A genus of hardy to frost tender, deciduous and evergreen shrubs and trees, usually slow growing, valued principally for their frequently scented, variably shaped, showy flowers most often in shades of cream, green, pink, purple, yellow or white. Cone-like fruits are produced in autumn. Well suited as specimens. Both flowers and foliage may be damaged by late frosts. Best in humus-rich, neutral to acidic soil although some species are tolerant of lime.

M. campbellii A hardy, deciduous tree with leaves of mid-green and of spreading habit in maturity. Cup and saucer-shaped flowers of white, crimson or rose-pink are produced on bare stems from late winter to spring. 15 × 10m/50 × 30ft

M. campbellii subsp. *mollicomata* Similar to *M. campbellii* but with pink to pink-purple flowers in spring. 15 × 10m/50 × 30ft

M. denudata (Lily tree) A hardy, deciduous shrub or tree with leaves of mid-green and of spreading habit. Cup-shaped flowers of pure white are produced on bare stems in spring. 10 × 10m/30 × 30ft

M. grandiflora 'Exmouth' A hardy, evergreen tree with leaves of light green, felted brown on the undersides, and producing large, scented, cup-shaped cream flowers from late summer to early autumn. 10 × 10m/30 × 30ft

M. kobus A hardy, deciduous tree with aromatic leaves of mid-green and producing goblet to saucer-shaped white flowers, stained pink at the base, in mid-spring. 12 × 10m/40 × 30ft

M. liliiflora 'Nigra' A hardy, deciduous shrub of compact habit with leaves of dark green and producing goblet-shaped, deep purple-red flowers in early summer and, occasionally, in autumn. 3 × 2.5m/10 × 8ft

M. × loebneri 'Leonard Messel' A hardy, deciduous tree of rounded habit with leaves of mid-green and producing star-shaped flowers of pale lilac-pink on bare stems in mid-spring. 8 × 6m/25 × 20ft

M. salicifolia (Willow-leafed magnolia) A hardy deciduous tree with mid-green leaves and scented white flowers in spring on bare branches. 10 × 5m/30 × 15ft

M. × soulangeana 'Alba Superba' A hardy, deciduous shrub or tree of upright habit with leaves of dark green and producing scented, goblet-shaped flowers of white, stained purple at the base, simultaneously with the emerging leaves in spring. 7 × 5m/22 × 15ft

M. × soulangeana 'Burgundy' Similar to *M. soulangeana* 'Alba Superba' but of spreading habit and with flowers of deep purple-pink. 6 × 6m/20 × 20ft

M. × soulangeana 'Lennei' Similar to *M. soulangeana* 'Burgundy' but with flowers of purple-pink, white on the insides. 6 × 6m/20 × 20ft

M. stellata (Star magnolia) A hardy, deciduous shrub or tree of spreading habit with leaves of mid-green and producing star-shaped, pure white flowers, occasionally tinged pink, on bare stems in early and mid-spring. 3 × 4m/10 × 12ft

M. wilsonii A hardy, deciduous shrub or tree of spreading habit with leaves of dark green, felted brown on the undersides, and producing cup-shaped, scented, hanging white flowers in late spring and early summer. 6 × 6m/20 × 20ft

Magnolia liliiflora 'Nigra'

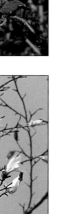

Magnolia salicifolia

Magnolia × *loebneri* 'Leonard Messel'

Magnolia × *soulangeana* 'Alba Superba'

Magnolia × *soulangeana* 'Burgundy'

Magnolia × *soulangeana* 'Lennei'

Magnolia wilsonii

Magnolia stellata

Mahonia aquifolium

Mahonia japonica

Mahonia × wagneri 'Moseri'

Malus 'Evereste'

Malus floribunda

Mahonia lomariifolia

MAHONIA

A genus of hardy to frost hardy, evergreen shrubs valued for their foliage, usually spiny edged, flowers, most often yellow and carried on racemes or panicles, and fruits. Best grown in partial shade although some species require full sun.

M. aquifolium (Oregon grape) A hardy shrub of suckering habit with bright green leaves, colouring red-purple over winter, and carrying racemes of yellow flowers in spring followed by blue-black berries. 1 × 1.5m/3 × 5ft

M. japonica A hardy shrub of upright habit with lance-shaped leaves of dark green and carrying racemes of scented, pale yellow flowers from late autumn to early spring followed by blue-purple berries. 2 × 3m/6 × 10ft

M. lomariifolia A frost hardy shrub of upright habit with leaves of dark green and carrying erect racemes of scented yellow flowers from late autumn to winter followed by blue-black berries. Protect from cold winds. 3 × 2m/10 × 6ft

M. × wagneri 'Moseri' A hardy shrub of upright habit with pale green leaves, tinged pink or red, and carrying racemes of yellow flowers in spring followed by blue-black berries. 1 × 1m/3 × 3ft

MALUS (Crab apple)

A genus of deciduous trees and shrubs cultivated mainly for their single, semi-double or double, frequently scented flowers as well as for their interesting, colourful fruits, most of which are edible. Within this genus are to be found cultivars of *M. × domestica*, commercial apples. Best in full sun although shade tolerant.

M. 'Evereste' A tree of conical shape with leaves of dark green. White flowers in spring are followed by orange-yellow fruits. 7 × 6m/22 × 20ft

M. floribunda (Japanese crab apple) A tree of spreading habit with leaves of dark green, pale pink flowers in mid and late spring followed by small yellow fruits. 10 × 10m/30 × 30ft

M. hupehensis A tree of spreading habit with leaves of dark green, scented white flowers in mid and late spring followed by cherry-red fruits. 12 × 12m/40 × 40ft

M. × moerlandsii 'Profusion' A tree of spreading habit with leaves of bronze-green, purple-red when young, and deep purple-pink flowers in late spring followed by purplish fruits. 10 × 10m/30 × 30ft

M. × robusta 'Red Sentinel' A tree of upright habit with leaves of dark green, white flowers in late spring followed by shiny red fruits lasting well into winter. 7 × 7m/22 × 22ft

M. × schiedeckeri 'Red Jade' A tree of weeping habit with shiny leaves of mid-green, white or pink tinged flowers in late spring followed by glossy red fruits. 4 × 6m/13 × 20ft

M. × zumi 'Golden Hornet' A tree of rounded habit with leaves of bright green, white flowers in late spring and golden fruits lasting well into winter. 10 × 8m/30 × 25ft

Malus hupehensis

Malus × schiedeckeri 'Red Jade'

Malus × moerlandsii 'Profusion'

Malus × robusta 'Red Sentinel'

Malus × zumi 'Golden Hornet'

MALVA (Mallow)

A genus of annuals, biennials and perennials grown for their showy flowers mainly of blue, pink, purple or white produced over a prolonged period. Best in full sun.

M. moschata f. *alba* A perennial of upright habit with leaves of mid-green, slightly musk scented, and producing white flowers from early summer to early autumn. 1m × 60cm/3 × 2ft

M. sylvestris mauritiana A low growing perennial of spreading habit producing flowers of deep purple from spring to autumn. 15cm × 1m/6in × 3ft

M. sylvestris 'Primley Blue' A perennial of bushy habit with leaves of dark green and producing pale, sky-blue flowers with deeper veining from late spring to early autumn. 1m × 60cm/3 × 2ft

Malva sylvestris mauritiana

Malva sylvestris 'Primley Blue'

Malva moschata f. *alba*

Matteuccia struthiopteris

Meconopsis cambrica

Meconopsis napaulensis

Melianthus major

Mentha gentilis 'Variegata'

Matthiola white perennial

Meconopsis grandis

Mentha suaveolens 'Variegata'

MATTEUCCIA

A genus of deciduous ferns valued for their distinctive 'shuttlecock' fronds. For humus-rich, damp, neutral to acidic soil in partial shade.

M. struthiopteris (Ostrich fern) A deciduous, rhizomatous fern producing mid-green sterile fronds in spring followed by dark brown, fertile fronds in late summer. 1.5 × 1m/5 × 3ft

MATTHIOLA (Stock)

A genus of hardy to frost hardy annuals and perennials, sometimes sub-shrubs, valued for their most often fragrant flowers mainly in pastel shades. Best in neutral to alkaline soil in sun.

M. fruticulosa A hardy perennial of dwarf habit with grey-green leaves and producing flowers varying from yellow to purple-violet in summer. 60 × 30cm/ 2 × 1ft

MECONOPSIS

A genus of annuals, biennials and deciduous or evergreen monocarpic perennials grown for their poppy-like flowers in humus-rich, damp, neutral to acidic soil.

M. cambrica (Welsh poppy) A deciduous perennial forming clumps of pale green leaves over which rise lemon to orange-yellow flowers from mid-spring to late summer. 45 × 30cm/1.5 × 1ft

M. grandis (Himalayan blue poppy) A deciduous perennial forming basal rosettes of mid-green leaves over which rise china to deep blue flowers in early summer. 1m × 60cm/3 × 2ft

M. napaulensis An evergreen perennial forming basal rosettes of yellow-green leaves over which rise cup-shaped flowers of pink to purple from late spring to midsummer. 2.6m × 60cm/8 × 2ft

MELIANTHUS

A genus of frost hardy to frost tender, evergreen shrubs noted for their grey-green, cut leaves and small, nectar producing flowers.

M. major (Honey bush) A half hardy shrub of spreading habit with grey-green leaves and racemes of crimson to brown-red flowers from late spring to midsummer. 2 × 1m/6 × 3ft

MENTHA (Mint)

A genus of aromatic perennials, occasionally annuals, mainly cultivated as culinary herbs. For poorish soil in full sun.

M. gentilis 'Variegata' (Ginger mint) A perennial of spreading habit with striped or spotted gold leaves borne on red-tinted stems. Lilac flowers in summer. 30cm × 1m/1 × 3ft

M. suaveolens 'Variegata' (Pineapple mint) A perennial of spreading habit with crinkled, cream-striped leaves. Pink-white flowers in summer. 1 × 1m/3 × 3ft

MERTENSIA

A genus of clump forming or spreading perennials noted for their tubular blue flowers. Smaller species are suitable for the rock garden or alpine house and require full sun.

M. pulmonarioides (Virginia cowslip) A perennial forming clumps of blue-green leaves and producing violet-blue or white flowers in spring. 45 × 30cm/1.5 × 1ft

MESPILUS (Medlar)

A genus of a single species of deciduous tree or large shrub most often grown as a specimen and valued for its flower, fruit and autumn colour.

M. germanica A deciduous tree of spreading habit with dark green leaves, colouring deep yellow in autumn, and producing pink-tinged, white flowers in late spring and early summer followed by edible, brown fruits. 6 × 8m/20 × 25ft

METASEQUOIA (Dawn redwood)

A genus of a single species of deciduous, coniferous tree producing linear leaves turning flame in autumn. Best in damp, well drained soil in sun but tolerant of water-logged conditions.

M. glyptostroboides A deciduous tree of conical habit with orange-brown, fibrous bark and leaves of mid-green, colouring in autumn, with both male and female cones. 20–40 × 5m/ 70–130 × 15ft

MEUM (Baldmoney)

A genus of a single species of perennial forming clumps of aromatic leaves and carrying umbels of starry flowers. Best in alkaline soil in sun.

M. athamanticum A perennial with leaves of light green and white or purple-tinted, tiny flowers in summer. 30 × 30cm/1 × 1ft

MILIUM

Genus of annual and perennial grasses with lance-shaped, yellow-green leaves grown mainly for their foliage effect.

M. effusum 'Aureum' (Bowles' golden grass) A perennial, semi-evergreen grass forming tufts of yellow-green leaves and producing gold spikelets from late spring to midsummer. 60 × 30cm/2 × 1ft

MIMOSA

A genus of frost tender annuals, evergreen perennials, shrubs and small trees grown for their attractive, pea-like flowers. Suitable as houseplants or for a warm conservatory or glasshouse.

M. pudica (Sensitive plant) A frost tender annual or short-lived perennial with leaves of grey-green and producing pink to lilac flowerheads in summer. 60 × 60cm/2 × 2ft

MIMULUS (Monkey flower)

A genus of hardy to frost tender annuals, perennials and evergreen shrubs grown for their unusually spotted flowers in contrasting colours. For humus-rich, damp soil or, in the case of tender species, in a cool glasshouse.

M. 'Orange Glow' A hardy perennial forming a carpet of mid-green leaves with yellow flowers with orange markings in summer. 20 × 20cm/8 × 8in

Mertensia pulmonarioides

Mespilus germanica

Meum athamanticum

Milium effusum 'Aureum'

Metasequoia glyptostroboides

Mimulus 'Orange Glow'

169

Miscanthus 'Silver Feather'

Moltkia suffruticosa

Monarda 'Cambridge Scarlet'

Monarda 'Croftway Pink'

Morina longifolia

Morus nigra

MISCANTHUS

A genus of hardy to frost hardy deciduous or evergreen perennial grasses grown for their attractive leaves and silky spikelets. For damp but well drained soil in sun.
M. 'Silver Feather' A hardy, deciduous perennial grass forming clumps of sword-like leaves of blue-green with silver-brown spikelets in autumn. 2.6 × 1.2m/8 × 4ft

MITELLA (Bishop's cap)

A genus of perennials of clump forming habit consisting of basal leaves and racemes of bell-shaped flowers in summer. Best in acidic to neutral soil.
M. breweri A low growing perennial forming clumps of mid-green leaves and carrying tiny yellow-green flowers in late spring and summer. 15 × 20cm/6 × 8in

MOLTKIA

A genus of hardy to frost hardy deciduous and evergreen perennials, shrubs and sub-shrubs grown for their tubular-shaped flowers of blue, purple or yellow. Best in full sun. Protect from an excess of winter wet.
M. suffruticosa A hardy, deciduous shrub of upright habit with leaves of dark green and bearing clusters of blue to violet-blue flowers in summer. 30 × 30cm/1 × 1ft

MOLUCCELLA (Bells of Ireland)

A genus of half hardy annuals and short-lived perennials flowering from summer to autumn and most used as summer bedding. Best in full sun.
M. laevis A half hardy annual with scalloped leaves of light green and carrying green cupped, white to purple-pink flowers in summer. 60 × 25cm/ 2ft × 10in

MONARDA (Bergamot)

A genus of annuals and rhizomatous perennials with aromatic leaves of dark green or tinged purple and producing whorls of sage-like flowers in summer and early autumn.
M. 'Croftway Pink' A perennial of clump forming habit with leaves of dark green and carrying china-pink flowers from midsummer to early autumn. *M.* 'Cambridge Scarlet' bears rich scarlet flowers. 1m × 45cm/3 × 1.5ft

MORINA

Genus of evergreen perennials with spiny leaves of shiny mid-green and carrying whorls of bracts with spikes of tubular flowers in pink, red, white or yellow. For poorish soil in full sun.
M. longifolia (Whorlflower) An evergreen perennial forming a rosette of basal leaves and producing spikes of white flowers arranged in tiers in midsummer. Flowers become tinged with pink and red after fertilization. 1m × 30cm/3 × 1ft

MORUS (Mulberry)

Genus of hardy to frost tender, deciduous shrubs and trees grown largely as specimens for their catkin-like flowers and edible fruits. For full sun out of the reach of cold winds.
M. nigra A hardy, deciduous tree with heart-shaped leaves of mid-green and producing green fruits, ripening to red then dark purple in late summer. 12 × 15m/40 × 50ft

Muscari aucheri

Mutisia ilicifolia

Muscari neglectum

MUSCARI (Grape hyacinth)
A genus of hardy to frost hardy, bulbous perennials grown for their mainly tubular or bell-shaped flowers in a variety of colours. Most effective when massed. Best in full sun.
M. aucheri A hardy, bulbous perennial with upright, narrow leaves of mid-green and carrying blue flowers, often pale above and dark below, in spring. 10 × 5cm/4 × 2in
M. neglectum A hardy, bulbous perennial with upright leaves of mid-green and dark blue flowers in spring. Suitable for naturalizing. 10–20 × 5cm/4–8 × 2in

MUTISIA
A genus of frost hardy to half hardy, evergreen climbers noted for their daisy-like flowers from summer to autumn. For well drained soil in full sun.
M. ilicifolia A frost hardy, evergreen climber with holly-like leaves and yellow-centred, pale pink flowers in summer and autumn. 3m/10ft

Myriophyllum aquaticum

Myrrhis odorata

MYRIOPHYLLUM (Milfoil)
A genus of hardy to frost hardy aquatic annuals and perennials grown principally for their attractive foliage and their oxygenating properties.
M. aquaticum (Parrot feather) A frost hardy, aquatic perennial with leaves of yellow-green beneath the surface and blue-green above. Yellow-green flowers are produced in summer. Indefinite spread

Myrtus communis

Myosotis sylvatica

MYOSOTIS (Forget-me-not)
Genus of annuals, biennials and perennials noted for their flowers of mostly blue, yellow or white. Low growing perennials are short-lived.
M. sylvatica A biennial or short-lived perennial forming tufts of grey-green leaves and carrying open bowl-shaped flowers of blue, occasionally white, in late spring and early summer.
15–30 × 15cm/6in–1ft × 6in

MYRRHIS (Sweet Cicely)
A genus of a single species of aromatic perennial grown for its attractive, ferny foliage and umbels of cow-parsley type flowers. Best in partial shade.
M. odorata A hollow stemmed perennial with leaves of bright green and carrying umbels of starry white flowers in late spring and early summer.
60 × 45cm/2 × 1.5ft

MYRTUS (Myrtle)
A genus of frost hardy, evergreen trees and shrubs of upright habit and grown for aromatic leaves and flowers. Position in a sunny, sheltered spot.
M. communis A frost hardy, evergreen shrub of upright habit with leaves of shiny dark green and producing white flowers in summer and early autumn followed by deep purple, near black fruits. 3 × 3m/10 × 10ft

Nandina domestica

NANDINA (Heavenly bamboo)

A genus of a single species of frost hardy, evergreen or semi-evergreen shrub cultivated for its flowers, foliage and fruit. For a sheltered spot in full sun.

N. domestica A frost hardy, evergreen or semi-evergreen shrub with lance-shaped leaves coloured red when new and also in winter. Starry white flowers are carried in midsummer to be followed by bright red fruits. 2 × 1.5m/6 × 5ft

Narcissus bulbocodium

Narcissus cyclamineus

Narcissus 'February Gold'

Narcissus 'Golden Ducat'

Narcissus 'Hawera'

Narcissus 'Flower Drift'

NARCISSUS (Daffodil)

A genus of hardy to half hardy, bulbous perennials from which numerous cultivars have been developed. The majority flower in spring and are at their best when massed. Most are tolerant of a wide range of soils and conditions. For horticultural purposes narcissus are grouped according to twelve divisions. These are: Division 1 Trumpet, Division 2 Large-cupped, Division 3 Small-cupped, Division 4 Double, Division 5 Triandrus, Division 6 Cyclamineus, Division 7 Jonquilla, Division 8 Tazetta, Division 9 Poeticus, Division 10 Wild Species, Division 11 Split-corona, and Division 12 Miscellaneous.

N. bulbocodium (Hoop-petticoat daffodil) A hardy, bulbous perennial belonging to Division 10. Deep yellow, funnel-shaped flowers, the trumpets of which are expanded, are produced in early spring. Suitable for naturalizing. 10–15cm/4–6in

N. cyclamineus A hardy, bulbous perennial belonging to Division 10. Golden-yellow flowers, with narrow waisted trumpets, are produced in early spring. 15–20cm/6–8in

N. 'February Gold' A hardy, bulbous perennial belonging to Division 6. Golden-yellow trumpet flowers are produced in spring. 30cm/1ft

N. 'Flower Drift' A hardy, bulbous perennial belonging to Division 4. Double flowers of egg-yolk yellow and white are produced in early and mid-spring. 45cm/1.5ft

N. 'Golden Ducat' A hardy, bulbous perennial belonging to Division 4. Double flowers of deep butter-yellow are produced in mid-spring. 45cm/1.5ft

N. 'Hawera' A frost hardy, bulbous perennial belonging to Division 5. Single stems carry several canary-yellow flowers in late spring. 18cm/7in

Narcissus 'Ice Follies'

Narcissus 'Jetfire'

Narcissus 'Mount Hood'

Narcissus 'Palmares'

N. 'Ice Follies' A hardy, bulbous perennial belonging to Division 2. Creamy-white, wide cupped trumpets, frilled at the end, are produced in mid-spring. 45cm/1.5ft

N. 'Jetfire' A hardy, bulbous perennial belonging to Division 6. Bright yellow flowers with orange trumpets are produced in early spring. 20cm/8in

N. 'Mount Hood' A hardy, bulbous perennial belonging to Division 1. Large white flowers with frilled trumpets of deep cream are produced in mid-spring. 45cm/1.5ft

N. 'Palmares' A hardy, bulbous perennial belonging to Division 11. Single flowers of pale apricot and creamy white, the corona split for half its length, are produced in spring. 45cm/1.5ft

N. 'Passionale' A hardy, bulbous perennial belonging to Division 2. Pure white flowers with rose-pink trumpets, slightly frilled at the end, are produced in mid-spring. 45cm/1.5ft

N. 'Peeping Tom' A hardy, bulbous perennial belonging to Division 6. Long trumpets of deep golden-yellow are produced in early and mid-spring. 20cm/8in

N. 'Petit Four' A hardy, bulbous perennial belonging to Division 4. Double flowers of apricot and white are produced in early and mid-spring. 45cm/1.5ft

N. poeticus var. *recurvus* A hardy, bulbous perennial belonging to Division 9. Pure white, scented flowers with yellow, red fringed centres, are produced in late spring and early summer. 30cm/1ft

N. pseudonarcissus 'Lobularis' A hardy, bulbous perennial belonging to Division 10. Pale lemon and deep yellow flowers are produced in early spring. Excellent for naturalizing. 30cm/1ft

Narcissus 'Passionale'

Narcissus 'Peeping Tom'

Narcissus pseudonarcissus 'Lobularis'

Narcissus 'Petit Four'

Narcissus poeticus var. *recurvus*

Narcissus 'Rip van Winkle'

Narcissus 'Roseworthy'

Narcissus 'Silver Chimes'

Narcissus 'Sir Winston Churchill'

N. 'Rip van Winkle' A hardy, bulbous perennial belonging to Division 4. Double flowers of yellow-green are produced in early spring. 15cm/6in

N. 'Roseworthy' A hardy, bulbous perennial belonging to Division 2. Petals of creamy-white surround a trumpet of pale peach on flowers produced in mid-spring. 30cm/1ft

N. 'Silver Chimes' A frost hardy, bulbous perennial belonging to Division 8. Clusters of fragrant flowers comprising creamy-white petals and pale lemon, cupped trumpets are produced in mid and late spring. 30cm/1ft

N. 'Sir Winston Churchill' A hardy, bulbous perennial belonging to Division 4. Fragrant double flowers of creamy-white and egg-yolk yellow are produced in early and mid-spring. 45cm/1.5ft

N. 'Sun Disc' A hardy, bulbous perennial belonging to Division 7. Circular flowers of mid-yellow are produced in mid-spring. 15cm/6in

N. 'Tête-à-tête' A hardy, bulbous perennial belonging to Division 12. Flowers comprising golden-yellow petals with deeper yellow trumpets are produced in early spring. 15cm/6in

N. 'Thalia' A hardy, bulbous perennial belonging to Division 5. Single stems carry generally two off-white flowers in mid-spring. 30cm/1ft

N. 'White Lion' A hardy, bulbous perennial belonging to Division 4. Double flowers of creamy-white and cream are produced in early and mid-spring. 45cm/1.5ft

N. 'White Marvel' A hardy, bulbous perennial belonging to Division 4. Double flowers of pale creamy-yellow are produced in late spring. 45cm/1.5ft

Narcissus 'Sun Disc'

Narcissus 'Tête-à-tête'

Narcissus 'White Lion'

Narcissus 'White Marvel'

Narcissus 'Thalia'

Nectaroscordum siculum

Neillia thibetica

NECTAROSCORDUM

A genus of bulbous perennials grown for their garlic scented, tubular hanging flowers produced over long, grooved leaves of mid-green.
N. siculum A bulbous perennial with sword-like leaves and producing creamy-white flowers flushed pink or purple-red and tinged green at the base in summer. 1.2m × 10cm/4ft × 4in

NEILLIA

A genus of deciduous shrubs and sub-shrubs of arching habit and carrying racemes of tubular flowers in spring and early summer.
N. thibetica A deciduous shrub of suckering habit forming a thicket of stems carrying bright green leaves and flowers of rose-pink in early summer. 2 × 2m/6 × 6ft

NELUMBO (Lotus)

Genus of half hardy to frost tender, rhizomatous aquatic perennials cultivated for their scented, water lily-like flowers. For shallow or deep water according to species.
N. lutea A frost tender, aquatic perennial with leaves of blue-green and carrying rose-type flowers of pale lemon-yellow in summer. 1m/3ft × indefinite spread

Nemesia caerulea

Nepeta nervosa

Nepeta 'Six Hills Giant'

NEMESIA

A genus of frost hardy to half hardy annuals, perennials and sub-shrubs grown mainly as summer bedding. For sandy, free-draining, slightly acidic soil in sun.
N. caerulea A half hardy perennial producing racemes of flowers in shades of pink, blue, lavender or white from early summer to autumn. 60 × 30cm/ 2 × 1ft

NEPETA (Catmint)

Genus of hardy to half hardy perennials, seldom annuals, often with aromatic leaves, frequently grey-green, and noted for their tubular flowers in shades of blue, purple, yellow or white. Attractive to bees.
N. nervosa A hardy perennial forming clumps of lance-shaped, grey-green leaves, slightly aromatic, and carrying spires of purple-blue, occasionally yellow, flowers from midsummer to early autumn. 45 × 30cm/1.5 × 1ft
N. 'Six Hills Giant' A hardy perennial forming clumps of narrow, aromatic grey-green leaves and carrying spires of lavender-blue flowers in summer. 1m × 60cm/3 × 2ft

Nerine bowdenii

Nerine flexuosa 'Alba'

Nerium oleander

NERINE

A genus of hardy to half hardy, bulbous perennials valued for their funnel-shaped, lily-like flowers followed by upright, basal leaves. For well drained soil in a sunny, sheltered situation.
N. bowdenii A frost-hardy, bulbous perennial comprising long, strap-shaped leaves and producing umbels of mid-pink flowers in autumn. 45 × 8cm/1.5ft × 3in
N. flexuosa 'Alba' A half hardy, bulbous perennial with long, strap-shaped leaves and producing umbels of white flowers in late autumn. 45 × 8cm/1.5ft × 3in

NERIUM (Oleander)

A genus of frost tender, evergreen shrubs or small trees valued for their colourful flowers and suitable for a cool conservatory. Many cultivars with both single and double flowers.
N. oleander A frost tender, evergreen shrub of spreading habit with pink, white or red flowers in summer over grey-green leaves. 2 × 1m/6 × 3ft

Nicandra physalodes

Nicotiana alata hybrid

NICANDRA (Shoo fly)

A genus of a single species of annual grown for its bell-shaped flowers followed by unusual brown berries surrounded with lantern-like calyces. Best in full sun.

N. physalodes An upright annual of vigorous habit producing a profusion of pale violet-blue flowers, with white throat, from summer to autumn followed by rounded berries. 1m × 30cm/3 × 1ft

NICOTIANA (Tobacco plant)

Genus of frost hardy to half hardy annuals, biennials, perennials and shrubs valued for their sometimes scented flowers in a range of mixed colours which are employed most often in summer bedding schemes.

N. alata hybrid A half hardy, rosette forming perennial, most widely grown as an annual, with scented flowers in summer which are white inside, green-yellow on the outside on the type plant; hybrids flower in many shades. 1m × 30cm/3 × 1ft

N. langsdorffii A half hardy, rosette forming annual with tubular flowers of lime-green in summer. 1m × 30cm/3 × 1ft

Nicotiana langsdorffii

Nigella damascena

Nomocharis pardanthina

Nothofagus betuloides

NIGELLA (Love-in-a-mist)

A genus of annuals of upright habit with feathery leaves and producing flowers in shades of blue, pink, yellow or white in summer. Best in full sun where they will self-seed.

N. damascena An annual with attractive, divided leaves of light green and carrying flowers of pale blue in summer. 45 × 23cm/1.5ft × 9in

NOMOCHARIS

A genus of bulbous perennials grown for their racemes of usually spotted, open saucer-shaped flowers in summer. For humus-rich, acid soil in part shade. Do not allow to dry out in hot periods.

N. pardanthina A bulbous perennial with lance-shaped leaves and pale pink or white flowers, spotted red-purple, in early summer. 1m × 10cm/3ft × 4in

NOTHOFAGUS (Southern beech)

A genus of hardy to frost hardy, deciduous or evergreen shrubs and trees cultivated mainly for their attractive habit and, in the case of deciduous species, for their autumn colour.

N. betuloides An evergreen hardy to frost-hardy tree of broadly conical shape with small glossy dark green leaves. 20 × 5m/70 × 15ft

Nymphaea 'Escarboucle'

NYMPHAEA (Water lily)

A genus of hardy to frost tender aquatic perennials grown mainly for their colourful flowers and attractive leaves held on the surface of the water. Nymphaea requires to be grown in submerged containers filled with fertile, loamy soil and planted to a depth in accordance with the size of the rhizome. Planting depths (PD) are broadly as follows: miniatures 23cm/9in; small 30cm/1ft; medium 45cm/1.5ft; large 1m/3ft.

N. 'Escarboucle' A hardy, aquatic perennial with rounded leaves of mid-green, brown spotted when young, and carrying dark pink-red, starry flowers in summer. PD 1m/3ft

N. 'Gonnère' A hardy, aquatic perennial with rounded leaves of mid-green and carrying scented, globe-like, double white flowers in summer. PD 45cm/1.5ft

N. 'James Brydon' A hardy, aquatic perennial with rounded bronze-green leaves and carrying cup-shaped, rose-red flowers in summer. PD 23–45cm/9in–1.5ft

N. 'Marliacea Chromatella' A hardy, aquatic perennial with leaves of olive-green, marked bronze, and carrying deep yellow flowers in summer. PD 45cm/1.5ft

N. 'Venusta' A hardy, aquatic perennial with leaves of dark green and carrying warm pink flowers in summer. PD 45cm–1m/1.5–3ft

Nymphaea 'Gonnère'

Nymphaea 'James Brydon'

Nymphaea 'Marliacea Chromatella'

Nymphaea 'Venusta'

Nuphar lutea

NUPHAR (Yellow pond lily)

A genus of hardy to frost hardy, deciduous aquatic perennials comprising creeping rhizomes and forming both surface and submerged leaves and rounded, surface flowers. Most suited to large ponds and lakes.

N. lutea A hardy, aquatic perennial with leaves of dark green and carrying golden-yellow flowers in summer. 2m/6ft spread

NYSSA (Tupelo)

A genus of deciduous trees cultivated mainly for their attractive foliage and the brilliance of their autumn leaf colour. Best in neutral to acidic soil out of the reach of cold winds.

N. sylvatica (Black gum) A deciduous tree of broadly columnar shape with leaves of dark green colouring flame in autumn. 20 × 10m/70 × 30ft

Nyssa sylvatica (autumn foliage)

Oenothera biennis

Oenothera missouriensis

Oenothera fruticosa 'Fireworks'

Olearia ilicifolia

Olearia macrodonta

Oenothera speciosa 'Pink Petticoats'

OENOTHERA (Evening primrose)

A genus of hardy to frost hardy annuals, biennials and perennials cultivated in the main for their usually scented short-lived flowers in shades of pink, yellow or white produced over a long period in summer. Small species are well suited to the rock garden. All prefer full sun and well drained soil.

O. biennis A hardy annual or biennial of upright habit forming rosettes of red veined, mid-green leaves. Scented, cup-shaped flowers of pale lemon, darkening with age, and opening in the evening, are produced from summer to autumn. 1m × 60cm/3 × 2ft

O. fruticosa 'Fireworks' A hardy perennial or biennial of upright habit with basal leaves flushed purple-brown and producing deep butter-yellow flowers, red in bud, from late spring to late summer. 60 × 30cm/2 × 1ft

O. missouriensis A hardy perennial of vigorous, spreading habit. Lance-shaped leaves of mid-green, white ribbed, carry golden-yellow, cup-shaped flowers in succession from late spring to early autumn. 15 × 45cm/6in × 1.5ft

O. speciosa 'Pink Petticoats' A hardy perennial of vigorous, spreading habit forming rosettes of mid-green leaves and carrying pink flowers with darker veining in succession from early summer to early autumn. 30 × 30cm/1 × 1ft

OLEA (Olive)

A genus of frost hardy, evergreen shrubs and trees noted for their edible fruits. For well drained, fertile soil in full sun out of the reach of drying winds. Well suited to a cool conservatory or glasshouse.

O. europaea A frost hardy, evergreen tree with leaves of grey-green, silver-grey on the undersides, with scented, cream flowers in summer followed by rounded fruits (olives). 10 × 10m/30 × 30ft

OLEARIA (Daisy bush)

A genus of hardy to frost tender evergreen shrubs and trees noted for their daisy-like flowers produced in spring and summer. For a position in full sun sheltered from cold winds. Frost tender species may be cultivated under glass and placed outside during summer months.

O. ilicifolia (Mountain holly) A hardy, evergreen shrub of spreading habit with sharply cut leaves of grey-green and producing corymbs of scented, white daisy-like flowerheads in summer. Position in a sheltered spot. 5 × 5m/15 × 15ft

O. macrodonta A hardy, evergreen shrub or small tree of upright habit with sharply cut, holly-type leaves of shiny, dark green. Corymbs of scented, white daisy-like flowerheads are produced in summer. 6 × 5m/20 × 15ft

O. phlogopappa A frost hardy, evergreen shrub of upright habit with shalllow cut leaves of grey-green, grey-white on the undersides, carrying corymbs of white or violet-blue flowerheads in spring and early summer. 2 × 2m/6 × 6ft

O. 'Waikariensis' A frost hardy, evergreen shrub of upright habit with lance-shaped leaves of mid-green and carrying corymbs of creamy-white flowerheads in summer. 3 × 5m/10 × 15ft

OMPHALODES (Navelwort)

A genus of annuals, biennials and perennials, some of which are semi-evergreen or evergreen, valued for their forget-me-not type flowers which are produced in spring and summer. For humus-rich soil in part shade.

O. cappadocica 'Cherry Ingram' An evergreen perennial of compact, clump forming habit carrying racemes of deep blue, starry flowers over mid-green, basal leaves in early spring.
25 × 45cm/10in × 1.5ft

O. verna 'Alba' A semi-evergreen perennial of clump forming habit with basal leaves of mid-green and carrying racemes of white, starry flowers in spring. 20 × 30cm/8in × 1ft

ONOCLEA

A genus of a single species of deciduous fern for cultivation in humus-rich, damp, acidic soil in partial shade.

O. sensibilis (Sensitive fern) A deciduous fern comprising upright, sterile fronds of light green in spring to be followed by fertile fronds in late summer. New fronds may appear slightly pink-bronze in spring. 60cm/2ft × indefinite spread

ONOPORDUM (Cotton thistle)

A genus of biennials forming rosettes of spiny leaves, the surfaces of which are covered with soft, grey hair. Large, thistle-like flowerheads are produced singly or in clusters in summer. Best in full sun in neutral to alkaline soil.

O. nervosum A biennial forming rosettes of silver-grey leaves over which are carried deep purple-pink flowerheads encased in spiny bracts in summer. Readily self-seeds. 2.5 × 1m/9 × 3ft

OPHIOPOGON (Lilyturf)

A genus of hardy to half hardy evergreen perennials valued in the main for their attractive, grass-like leaves and racemes of small flowers followed by shiny fruits. Best in slightly acidic soil.

O. planiscapus 'Nigrescens' A hardy perennial of spreading habit with strap-shaped, tapering leaves of near black and carrying palest purple flowers in summer followed by blue-black fruit. 20 × 30cm/8in × 1ft

Olearia phlogopappa

Olearia 'Waikariensis'

Omphalodes cappadocica 'Cherry Ingram'

Omphalodes verna 'Alba'

Onopordum nervosum

Onoclea sensibilis

Ophiopogon planiscapus 'Nigrescens'

Origanum laevigatum

Origanum laevigatum 'Hopley's'

Ornithogalum umbellatum

ORIGANUM (Marjoram)

A genus of hardy to frost hardy perennials and deciduous and evergreen sub-shrubs noted for their aromatic leaves, much used for culinary purposes, as well as for their tubular flowers carried amidst coloured bracts. Best in poorish alkaline soil in full sun.

O. laevigatum A hardy perennial with upright stems of wine-red and deep green leaves. Whorls of purple-pink flowers surrounded by purple-red bracts are carried from late spring to autumn. 60 × 45cm/2 × 1.5ft

O. laevigatum 'Hopley's' Similar to *O. laevigatum* but with flowers of deep pink. 60 × 45cm/2 × 1.5ft

ORNITHOGALUM (Star of Bethlehem)

A genus of hardy to frost tender, bulbous perennials cultivated for their corymbs of starry, occasionally scented, flowers in spring and summer.

O. umbellatum A hardy, bulbous perennial carrying starry white flowers, striped green on the outsides, in early summer. 10–30cm × 10cm/4in–1ft × 4in

Orontium aquaticum

Osmanthus × *burkwoodii*

Osmanthus delavayi

ORONTIUM (Golden club)

A genus of a single species of aquatic perennial. Suitable for the margins of pond or stream.

O. aquaticum A rhizomatous, aquatic perennial with floating or submerged leaves of mid-green, tinged purple on the undersides, and carrying bright yellow flowers borne at the tips of white spadices from late spring to midsummer. 30 × 60cm/1 × 2ft

OSMANTHUS

A genus of hardy to frost tender, evergreen shrubs and small trees grown mainly for their leaves, most often sweetly scented flowers, and fruits. Tender species may be cultivated under glass.

O. × *burkwoodii* A hardy, evergreen shrub of dense habit. Shiny, dark green leaves, lightly toothed, are complemented with clusters of scented, white, tubular flowers in spring. 3 × 3m/10 × 10ft

O. delavayi A hardy, evergreen shrub of rounded habit with arching stems. Shiny, dark green leaves are accompanied with highly scented, tubular white flowers in spring followed by blue-black fruits. 4 × 4m/12 × 12ft

Osmunda regalis

OSMUNDA

A genus of deciduous ferns for humus-rich, moist, acidic soil in partial shade.
O. regalis prefers moisture retentive soil in a sunny situation.
O. regalis (Royal fern) A deciduous fern producing light green sterile fronds in spring to be followed by partially fertile fronds in summer with tassel-like tips consisting of rust coloured sporangia. 2 × 4m/6 × 12ft

Osteospermum 'Buttermilk'

Osteospermum 'Whirligig'

Osteospermum jucundum var. *compactum*

OSTEOSPERMUM (African daisy)

A genus of hardy to frost tender, evergreen sub-shrubs, perennials and annuals valued for their daisy-like flowers borne in profusion from spring to autumn. Many named cultivars cover a wide range of colours. For a sheltered position in full sun.
O. 'Buttermilk' A half hardy sub-shrub of upright habit with lance-shaped leaves of mid-green and carrying white and primrose-yellow flowers, bronze-yellow on the reverse, from late spring to autumn. 60 × 60cm/2 × 2ft
O. jucundum var. *compactum* A frost hardy sub-shrub of compact habit with leaves of grey-green and carrying mauve-pink flowers, deeper on the reverse, from late spring to autumn. 20 × 30cm/8in × 1ft
O. 'Whirligig' A half hardy sub-shrub of spreading habit with leaves of grey-green and carrying flowers made up of distinctive, spoon-shaped white petals, slate-blue on the reverse, from late spring to autumn. 60 × 60cm/2 × 2ft

Othonna cheirifolia

Oxalis articulata

Ozothamnus ledifolius

OTHONNA

A genus of hardy to frost tender, evergreen or deciduous succulent perennials and shrubs noted for their fleshy leaves and daisy-like, mainly yellow, flowers.
O. cheirifolia A frost hardy, evergreen shrub with branching stems of fleshy, pale grey-green leaves. Yellow flower-heads in summer. Best in well drained soil in full sun. 30 × 60cm/1 × 2ft

OXALIS (Shamrock)

Genus of hardy to frost tender, bulbous, rhizomatous or tuberous annuals and perennials, some of which may become invasive, valued for their flowers and clover-like foliage. For sun or part shade according to species.
O. articulata A low growing, hardy perennial with mauve-pink flowers from late spring to late summer. Tolerant of most situations. 20 × 20cm/8 × 8in

OZOTHAMNUS

A genus of hardy to half hardy, evergreen shrubs and woody based perennials grown for their aromatic foliage and their corymb-like flowerheads.
O. ledifolius A frost hardy, evergreen shrub of compact habit with linear leaves of deep green, yellow and downy on the undersides; white flowerheads in early summer. 1 × 1m/3 × 3ft

P

Pachysandra terminalis

Pachysandra terminalis 'Variegata'

PACHYPHRAGMA

A genus of a single species of semi-evergreen, rhizomatous perennial with leaves of a shiny, deep green, dulling with age. Suitable as ground cover in damp soil in partial shade.

P. macrophyllum A semi-evergreen perennial forming basal clusters of scalloped leaves with flat corymbs of cross-shaped white flowers in early spring. Fruits follow. 30 × 60cm/1 × 2ft

PACHYSANDRA

A genus of evergreen or semi-evergreen perennials and sub-shrubs with leaves of grey-green to dark green, or variegated, and carrying small, petalless flowers in spring or early summer. Suitable as ground cover.

P. terminalis An evergreen perennial of spreading habit with shiny leaves of deep green and carrying spikes of tiny white flowers in early summer. 20cm/8in × indefinite spread

P. terminalis 'Variegata' Similar to *P. terminalis* but less vigorous and with leaves margined in white. 25 × 60cm/10in × 2ft

PAEONIA (Peony)

Genus of hardy to frost hardy perennials and deciduous shrubs or sub-shrubs valued for their attractive, finely cut leaves and large saucer to cup-shaped flowers, single, semi-double, double, and anemone-form, in a wide range of colours. Best in humus-rich, damp but well drained soil. Long lived, peonies are inclined to resent disturbance and may take time to settle when newly planted.

P. delavayi (Tree peony) A hardy, deciduous shrub with leaves of dark green, blue-green on the undersides, and producing single, deep red flowers in early summer. 2 × 1.2m/6 × 4ft

P. delavayi var. *ludlowii* A hardy, deciduous shrub with leaves of bright green and producing large, single, brilliant yellow flowers in late spring. 2.5 × 2.5m/8 × 8ft

P. lactiflora 'Bowl of Beauty' A hardy perennial with leaves of mid-green producing anemone-form, deep pink flowers with creamy centres in early summer. 1 × 1m/3 × 3ft

P. lactiflora 'Docteur H. Barnsby' A hardy perennial with leaves of mid-green and producing double, velvet-red flowers in early summer. 1 × 1m/3 × 3ft

Paeonia delavayi

Paeonia delavayi var. *ludlowii*

Paeonia lactiflora 'Bowl of Beauty'

Paeonia lactiflora 'Docteur H. Barnsby'

Paeonia lactiflora 'Monsieur Jules Elie'

Paeonia × lemoinei 'Souvenir de Maxime Cornu'

Paeonia mascula subsp. arietina

Paeonia mlokosewitschii

P. lactiflora 'Monsieur Jules Elie' A hardy perennial with leaves of dark green and producing large, double, deep rose-red flowers in early summer. 1 x 1m/3 x 3ft

P. × lemoinei 'Souvenir de Maxime Cornu' (Tree peony) A hardy, deciduous shrub with divided leaves of mid-green producing scented, double flowers of orange-gold in early summer. 2 × 1.5m/6 × 5ft

P. mascula subsp. *arietina* A hardy perennial with leaves of blue-green, divided into narrow leaflets, and producing single reddish-pink flowers in early summer. 60 × 60cm/2 × 2ft

P. mlokosewitschii A hardy perennial with divided leaves of grey-green producing single, pale, lemon-yellow flowers in late spring and early summer. 75 × 75cm/2.5 × 2.5ft

P. officinalis 'Rosea Plena' A hardy perennial with divided leaves of dark green, paler on the undersides, and producing large, double flowers of rose-pink in early and mid-summer. 75 × 75cm/2.5 × 2.5ft

P. suffruticosa 'Sitifukujin' (Tree peony) A hardy, deciduous shrub with leaves of dark green producing semi-double, pink-crimson flowers in early summer. 2 × 2m/6 × 6ft

P. veitchii var. *woodwardii* A hardy perennial with divided leaves of dark green, hairy on the undersides, and producing pale, rose-pink flowers, darker in bud, in late spring and early summer. 30 × 30cm/1 × 1ft

Paeonia officinalis 'Rosea Plena'

Paeonia suffruticosa 'Sitifukujin'

Paeonia veitchii var. woodwardii

PANDOREA

A genus of frost tender, evergreen climbers, valued for their foliage and scented, tubular flowers. Position in full sun in damp but well drained soil.

P. pandorana (Wonga wonga vine) A frost tender (but may survive temperatures of 0°C/32°F for short periods), twining climber with pinnate leaves and producing creamy-yellow flowers, spotted red-purple, in winter and spring. 6m/20ft

Papaver orientale 'Charming'

Papaver rhoeas Shirley series

PAPAVER (Poppy)

A genus of hardy to frost hardy, annuals, biennials and perennials, some of which may be considered as weeds, grown largely for their saucer, cup or bowl-shaped flowers in a wide range of colours and markings. Best in full sun.

P. orientale 'Charming' A hardy perennial forming clumps of toothed leaves with flowers of blush lilac-pink from late spring to mid-summer. 60 × 60cm/2 × 2ft

P. rhoeas Shirley Series A hardy annual. Flowers, in the colour range of orange, pink, red or yellow, may be single, semi-double or double. 60 × 30cm/2 × 1ft

P. somniferum Peony-flowered Series A hardy annual. Flowers, in shades of pink, purple, red or white, are large, frilly and double. 1m × 30cm/3 × 1ft

Papaver somniferum Peony-flowered series

PARADISEA (St. Bruno's lily)

A genus of perennials forming clumps of grey-green, basal leaves and grown for their racemes of scented, tubular flowers which are excellent for cutting. For humus-rich, damp soil in sun or light shade.

P. liliastrum A perennial with tapering, grass-like leaves and producing white flowers with pronounced yellow anthers in late spring or early summer. 45 × 30cm/1.5 × 1ft

Parahebe catarractae

PARAHEBE

Genus of hardy to frost hardy evergreen or semi-evergreen sub-shrubs and perennials grown for their upright racemes of small, saucer-shaped flowers in blue, lilac, pink or white, often with contrasting markings. Best in full sun.

P. catarractae A hardy, evergreen shrub with small, oval mid-green leaves and racemes of white, purple-veined flowers in summer. 30 × 30cm/1 × 1ft

PARIS

A genus of rhizomatous perennials with upright stems carrying variable leaves of mid to dark green, and supporting wheel-shaped flowers followed by fruit capsules. For rich soil in part shade.

P. quadrifolia An erect perennial carrying whorls of mid-green leaves bearing solitary, star-like, green and white flowers in late spring followed by blue-black seed capsules. 30 × 30cm/1 × 1ft

Parthenocissus henryana

Parthenocissus quinquefolia (autumn foliage)

Parrotia persica

PARROTIA

A genus of a single species of deciduous tree noted for its attractive foliage, peeling bark and the brilliance of its autumn leaf colour. Best autumn colour is achieved when grown in acidic soil.

P. persica (Persian ironwood) A deciduous tree forming spreading branches based on a short trunk of peeling grey and fawn bark. 8 × 10m/ 25 × 30ft

PARTHENOCISSUS (Virginia creeper)

Genus of principally hardy, deciduous climbers cultivated for their attractive leaves, lobed or fully divided, which become brightly coloured in autumn. The majority of species will self-cling to a support by means of disc-like suckers. Well suited to grow against a wall or through a large tree.

P. henryana (Chinese Virginia creeper) A mainly hardy climber with divided leaves of mid-green, veined white, colouring brilliant red in autumn. Best in partial shade in a sheltered situation. 10m/30ft

P. quinquefolia A hardy climber of vigorous habit. Divided, dull, mid-green leaves colour vibrant red in autumn. 15m/50ft

Passiflora antioquiensis

Passiflora caerulea

Paulownia tomentosa

Trailing pelargoniums

Zonal pelargoniums

PASSIFLORA (Passion flower)

A genus of half hardy to frost tender, evergreen or semi-evergreen climbers valued for their striking and unusual flowers and, on some species, their fleshy, edible fruits in autumn. Water well during prolonged dry periods.

P. antioquiensis (Banana passion fruit) A frost tender climber with lobed leaves of mid to dark green and carrying long-tubed flowers, opening wide at the end, of brilliant rose-red, occasionally pink, in summer. Yellow fruits follow. 5m/15ft

P. caerulea A frost hardy climber with deep green divided leaves and carrying bowl-shaped flowers of white, sometimes flushed pink, with coronas of purple, blue and white from summer to autumn. Orange-yellow fruits follow. 10m/30ft

PAULOWNIA (Foxglove tree)

A genus of hardy to frost hardy, deciduous trees grown mainly for their large leaves and foxglove-like flowers which appear before the emergence of new foliage. Best in full sun. In cold areas hard prune each spring for resulting large leaves.

P. tomentosa A hardy tree of columnar habit with large, hairy leaves of light green and producing panicles of scented mauve flowers in late spring. 12 x 10m/40 x 30ft

PELARGONIUM (Geranium)

A genus of frost tender, mainly evergreen perennials widely cultivated as annuals and grown for their brightly coloured flowers which are borne almost continuously throughout summer. Frequently employed in bedding schemes and for containers. Pelargoniums fall into four main groups: Zonal – rounded leaves with distinctive markings and single, semi-double or double flowers. Regal – rounded to oval, serrated leaves and trumpet-shaped flowers. Ivy-leafed – trailing plants with rounded, lobed leaves and zonal-type flowers. Scented-leaved and species – fragrant leaves and small, often starry flowers. For neutral to alkaline soil in full sun.

Trailing pelargoniums Frost tender, evergreen perennials of trailing habit with mainly lobed, fleshy leaves of mid-green and producing clusters of single, semi-double or double flowers in shades of mauve, red, pink, purple or white in summer.

Zonal pelargoniums Frost tender, evergreen perennials of bushy, upright habit with rounded leaves, frequently marked bronze-green or maroon, and producing single, semi-double or double flowers in shades of orange, red, pink, purple, white and rarely yellow in summer. To 60cm/2ft height

P. 'Lord Bute' A frost tender, evergreen perennial belonging to the Regal group. Clusters of deep red-black flowers appear over serrated leaves of light to mid-green in summer. 45 × 30cm/1.5 × 1ft

P. 'Mabel Grey' A frost tender, evergreen perennial belonging to the Scented-leaved group. Clusters of pale lilac and purple flowers are carried over lemon-scented, veined leaves of mid-green in summer. 1m × 60cm/3 × 2ft

P. 'Madame Layal' A frost tender, evergreen perennial classified as Angel group but similar to Regal. Clusters of single flowers of deep purple and lilac are carried over lightly serrated leaves of mid to dark green in summer. 30 × 30cm/1 × 1ft

P. 'Roller's Pioneer' A frost tender, evergreen perennial belonging to the Ivy-leaved group. Clusters of deep, velvet-red semi-double flowers are carried over marbled leaves in summer. Trailing to 60cm/2ft

P. 'Elsie Hickman' A frost tender, evergreen perennial belonging to the Regal group. Clusters of rich, velvet-red and mid-pink flowers are carried over serrated leaves of mid to dark green in summer. 60 × 60cm/2 × 2ft

Pelargonium 'Lord Bute'

Pelargonium 'Madame Layal'

Pelargonium 'Mabel Grey'

Pelargonium 'Roller's Pioneer'

Pelargonium 'Elsie Hickman'

PENNISETUM

A genus of hardy (to − 10°C/14°F) to frost tender annual and perennial grasses with linear leaves and cultivated for their attractive spikelets in summer and autumn. For light, well drained soil in a position in full sun.

P. orientale A frost hardy, deciduous perennial grass with arching leaves of deep green and bearing soft, bristly spikelets of pink in mid and late summer. 60 × 75cm/2 × 2.5ft

Penstemon 'Blackbird'

Penstemon 'Chester Scarlet'

Penstemon davidsonii var. *menziesii*

Penstemon 'Edithiae'

Penstemon 'Apple Blossom'

PENSTEMON

Genus of hardy to half hardy, mostly semi-evergreen annuals, perennials, sub-shrubs and shrubs valued for their most often tubular-type flowers in a wide range of colours and borne from spring until autumn according to species. For full sun in fertile, well drained soil.

P. 'Apple Blossom' A hardy perennial with narrow leaves of mid-green and bearing tubular flowers of pale pink with white throats from midsummer to mid-autumn. 60 × 60cm/2 × 2ft

P. 'Blackbird' A hardy/frost hardy perennial with narrow leaves of mid-green and bearing tubular flowers of deep wine-red from midsummer to mid-autumn. 60 × 60cm/2 × 2ft

P. 'Chester Scarlet' A hardy/frost hardy perennial with narrow leaves of mid-green and bearing tubular flowers of bright scarlet from midsummer to mid-autumn. 60 × 45cm/2 × 1.5ft

P. davidsonii var. *menziesii* A hardy, semi-evergreen sub-shrub of creeping habit with rounded leaves of mid-green and bearing racemes of tubular, pale violet and pink flowers in summer. 15 × 20cm/6 × 8in

P. 'Edithiae' A hardy perennial with narrow leaves of mid-green and bearing tubular flowers of pale violet-mauve in late spring and early summer. 30 × 30cm/1 × 1ft

P. glaber A hardy, semi-evergreen sub-shrub with narrow leaves of mid-green and bearing tubular flowers of blue and pink in summer. 45 × 60cm/1.5 × 2ft

P. 'Joy' A hardy/frost hardy perennial with narrow leaves of mid-green and bearing tubular flowers of warm pink with lighter throats from midsummer to mid-autumn. 60 × 45cm/2 × 1.5ft

Penstemon glaber

Penstemon 'Joy'

Perovskia atriplicifolia

Persicaria bistorta 'Superba'

PEROVSKIA (Russian sage)

A genus of deciduous sub-shrubs grown mainly for their aromatic foliage of grey-green as well as for their spires of blue flowers borne on the current season's growth. Best in full sun. Tolerant of dry chalk.

P. atriplicifolia A sub-shrub of upright habit with deep cut leaves of grey-green and carrying small, tubular flowers of violet blue in late summer and early autumn. 1.2 × 1m/4 × 3ft

Persicaria campanulata

Persicaria vacciniifolia

PERSICARIA

A genus of hardy to frost hardy, deciduous, semi-evergreen or evergreen annuals, perennials and seldom sub-shrubs, many with good autumn leaf colour, grown mainly for their spikes or panicles of pink, red or white flowers and, in some species, distinctive fruits. Certain species may be considered invasive. Tolerant of most situations including, in the case of *P. bistorta*, dry soil.

P. bistorta 'Superba' A hardy, semi-evergreen perennial of clump forming habit with veined leaves of mid-green and carrying cylinder-like spikes of mid-pink flowers from early summer to mid-autumn. 75 cm × 1m/2.5 × 3ft

P. campanulata A hardy, deciduous or semi-evergreen perennial forming basal clumps of hairy, grey-green leaves, usually whitish on the undersides, and carrying panicles of scented pink or white flowers from midsummer to mid-autumn. 1 × 1m/3 × 3ft

P. vacciniifolia A hardy, semi-evergreen perennial of creeping habit with reddish stems and shiny leaves of mid-green. Bell-shaped flowers of deep pink, opening paler, are carried on upright spikes in late summer and autumn. 20 × 45cm/8in × 1.5ft

Petasites japonicus var. *giganteus*

PETASITES (Butterbur)

A genus of hardy to frost hardy, rhizomatous perennials, some of which may be considered as invasive, grown mainly for their heart to kidney-shaped leaves as a form of ground cover at the margins of ponds and streams.

P. japonicus var. *giganteus* An invasive hardy perennial for semi-shade with large, kidney-shaped, basal leaves and producing corymbs of yellow-white flowerheads surrounded by pale green bracts in late winter before the emergence of new leaves. 1.1m/3.5ft × indefinite spread

PETUNIA

Genus of half hardy perennials, widely cultivated as annuals, from which have been raised numerous named hybrids. Petunias are grown for their brightly coloured flowers which are mainly borne in summer and autumn. Best in a sunny position out of the reach of drying winds.

Petunia hybrids Half hardy perennials with leaves of mid to dark green and producing single or double, saucer or trumpet-type flowers in a range of colours to include pink, purple, red, violet, violet-blue, white or yellow, many of which are veined, striped or with throats of contrasting colours, from early summer to late autumn. 30–45 × 30cm–1m/1–1.5 × 1–3ft

Petunia hybrids

Phalaris arundinacea 'Picta'

PHALARIS

A genus of hardy to frost hardy, perennial grasses with leaves of light to mid-green, often variegated, and producing spikelets of one to three flowers. Tolerant of most situations.
P. arundinacea 'Picta' (Gardeners' garters) A hardy, perennial grass with mid-green leaves striped white and pale green spikelets in early and midsummer. Invasive. 1m/3ft × indefinite spread

Philadelphus coronarius 'Aureus'

Philadelphus 'Manteau d'Hermine'

Philadelphus 'Sybille'

Phlomis fruticosa

Philadelphus 'Belle Etoile'

PHILADELPHUS (Mock orange)

A genus of hardy to frost hardy, deciduous shrubs valued principally for their most often scented, single, semi-double and double flowers as well as for their attractive habit. Best in full sun although tolerant of some shade.
P. 'Belle Etoile' A hardy shrub of arching habit with tapering leaves of mid-green and producing single, cup-shaped, highly scented, white flowers, pale purple at the centre, in late spring and early summer. 2 × 2.5m/6 × 8ft
P. coronarius 'Aureus' A hardy shrub of upward habit with leaves of golden-yellow becoming yellow-green in summer and single, scented, creamy-white flowers in early summer. 2.5 × 1.5m/8 × 5ft
P. 'Manteau d'Hermine' A hardy shrub of compact habit with pale to mid-green leaves and double, highly scented, creamy-white flowers in early and midsummer. 75cm × 1.5m/2.5 × 5ft
P. 'Sybille' A hardy shrub of arching habit with leaves of mid-green and producing single, cup-shaped, scented, white flowers, marked with purple at the centre, in early or midsummer. 1.2 × 2m/4 × 6ft

PHLOMIS

A genus of hardy to frost hardy, evergreen perennials, sub-shrubs and shrubs noted for their conspicuous, hooded flowers, usually carried in whorls, and for their attractive foliage, most often pale green or grey-green. For fertile, well drained soil in full sun.
P. fruticosa (Jerusalem sage) A largely hardy, evergreen shrub forming a mound of upward shoots of sage-like, crinkled, grey-green leaves, woolly on the undersides. Deep, butter-yellow flowers are produced in early and midsummer.
1 × 1.5m/3 × 5ft
P. italica A frost hardy shrub of upright habit with grey-green, woolly leaves and producing lilac-pink flowers in midsummer. 60 × 60cm/2 × 2ft
P. russeliana A hardy perennial with hairy leaves of mid-green over which hooded flowers of pale creamy-yellow are carried in early summer although also at other times. 1m × 75cm/3 × 2.5ft

Phlomis russeliana

Phlox divaricata 'May Breeze'

Phlox adsurgens 'Wagon Wheel'

Phlox bifida

Phlox carolina 'Bill Baker'

Phlox paniculata 'Fujiyama'

PHLOX

A genus of hardy to half hardy annuals and perennials, some of which are evergreen, grown mainly for their brightly coloured flowers in a wide range of colours. Smaller species are well suited to the rock garden or alpine house whilst taller growing, 'border' phlox are tolerant of many garden situations. Some species thrive best in acid soil.

P. adsurgens 'Wagon Wheel' A hardy, semi-evergreen perennial of creeping, low growing habit with pale to mid-green leaves. Salmon-pink flowers, divided to resemble the spokes of a wheel, are produced in late spring and early summer. Best in acid soil and part shade. 30 × 30cm/1 × 1ft

P. bifida (Sand phlox) A hardy, evergreen perennial forming mounds of slender leaves and producing scented, starry, lavender-blue to white flowers in late spring and early summer. Prefers full sun but will tolerate slight shade. 20 × 15cm/8 × 6in

P. carolina 'Bill Baker' A hardy perennial of upright habit with leaves of bright green producing pink flowers in early summer. For sun or part shade. 45 × 30cm/1.5 × 1ft

P. divaricata 'May Breeze' A hardy, semi-evergreen perennial of upright habit with leaves of mid-green and producing the palest pink to white flowers in early summer. Best in partial shade. 30 × 45cm/1 × 1.5ft

P. drummondii (Annual phlox) A frost hardy annual of upright to spreading habit. Flowers, in the colour range lavender-blue, pink, purple, red or white, often paler on the insides and marked at the bases of the petal lobes, are produced in late spring. For full sun. 10–45 × 30cm/4in–1.5 × 1ft

P. paniculata 'Fujiyama' A hardy perennial of upright habit with narrow leaves of mid-green and producing scented, white flowers in summer to early autumn. For sun or part shade. 75 × 60cm/2.5 × 2ft

P. stolonifera A hardy perennial of creeping habit with leaves of dark green and producing pale to deep purple flowers in early summer. Best in acid soil and part shade. 15 × 30cm/6in × 1ft

P. subulata 'Betty' A hardy, evergreen perennial forming cushions of bright green leaves and carrying cerise-pink flowers in late spring and early summer. Best in full sun. 15 × 45cm/6in × 1.5ft

P. subulata 'Emerald Cushion' A hardy, evergreen perennial forming cushions of bright green leaves and carrying pale mauve-pink flowers in late spring and early summer. Best in full sun. 15 × 45cm/6in × 1.5ft

Phlox stolonifera

Phlox subulata 'Betty'

Phlox subulata 'Emerald Cushion'

Phormium cookianum 'Dazzler'

Phormium tenax

Phormium tenax (flowers)

PHORMIUM

A genus of frost hardy to half hardy evergreen perennials forming clumps of linear leaves ranging in colour from yellow-green to dark green, often striped. Cultivars, of which there are a number, are valued for their coloured and variegated foliage. Panicles of flowers are produced in summer. Position in well drained soil in full sun. In cold areas, apply a thick mulch in winter.

P. cookianum 'Dazzler' A frost hardy perennial with arching leaves variably striped bronze-red and green and producing tubular yellow-green flowers in summer. 1 × 1m/3 × 3ft

P. tenax A frost hardy perennial with stiff, upright leaves of dark green, blue-green on the undersides, and producing tubular dull-red flowers in summer. 4 × 2m/12 × 6ft

Photinia × fraseri 'Red Robin'

Phuopsis stylosa 'Purpurea'

Phygelius aequalis 'Yellow Trumpet'

PHOTINIA

A genus of hardy to frost hardy, deciduous and evergreen shrubs and trees valued for their attractive foliage, their flowers and fruit.

P. × fraseri 'Red Robin' A frost hardy, evergreen shrub of compact habit with leathery leaves of dark green, shiny red or bronze when young. Small white flowers are produced in mid and late spring. 5 × 5m/15 × 15ft

PHUOPSIS

A genus of a single species of mat-forming perennial grown for its whorls of narrow, light green leaves and its tubular-shaped, scented flowers carried in clusters throughout the summer.

P. stylosa 'Purpurea' A mat forming perennial with musk-scented leaves and carrying rounded heads of purple flowers for a prolonged period in summer. 15 × 45cm/6in × 1.5ft

PHYGELIUS (Cape figwort)

A genus of frost hardy, evergreen shrubs or sub-shrubs grown for their colourful, tubular flowers carried over a long period throughout summer and early autumn. In cold areas treat as herbaceous perennials, cutting back to ground level in spring. Best in a sheltered spot in full sun.

P. aequalis 'Yellow Trumpet' A frost hardy shrub of suckering habit with light green leaves and producing pale, creamy-yellow flowers in summer. 1 × 1m/3 × 3ft

PHYSALIS (Ground cherry)

Genus of hardy to frost hardy annuals and perennials grown mainly for their tiny, insignificant, bell-shaped flowers which are followed by rounded, red berries enclosed in most striking orange to scarlet calyces, often used in dried arrangements. Inclined to become invasive.

P. alkekengi (Chinese lanterns) A hardy, rhizomatous perennial of spreading habit with triangular to diamond-shaped leaves, cream flowers in midsummer followed by brilliant orange-red berries enclosed in papery red calyces. 75cm × 1m/2.5 × 3ft

PHYSOCARPUS

A genus of deciduous shrubs noted for their peeling bark, their attractive foliage and corymbs of cup-shaped, white flowers. Best in acidic soil which is well drained in sun or part shade.

P. opulifolius (Ninebark) A compact shrub of suckering habit with leaves of mid-green, white flowers tinged pink in early summer, and clusters of bladder-like, green-red fruits. 3 × 5m/10 × 15ft

Physalis alkekengi (calices)

Physostegia virginiana 'Variegata'

PHYSOSTEGIA (Obedient plant)

A genus of hardy to frost hardy, rhizomatous perennials of upright habit grown for their tubular flowers in shades of pink, purple or white which, if moved, remain in position giving rise to the common name of obedient plant. Best in soil which does not dry out.

P. virginiana 'Variegata' A hardy perennial with grey-green leaves, margined with white, and producing magenta-pink flowers from midsummer to early autumn. 60 × 60cm/2 × 2ft

Picea abies 'Gregoryana'

Picea glauca var. *albertiana* 'Conica'

Picea breweriana

PICEA (Spruce)

A genus of hardy to frost hardy, evergreen coniferous trees noted for their whorled branches and needle-like leaves. Female cones ripen throughout the season from green or red to purple or brown; male cones are yellow to red-purple. Picea species are valued as specimens, many of which are dwarf, or to form shelter belts. Best in neutral to acid soil in full sun.

P. abies 'Gregoryana' A hardy shrub or small tree of dwarf habit with forward pointing leaves of fresh green. Well suited to the rock garden. 75 × 75cm/2.5 × 2.5ft

P. abies 'Little Gem' Similar to *P. abies* 'Gregoryana'. 1 × 1m/3 × 3ft

P. breweriana (Brewer's spruce) A hardy, slow growing tree of columnar habit with weeping branchlets and leaves of deep green, green-white on the undersides, and cylinder-shaped, reddish-brown, female cones. 10 × 3m/30 × 10ft

P. glauca var. *albertiana* 'Conica' A hardy, conical shrub or small tree of dwarf habit with fresh green, outward facing leaves and green, ripening to brown, female cones. 2–6 × 1–2.5m/6–20 × 3–8ft

P. pungens glauca 'Procumbens' A hardy shrub or small tree of prostrate habit with outwardly curving, narrow leaves of grey-blue and green, ripening to pale brown, female cones. Well suited to the rock garden. 15cm × 1m/6in × 3ft

Picea abies 'Little Gem'

Picea pungens glauca 'Procumbens'

Pieris japonica 'Little Heath'

Pieris japonica 'Mountain Fire'

Pieris 'Flamingo'

PIERIS

A genus of hardy to frost hardy, evergreen shrubs valued for their attractive, shiny leaves of mid to deep green most often brilliantly coloured when young. Small, urn-shaped flowers are carried in spring. For humus-rich, damp but well drained, acidic soil in full sun or light shade. Position out of the reach of drying winds.
P. 'Flamingo' A hardy shrub with shiny leaves of deep green and hanging panicles of dark pink flowers, red in bud, in late winter and early spring. 4 × 3m/12 × 10ft
P. japonica 'Little Heath' A hardy shrub of dwarf habit with leaves of pale green, margined with white, and tinged pink when young. Pink flowers in late winter and early spring. 60 × 60cm/2 × 2ft
P. japonica 'Mountain Fire' A hardy shrub with leaves of mid-green, brilliant red when young, and hanging panicles of creamy flowers in late winter and early spring. 1.5 × 1.5m/5 × 5ft

PILEOSTYGIA

A genus of largely hardy (to −10°C/14°F), evergreen climbers cultivated for their attractive foliage and cup or star-shaped, white flowers. Suitable for wall training.
P. viburnoides A frost hardy, evergreen climber with leathery leaves of mid-green and bearing starry white flowers in late summer and autumn. 6m/20ft

PINUS (Pine)

A genus of hardy to frost hardy, evergreen, coniferous trees and shrubs noted for fissured bark, for their needle-like leaves in shades of green and for male and female cones. Well suited as specimens or to form wind breaks. Small, slow growing species may be grown in the rock garden. Best in full sun.
P. mugo (Dwarf mountain pine) A hardy shrub or small tree of spreading habit with grey, scaly bark and leaves of deep and bright green. Dark brown female cones are produced. 3.5 × 5m/11 × 15ft
P. pinea (Umbrella pine) A hardy tree of domed shape in maturity with bark of orange-brown. Young leaves of blue-green colour to a shiny green over a period of years. Brown female cones are produced. 15–20 × 6–12m/50–70 × 20–40ft
P. radiata (Monterey pine) A hardy fast-growing tree of conical habit maturing to a domed shape with deeply ridged, black bark. Shiny, bright green leaves are accompanied with yellow-brown, female cones. 25–40 × 8–12m/80–130 × 25–40ft
P. wallichiana (Blue pine) A hardy vigorous tree of conical habit maturing to a domed shape with smooth, grey bark later becoming scaly. Grey-green to blue-green leaves are accompanied with green, female cones ripening to brown. 20–35 × 6–12m/70–120 × 20–40ft

Pinus mugo

Pinus pinea

Pinus radiata

Pinus wallichiana

Piptanthus nepalensis

Pistia stratiotes

Pittosporum tenuifolium 'James Stirling'

Pittosporum tenuifolium 'Silver Queen'

PIPTANTHUS

A genus of frost hardy, deciduous or semi-evergreen shrubs grown for their attractive foliage and pea-like flowers. Well suited to wall training. Afford shelter from drying winds in cold areas.

P. nepalensis (Evergreen laburnum) A frost hardy, deciduous or semi-evergreen shrub of upright habit with leaves of blue-green, blue-white on the undersides. Mid-yellow, pea-like flowers are produced in racemes in late spring and early summer followed by hanging seed pods. 2.5 × 2m/8 × 6ft

PISTIA (Water lettuce)

A genus of a single species of frost tender, evergreen, floating aquatic perennial largely grown as an ornamental plant on account of its attractive leaves and coloured roots. Grow on the water's surface in full sun. Overwinter in a frost free environment.

P. stratiotes A frost tender, evergreen, floating aquatic perennial with striking, wedge-shaped leaves of light, glaucous-green borne in rosettes. Inconspicuous white flowers appear throughout the year. 10cm/4in × indefinite spread

PITTOSPORUM

A genus of frost hardy to frost tender, most often evergreen shrubs and trees grown mainly for their attractive form, their leaves, frequently coloured or variegated, and their usually scented flowers. For sun or part shade in a sheltered position although cultivars with variegated or purple foliage are best in full sun.

P. tenuifolium 'James Stirling' A frost hardy, large shrub or small tree with dark brown to black stems carrying shiny leaves, slightly waved at the edges, of light to mid-green. Scented, deep red-black flowers are produced in late spring and early summer. 4–10 × 2–5m/12–30 × 6–15ft

P. tenuifolium 'Silver Queen' A frost hardy shrub of compact habit with dark stems carrying grey-green leaves with irregular edging of white flushed pink. Flowers as for the species. 1–4 × 2m/3–12 × 6ft

P. tenuifolium 'Tom Thumb' A frost hardy shrub of dwarf habit with dark stems carrying deep bronze leaves flushed purple. Flowers as for the species. 1m × 60cm/3 × 2ft

PLANTAGO (Plantain)

A genus of hardy to frost tender annuals, biennials, evergreen perennials and shrubs many of which are invasive and considered as weeds. For neutral to acid soil in full sun.

P. nivalis A hardy perennial forming neat rosettes of lance-shaped, hairy, silver-green leaves with spikes of grey-brown flowers in summer. 2.5 × 8cm/1 × 3in

PLATANUS (Plane)

Genus of hardy to half hardy, deciduous trees grown for their imposing form, their large leaves, colouring in autumn, and their interesting, flaking bark. Best in full sun.

P. × hispanica (London plane) A hardy, deciduous tree of columnar habit with flaking bark of brown, cream and grey and leaves of bright green. Fruits, ripening to brown, are carried in clusters through autumn into winter. 30 × 20m/100 × 70ft

Pittosporum tenuifolium 'Tom Thumb'

Platycodon grandiflorus mariesii

PLATYCODON (Balloon flower)

A genus of a single species of variable perennial forming clumps of blue-green leaves and carrying clusters of bell-shaped flowers in shades of blue, purple or white in late summer.

P. grandiflorus mariesii A perennial of clump forming habit with lance-shaped leaves of blue-green and carrying pale violet-blue flowers, balloon-shaped in bud, in late summer. 60 × 30cm/2 × 1ft

Pleione hookeriana

Plumbago capensis

PLEIOBLASTUS (Bamboo)

A genus of evergreen bamboos grown for their attractive, linear to lance-shaped leaves, often marked or variegated, and their hollow canes. Most suited to clearings in the woodland or wild garden. Variegated cultivars are best in full sun.
P. variegatus An evergreen bamboo with variegated, linear leaves of deep green with cream stripe and producing hollow, pale green canes.
75cm × 1.2m/2.5 × 4ft

PLEIONE

A genus of half hardy, although some species may prove to be frost hardy, deciduous bulbous orchid grown mainly as houseplants or in a cool alpine or glasshouse. Usually solitary flowers are produced at various times of year.
P. hookeriana A half hardy, deciduous orchid carrying solitary flowers of blush pink to purple with pink to white lips in summer. 10 × 15cm/4–6in

PLUMBAGO (Leadwort)

A genus of half hardy to frost tender annuals, perennials and evergreen shrubs and climbers valued for their blue, red or white flowers. In cold areas well suited to cultivation in a cool or temperate conservatory or glasshouse. Outdoors position in full sun.
P. capensis A half hardy, evergreen shrub grown most often as a climber. Matt green leaves, occasionally blue-grey, are accompanied with tubular flowers of sky-blue from summer to late autumn.
3–6 × 1–3m/10–20 × 3–10ft

PODOCARPUS

A genus of hardy to frost tender, evergreen coniferous trees and shrubs principally grown for their variably shaped, spiral arrangement of leaves. Plum-shaped fruits are borne where male and female plants are grown together. Tolerant of many situations and conditions.
P. alpinus A hardy shrub of spreading habit with narrow leaves of dull green, marked grey on the undersides, carrying cone-like flowers in summer. Red fruits are produced on female plants in autumn. 2 × 2m/6 × 6ft

Polemonium caeruleum

PODOPHYLLUM

A genus of hardy to frost hardy rhizomatous perennials grown for foliage, flower and fruit. For humus-rich, damp soil in full or part shade.
P. peltatum (American mandrake) A hardy perennial of creeping habit with shiny leaves and producing cup-shaped, scented, waxy, pale pink or white flowers from mid-spring to early summer. Yellow-green fruits in autumn. 45 × 1.2m/1.5 × 4ft

POLEMONIUM (Jacob's ladder)

A genus of generally clump forming annuals and perennials cultivated for their variously shaped flowers in shades of blue, mauve, pink or white, sometimes purple and yellow, produced in spring and summer.
P. caeruleum A perennial of clump forming habit carrying bell-shaped, lavender-blue flowers, occasionally white, on tall stems in early summer. 30–90 × 30cm/1–3 × 1ft
P. 'Hopley's' A perennial of clump forming habit carrying cup-shaped, pale lilac and mauve flowers in late spring and early summer. 45 × 45cm/1.5 × 1.5ft
P. 'Lambrook Mauve' A perennial of clump forming habit carrying cup-shaped, lilac-blue flowers in late spring and early summer. 45 × 45cm/1.5 × 1.5ft

Polemonium 'Lambrook Mauve'

POLYGONATUM (Solomon's seal)

A genus of hardy to frost hardy, rhizomatous perennials grown mainly for their foliage, carried on arching stems and colouring yellow in autumn, and their largely hanging, most often tubular or bell-shaped flowers in cream or white, occasionally pink, with green markings. For damp soil in full or part shade.
P. × hybridum A hardy perennial with arching stems carrying ribbed leaves of mid-green with cream and green, tubular flowers in late spring followed by small, blue-black fruits.
1.2m × 30cm/4 × 1ft

POLYGONUM

A genus of perennials mostly reclassified as *Persicaria* or *Fallopia*.
P. baldschuanicum (syn. *Fallopia baldschuanicum*) (Russian vine) A hardy, deciduous climber of vigorous or rampant habit with heart-shaped leaves of deep green and carrying panicles of funnel-type white flowers, tinted pinkish, in late summer and autumn. 12m/40ft

POLYPODIUM

A genus of hardy to frost tender, mainly evergreen ferns. Best in humus-rich, well drained soil in sun or light shade.
P. cambricum A hardy, deciduous fern with fronds of mid-green. New fronds emerge in late summer, dying back in spring.
15–60cm/6in–2ft × indefinite spread

Polygonatum × hybridum

Polygonum baldschuanicum

Polystichum setiferum 'Plumodivisilobum'

POLYSTICHUM (Shield fern)

A genus of hardy to frost tender, mainly evergreen ferns grown for their attractive fronds emerging most often from 'shuttlecock' crowns. For humus-rich, well drained soil in full or partial shade.
P. setiferum 'Plumodivisilobum' (Soft shield fern) A hardy, evergreen fern with fronds of deep green along the midribs of which are frequently to be found bulbils.
60 × 60cm/2 × 2ft

PONCIRUS (Japanese bitter orange)

A genus of a single species of deciduous shrub or small tree of open habit and grown for its scented white flowers and orange-like fruit. Best in full sun out of the reach of drying winds.
P. trifoliata A deciduous shrub or small tree with rigid stems lined with spines. Dark green leaves colour yellow in autumn. Scented white flowers in late spring and early summer followed by green, ripening to orange, fruits. 5 × 5m/15 × 15ft

Poncirus trifoliata

PONTEDERIA (Pickerel weed)

A genus of hardy to frost hardy, aquatic perennials for the margins of pond or stream. Spikes of usually blue flowers rise over clumps of fresh green leaves in summer and early autumn. Best in full sun in a maximum of 12cm/5in of water.
P. cordata A hardy, aquatic perennial with shiny floating or submerged leaves and producing spikes of tubular blue flowers in late summer. 1m x 60cm/3 x 2ft

POPULUS (Poplar)

Genus of largely deciduous trees valued for the rapidity of their growth and their ability to tolerate a wide range of soils and situations. Excellent as windbreaks or as specimens. Avoid planting close to buildings on account of vigorous root systems.
P. × candicans 'Aurora' A deciduous tree of columnar habit with heart-shaped leaves of dark green splashed white, cream and pink. Female catkins in early spring.
15 × 6m/50 × 20ft
P. nigra var. *italica* (Lombardy poplar) A deciduous tree of narrow, columnar habit with leaves of shiny, dark green. Male catkins in spring. 30 × 5m/100 × 15ft
P. tremula (Common aspen) A deciduous tree of spreading habit with leaves of dark green, bronze when new, colouring yellow in autumn. Leaves tremble and rattle in wind. Male and female catkins in early spring. 20 × 10m/70 × 30ft

Populus × candicans 'Aurora'

Potentilla nepalensis 'Miss Willmott'

Potentilla fruticosa 'Elizabeth'

Pratia pedunculata

POTENTILLA (Cinquefoil)

A genus of mainly perennials and shrubs, but also some annuals and biennials, grown largely for their attractive flowers in a wide range of colours to include shades of orange, pink, red, white or yellow produced from spring to autumn. Fairly tolerant of soil and situation but best in full sun.

P. fruticosa A deciduous shrub of compact, bushy habit with small, dark green leaves and producing saucer-shaped, yellow flowers from late spring to early autumn.

P. fruticosa 'Elizabeth' has bright, lemon-yellow flowers. 1 × 1.5m/3 × 5ft

P. nepalensis 'Miss Willmott' A perennial of clump forming habit with leaves of mid-green and bearing cherry-pink flowers with darker centres in summer. 45 × 60cm/1.5 × 2ft

PRATIA

A genus of hardy to frost hardy, evergreen perennials of spreading habit. Hardy species require damp soil in part or full shade although *P. pedunculata* is tolerant of dry conditions.

P. pedunculata A hardy perennial of carpeting habit with rounded leaves of mid-green and starry, bluish-white flowers throughout summer. 1.5cm/1½in × indefinite spread

PRIMULA

A genus of hardy to frost tender mainly perennials, some of which are evergreen, noted for their pale to deep green leaves forming basal rosettes and for their attractive flowers, shaped variously, which may be set among the leaves or carried on slender to thick stalks. Cultivation requirements vary according to species but most are best in humus-rich, damp soil in part shade. A complex genus, for ease of reference primula may be broadly grouped as follows: Auricula – evergreen with umbels of flat-faced flowers above smooth foliage often with white farina. Candelabra – deciduous or semi-evergreen with whorls of flowers arranged in tiers on stout stems. Primrose-Polyanthus – deciduous, semi-evergreen and evergreen flowering in winter and spring and often grown as biennials for containers and bedding schemes.

P. auricula hybrid A hardy, evergreen perennial forming rosettes of pale green, toothed leaves over which are carried white centred flowers of plum-purple in spring. For sun or part shade or for the alpine house. 20 × 25cm/8 × 10in

P. Crescendo Red A hardy, semi-evergreen perennial of the Primrose-Polyanthus group forming rosettes of veined, dark green leaves with yellow-centred, red flowers in late winter and spring. For sun or part shade. 20 × 25cm/8 × 10in

P. denticulata (Drumstick primula) A hardy, deciduous perennial forming rosettes of toothed, mid-green leaves, mealy-white on the undersides, over which are carried rounded umbels of tightly packed, tubular, purple flowers in spring. *P.d.* var. *alba* has white flowers. For sun or part shade. 45 × 45cm/1.5 × 1.5ft

Primula denticulata

Primula auricula hybrid

Primula Crescendo Red

Primula florindae

Primula 'Dusky Lady'

Primula elatior

P. 'Dusky Lady' A hardy, semi-evergreen perennial forming rosettes of purplish-green leaves over which are carried deep, wine-red flowers in spring. For sun or part shade. 15 × 30cm/6in × 1ft

P. elatior (Oxlip) A hardy semi-evergreen or evergreen perennial forming rosettes of scalloped leaves of mid-green over which are carried tubular, yellow flowers on stout stems in spring and summer. Best in neutral to acid soil in part shade. 30 × 25cm/1ft × 10in

P. florindae (Giant cowslip) A hardy, deciduous perennial forming rosettes of toothed leaves of mid-green over which are carried umbels of scented, tubular, sulphur-yellow flowers in summer. For full sun or part shade. 1 × 1m/3 × 3ft

P. 'Gigha' A hardy, semi-evergreen perennial forming rosettes of veined leaves of pale green over which are carried yellow centred, white flowers in spring. For sun or part shade. 20 × 25cm/8 × 10in

P. Gold Laced Group Hardy, semi-evergreen or evergreen perennials belonging to the Primrose-Polyanthus group with leaves of mid-green over which are carried umbels of gold centred and margined darkest red to near black flowers in spring. Best in neutral to acid soil in part shade or for the alpine house. 25 × 30cm/10in × 1ft

P. 'Guinevere' A hardy, evergreen perennial forming rosettes of finely toothed leaves of dark bronze over which are carried yellow centred, pale purple-pink flowers in spring. Best in neutral to acid soil in part shade. 12 × 25cm/5 × 10in

P. Hose in Hose A hardy, semi-evergreen perennial forming rosettes of veined leaves of mid-green over which are carried double flowers, by which one flower is duplicated into the throat of another, of pale primrose with darker centre in spring. For sun or part shade. 20 × 25cm/8 × 10in

Primula 'Gigha'

Primula 'Guinevere'

Primula Gold Laced Group

Primula Hose in Hose

Primula helodoxa

Primula japonica

Primula japonica 'Postford White'

Primula pulverulenta

Primula sieboldii

Primula sieboldii alba

Primula 'Miss Indigo

P. helodoxa A hardy, deciduous perennial belonging to the Candelabra group forming rosettes of mid-green leaves over which are carried whorls of golden-yellow flowers arranged in tiers on stout stems in late spring and early summer. Well suited to the bog garden. For moist soil in part shade. 1m × 30cm/3 × 1ft

P. japonica (Japanese primula) A hardy, deciduous perennial forming rosettes of finely toothed, veined leaves of light green over which are carried whorls of pale red to red-purple to white flowers in spring. For neutral to acid soil in part shade. 45 × 45cm/1.5 × 1.5ft

P. japonica 'Postford White' Similar to *P. japonica* but with red centred, white flowers. 45 × 45cm/1.5 × 1.5ft

P. 'Miss Indigo' A hardy, semi-evergreen perennial forming rosettes of veined leaves of mid-green over which are carried double flowers of dark, rich purple with white tips in spring. For part shade. 20 × 30cm/8in × 1ft

P. pulverulenta A hardy, deciduous perennial forming rosettes of finely toothed leaves of mid-green over which are carried whorls of deep red or red-purple flowers arranged in tiers on white-powdered stems in late spring and early summer. For moist soil in part shade. 60cm–1m × 30–45cm/2–3 × 1–1.5ft

P. sieboldii A hardy, deciduous perennial forming rosettes of downy, light green leaves over which are carried white centred flowers of rose-violet to lilac-purple, or crimson, in late spring and early summer. For moist soil in part shade. 30 × 45cm/1 × 1.5ft

P. sieboldii alba Similar to *P. sieboldii* but with pure white flowers. 30 × 45cm/1 × 1.5ft

P. 'Snow Cushion' A hardy, evergreen perennial forming rosettes of light green leaves over which are carried pure white flowers in spring. For sun or part shade. 10 × 20cm/4 × 8in

Primula 'Snow Cushion'

Primula veris

P. veris (Cowslip) A hardy, semi-evergreen or evergreen perennial forming rosettes of sometimes scalloped leaves of mid-green over which are carried umbels of scented flowers of deep yellow in spring. For sun or part shade.
25 × 25cm/10 × 10in
P. vialii A hardy, deciduous perennial forming rosettes of toothed, slightly hairy leaves of mid-green over which are carried poker-like spikes of tubular flowers, crimson in bud, opening to violet-purple in summer. For neutral to acid soil in part shade. 30–60 × 30cm/1–2 × 1ft
P. vulgaris (Primrose) A hardy, semi-evergreen or evergreen perennial forming rosettes of veined leaves of bright green over which are carried clusters of palest yellow flowers in spring. For sun or part shade in moist soil. 20 × 30cm/8in × 1ft
P. vulgaris 'Lilacina Plena' Similar to *P. vulgaris* but with double flowers of pale lilac, deeper at the centre. 20 × 30cm/8in × 1ft
P. vulgaris subsp. *sibthorpii* Similar to *P. vulgaris* but with wedge-shaped leaves and yellow centred flowers usually of lilac, purple, red, rose-pink or white.
20 × 30cm/8in × 1ft
P. vulgaris 'Viridis' Similar to *P. vulgaris* but with yellow centred flowers of light green. 20 × 30cm/8in × 1ft
P. 'Wanda' A hardy, semi-evergreen or evergreen perennial forming rosettes of deep purplish-green leaves over which are carried clusters of yellow centred, purple flowers in spring. Tolerant of both sun and shade. 15 × 30cm/6in × 1ft

Primula vialii

Primula vulgaris

Primula vulgaris subsp. *sibthorpii*

Primula vulgaris 'Lilacina Plena'

Prunella grandiflora 'Pink Loveliness'

PRUNELLA (Self-heal)
A genus of semi-evergreen perennials of spreading, vigorous habit cultivated for their upward spikes of tubular flowers in white, pink or violet. Attractive to bees. Tolerant of most soils and situations.
P. grandiflora 'Pink Loveliness' A perennial of spreading habit with leaves of dark green and producing whorls of clear pink flowers in summer.
15cm × 1m/6in × 3ft

Primula vulgaris 'Viridis'

Primula 'Wanda'

Prunus 'Amanogawa'

Prunus 'Kanzan'

Prunus laurocerasus

Prunus lusitanica

Prunus mume 'Beni-chidori'

Prunus 'Accolade'

Prunus cerasifera 'Pissardii'

PRUNUS (Ornamental cherry)

Genus of hardy to frost hardy, deciduous and evergreen trees and shrubs of upright and rounded habit, sometimes spreading, grown for their usually saucer, bowl or cup-shaped flowers, single, semi-double and double, in shades of pink, red or white. Flowers are most often followed by fruit and the genus includes *P.* × *domestica* (plum), *P. dulcis* (almond) and *P. persica* (peach). Many species are suitable as specimen trees, a number of which are ideal for the smaller garden. Most species are best in full sun.

P. 'Accolade' A hardy, deciduous tree of spreading habit with tapering leaves of deep green and clusters of semi-double, pale pink flowers, darker in bud, in early spring. 8 × 8m/25 × 25ft

P. 'Amanogawa' A hardy, deciduous tree of upright habit with emerging leaves of bronze-yellow colouring red and yellow from green in autumn. Clusters of semi-double, scented, pale pink flowers in late spring. 8 × 4m/25 × 12ft

P. cerasifera 'Pissardii' A hardy, deciduous tree of rounded habit with leaves of deep purple-red and single, pale pink flowers, fading to white, on bare stems in early spring. 10 × 10m/30 × 30ft

P. 'Kanzan' A hardy, deciduous tree of upright habit, spreading with age, with leaves of deep green, emerging bronze, and double, sugar-pink flowers in mid and late spring. 10 × 10m/30 × 30ft

P. 'Kursar' A hardy, deciduous tree of spreading habit with leaves of deep green, emerging bronze, and single flowers of mid-pink, darker at the centre, on bare stems in early spring. 8 × 8m/25 × 25ft

P. laurocerasus (Cherry laurel) A hardy, evergreen shrub, spreading with age, with oblong, shiny leaves of dark green, paler on the undersides, and racemes of scented white flowers in spring followed by red fruits ripening to black. 8 × 10m/25 × 30ft

P. lusitanica (Portugese laurel) A hardy/frost hardy, evergreen shrub or tree with shiny leaves of dark green and racemes of scented white flowers in early summer followed by red fruits. 6–10 × 5m/20–30 × 15ft

P. mume 'Beni-chidori' A hardy, deciduous tree of upright habit with tapering leaves of deep green and single, dark pink flowers on bare stems in late winter and early spring. 2.5 × 2.5m/8 × 8ft

Prunus 'Kursar'

Prunus 'Taoyame'

P. 'Taoyame' A hardy deciduous spreading tree with leaves, first bronze then greening, then red/orange in autumn, and semi-double scented pink flowers in spring. 5 × 8m/15 × 25ft

P. 'Taihaku' (Great white cherry) A hardy, deciduous tree of spreading habit with leaves of deep green, emerging bronze, and clusters of single white flowers in mid-spring. 8 × 10m/25 × 30ft

P. tenella 'Fire Hill' A hardy, deciduous shrub of upright habit with leaves of shiny deep green and clusters of very dark pink flowers in mid and late spring. 1.5 × 1.5/5 × 5ft

Prunus 'Shirotae'

Prunus Pendula 'Pendula Rosea'

Prunus Persica Hybrid

Prunus 'Pink Shell'

Prunus × *Subhirtella* 'Autumnalis Rosea'

Prunus 'Taihaku'

Prunus Tenella 'Fire Hill'

Pseudolarix amabilis (autumn foliage)

Pterostyrax hisipida

Pulmonaria officinalis 'Bowles' Blue'

PSEUDOLARIX (Golden larch)

A genus of a single species of deciduous, coniferous tree grown largely for its autumn colour of golden-orange and its male and female cones. Well suited as a specimen in acid to neutral soil in a sheltered situation in full sun.
P. amabilis A deciduous, coniferous tree of conical habit with furrowed grey bark and leaves of soft, green, colouring well in autumn. 15 × 6m/50 × 20ft

PTEROSTYRAX

A genus of deciduous trees or shrubs of spreading habit and grown for their peeling, aromatic bark, leaves of pale green, scented white flowers and ribbed or winged fruits. For neutral to acid soil in sun or part shade.
P. hispida (Epaulette tree) A deciduous tree or shrub producing bell-like, scented, white flowers in summer. 15 × 12m/50 × 40ft

Pulmonaria officinalis 'Sissinghurst White'

Pulmonaria rubra 'Redstart'

Pulmonaria longifolia

PULMONARIA (Lungwort)

A genus of deciduous or evergreen perennials of low growing habit valued for their late winter and spring flowers, most often funnel-shaped and in the colour range of blue, red, pink, purple, violet or white, and their hairy, basal leaves frequently spotted white or silver. For humus-rich, damp soil in total or partial shade although P. officinalis is tolerant of sun.
P. longifolia A hardy, deciduous perennial of clump forming habit with lance-shaped leaves of deep green spotted silver-white. Funnel-shaped flowers of blue to blue-purple are produced from late winter to late spring. 30 × 45cm/1 × 1.5ft
P. officinalis 'Bowles Blue' A hardy, evergreen perennial of clump forming habit with leaves of mid-green, spotted silver-white, and producing funnel-shaped flowers of lilac-blue with darker eye in spring. 30 × 45cm/1 × 1.5ft
P. officinalis 'Sissinghurst White' A hardy, evergreen perennial of clump forming habit with leaves of mid-green, heavily spotted white, and producing white, funnel-shaped flowers in spring. 30 × 45cm/1 × 1.5ft
P. rubra 'Redstart' A hardy, evergreen perennial of clump forming habit with leaves of matt green and producing funnel-shaped flowers of deep coral-red in late winter and early spring. 30cm × 1m/1 × 3ft

PULSATILLA

A genus of deciduous perennials of clump forming habit grown mainly for their attractively cut, fern-like foliage and their most often silky, bell or cup-shaped flowers followed by striking seedheads. Well suited to the rock garden or alpine house. For well drained soil in full sun.

P. vulgaris (Pasque flower) A perennial of clump forming habit with divided leaves of light green and carrying upright, purple, bell-shaped flowers in spring. 20 × 20cm/8 × 8in.

P. vulgaris var. *rubra* Similar to *P. vulgaris* but with flowers of wine red. 20 × 20cm/8 × 8in

PUNICA (Pomegranate)

A genus of frost hardy shrubs or trees of rounded habit and cultivated for their brilliant red flowers and edible fruits. Best in full sun in a sheltered situation.

P. granatum A frost hardy, somewhat spiny shrub with leaves of bright green, copper when young, and funnel-shaped flowers of orange-red in summer followed by edible fruits. 30cm–1m × 30cm–1m/1–3 × 1–3ft

PUSCHKINIA

A genus of single species of bulbous perennial closely related to *Scilla*. Racemes of pale blue flowers with deeper stripe are produced in spring. Well suited to the rock garden.

P. scilloides var. *libanotica* A small, bulbous perennial with linear, basal leaves and producing ice-white flowers, striped blue, in spring. 20 × 5cm/8 × 2in

PYRACANTHA (Firethorn)

A genus of hardy to frosty hardy, evergreen shrubs, sometimes trees, of upright and spreading habit and grown for their foliage, flowers and fruits of orange, yellow and red in autumn. Suitable as specimens, as a hedge or for wall training.

P. 'Mohave' A hardy/frost shrub of vigorous habit with leaves of dark green and hawthorn like white flowers in early summer followed by long lasting red berries. 4 × 5m/12 × 12ft

PYRUS (Pear)

A genus of largely deciduous trees and shrubs grown mainly for their form, flowers and fruit, some of which are edible as in the case of the numerous cultivars bred for the production of pears. Ornamental species are well suited as specimens. Best in full sun.

P. salicifolia 'Pendula' A deciduous tree of weeping habit with willow-like leaves of silver-grey and carrying small, creamy-white flowers in spring followed by pear-like green, inedible fruits. 5 × 4m/15 × 12ft

Pusatilla Vulgaris

Pulsatilla Vulgaris Var. *Rubra*

Puschkinia Scilloides Var. *Libanotica*

Pyracantha Rogersiana 'Flava'

Pyracantha 'Mohave'

Pyrus Salicifolia 'Pendula'

Quercus coccinea (autumn foliage)

Quercus cerris

QUERCUS (Oak) A genus of hardy to frost hardy, deciduous, semi-evergreen trees and shrubs grown principally for form and foliage. Leaves, which may be whole, lobed or toothed are accompanied by male and female flowers, in the form of catkins, followed by acorns, nuts held in scaly cups. Tolerant of both sun and shade, although evergreen species are best in full sun.

Q. cerris (Turkey oak) A hardy, deciduous tree of spreading habit with deeply lobed or toothed leaves of dark green, paler on the undersides, and colouring yellow in autumn. Acorn nuts are held in scaly cups. 30 × 23m/100 × 80ft

Q. coccinea (Scarlet oak) A hardy, deciduous tree of rounded habit with scaly grey-brown bark and shiny leaves of deep green colouring brilliant red in autumn. Acorn nuts are almost spherical. For lime free soil. 20 × 15m/70 × 50ft

Ramonda myconi

RAMONDA

A genus of evergreen perennials grown for their leaves, often hairy and crinkled and varied in shape and colour, and flat or flattened cup-shaped flowers produced in late spring and early summer. Well suited to the rock garden, the alpine house or for crevices in walls and paving. Best in part shade.

R. myconi An evergreen perennial forming rosettes of moderately crinkled, deep green leaves and producing outwardly facing, violet blue flowers with distinctive yellow anthers in late spring and early summer. 10 × 20cm/ 4 × 8in

Ranunculus ficaria 'Brazen Hussy'

Ranunculus ficaria flore-pleno

RANUNCULUS (Buttercup)

A genus of largely hardy annuals, biennials and deciduous, occasionally evergreen perennials cultivated for their generally bowl or cup-shaped flowers most often yellow but also orange, pink, red or white. Tolerant of a wide range of soils and situations although some species have specific requirements.

R. ficaria 'Brazen Hussy' A hardy, tuberous, deciduous perennial forming basal leaves of shiny bronze-chocolate-brown and producing glossy, cup-shaped flowers of golden-yellow in early spring. Summer dormant. For part or full shade. 5 × 30cm/2in × 1ft

R. ficaria flore-pleno A hardy, tuberous, deciduous perennial forming basal leaves of shiny deep green and producing double, clear yellow flowers in early to mid spring. For part of full shade. 5 × 30cm/2in × 1ft

RAOULIA

A genus of hardy (to around −10°C/ 14°F), evergreen perennials or sub-shrubs forming mats of silvery leaves with disc-shaped flowerheads. Well suited to the rock garden. For well drained, gritty soil in a cool situation.

R. australis A hardy, evergreen perennial with sulphur-yellow flowerheads in summer. 1 × 30cm/^{1}/2in × 1ft

REHMANNIA

A genus of frost tender or half-hardy perennials, sometimes treated as biennials, grown for foxglove-type flowers over basal rosettes of lobed or toothed, heavily veined, hairy leaves. Best in a sheltered site in full sun.

R. elata (Chinese foxglove) A half-hardy perennial with flowers of cerise pink to pink-purple from summer to autumn. 1m × 45cm/3 × 1.5ft

Rhamnus alaternus 'Argenteovariegata'

RHAMNUS (Buckthorn)

A genus of hardy to frost hardy, deciduous and evergreen shrubs and trees grown principally for their foliage, colouring in autumn on some deciduous species, and for their decorative fruits which follow tiny, sometimes scented, hermaphrodite flowers.

R. alaternus 'Argenteovariegata' A frost hardy, evergreen shrub of spreading habit with leaves of grey-green, margined white, and producing yellow-green flowers in late spring and early summer followed by red fruits ripening to black. 5 × 4m/15 × 12ft

Rhodanthemum hosmariense

Rhodiola rosea

RHODIOLA

A genus of perennials grown for their fleshy, grey-green leaves and starry flowers of green, orange, red or yellow. Best in full sun.

R. rosea A perennial of clump forming habit producing purple stems carrying glaucous leaves of grey-green, tipped red, terminating in corymb-like flowerheads of acid green opening from pink buds. 30 × 20cm/1ft × 8in

Rheum palmatum

RHEUM (Rhubarb)

A genus of rhizomatous perennials grown mainly for their large, ornamental leaves and imposing flower panicles which are followed by small, brown fruits. Most species thrive best in moist soil and are particularly effective at the water's edge. Confusion should not be made with *R.* × *hybridum*, grown for its edible stalk.

R. palmatum (Chinese rhubarb) A rhizomatous perennial forming a large rootstock from which emerge thick stalks carrying toothed leaves of dark green, the undersides of which are red, and panicles of creamy green to deep red, starry flowers in early summer. 2.5 × 1.8m/8 × 6ft

RHODANTHEMUM

A genus of frost hardy (to around −10°C/14°F) perennials and sub-shrubs grown largely for their solitary, daisy-like flowerheads. Well suited to the rock garden. Best in sun.

R. hosmariense A frost hardy sub-shrub of spreading habit with leaves of silver and producing white, yellow centred flowerheads from spring to autumn. 10–30 × 30cm/4in–1ft × 1ft

RHODOCHITON

A genus of frost tender, deciduous perennial climbers grown for their unusual flowers and lightly toothed leaves. In cold areas treated as annuals raised from ripe seed.

R. atrosanguineus A frost tender, perennial climber with heart shaped leaves of deep green and bearing near black to red-purple, tubular flowers with pink-mauve calyces from summer to autumn. 3m/10ft

Rhodochiton atrosanguineus

Rhododendron arboreum hybrid

Rhododendron barbatum

Rhododendron 'Bric-A-Brac'

Rhododendron 'Elizabeth'

Rhododendron 'Hino-Mayo'

Rhododendron 'John Cairns'

RHODODENDRON

A genus of hardy to frost tender, deciduous and evergreen shrubs and trees varying greatly in habit and from which have been developed numerous hybrids. Most have lance-shaped leaves of mid to dark green, some of which are covered with an indumentum, a wooly covering of tiny hairs or scales. Rhododendrons are valued for their showy, often scented flowers which are carried singly or in trusses and, in the case of some deciduous species or hybrids, for autumn colour. Rhododendrons thrive best in humus-rich, acid soil in light shade. Dwarf species will tolerate full sun.

R. arboreum hybrid A frost hardy, evergreen tree with leaves of dark green, the undersides of which are covered with a light brown indumentum, and carrying trusses of tubular-shaped, sugar-pink flowers in early spring. 12 × 4m/40 × 12ft

R. barbatum A hardy, evergreen shrub or small tree with leaves of dark green and red-purple, peeling bark. Tubular-shaped, scarlet flowers are carried in early spring. 6 × 6m/20 × 20ft

R. 'Bric-a -Brac' A hardy, evergreen shrub with deep green leaves and funnel-shaped, white flowers, cream in bud, in late winter and early spring. 1.5 × 1.5m/ 5 × 5ft

R. 'Elizabeth' A hardy, evergreen shrub of compact habit with small leaves of dark green and carrying funnel-shaped, bright red flowers in spring. Tolerant of sun. 1 × 1m/3 × 3ft

R. 'Hino-Mayo' A hardy, evergreen shrub of compact habit with small leaves of dark green and carrying funnel-shaped, bright pink flowers from mid-spring to midsummer. Tolerant of sun. 1.5 × 1.5m/5 × 5ft

R. 'John Cairns' A hardy, evergreen shrub of compact habit with small leaves of dark green and carrying funnel-shaped, orange-red flowers in spring. Best in full sun. 1.5 × 1.5/5 × 5ft

R. 'Lem's Cameo' A hardy, evergreen shrub with leaves of dark green, bronze when young, and carrying funnel-shaped, peach flowers, spotted red at the throat, and fading to apricot-cream in spring. 2.2 × 2.2m/7 × 7ft

R.luteum A hardy, deciduous shrub with slightly hairy leaves of mid-green and carrying scented, funnel-shaped yellow flowers in late spring and early summer. Best in full sun. 4 × 4m/12 × 12ft

R. moupinense A hardy, evergreen shrub of compact habit with shiny leaves of dark green, paler on the undersides, and carrying funnel-shaped, white or pink flowers, often spotted purple inside, in late winter and early spring. 1.2 × 1.2m/4 × 4ft

R. mucronulatum 'Cornell Pink' A hardy, deciduous shrub with leaves of dark green and carrying funnel-shaped, pink flowers from midwinter to early spring. Best in full sun. 2.5 × 2.5m/8 × 8ft

R. 'Olive' A hardy, evergreen shrub with small leaves of mid-green, lighter on the undersides, and carrying trusses of funnel-shaped, mauve-pink flowers, spotted darker on the insides, in early spring. 1.2 × 1m/4 × 3ft

R. ponticum A hardy, evergreen shrub of vigorous habit with shiny leaves of dark green, paler on the undersides, and carrying purplish flowers, occasionally white, in late spring and early summer. 6 × 6m/20 × 20ft

R. 'Praecox' A hardy, evergreen shrub with small leaves of dark green and carrying funnel-shaped, rose-purple flowers in late winter and early spring. Best in full sun. 1.2 × 1.2m/4 × 4ft

R. racemosum A hardy, evergreen shrub with leaves of mid-green, glaucous on the undersides, and carrying trusses of funnel-shaped, pink, rose or white flowers in early and mid-spring. 2 × 2m/6 × 6ft

R. 'Seta' A hardy, evergreen shrub with small leaves of dark green and carrying tubular-shaped, pale pink flowers, striped darker on the outsides, in early spring. 1.2 × 1.2m/4 × 4ft

R. williamsianum white form A hardy, evergreen shrub with leaves of bright green, glaucous on the undersides and brown when young, and carrying bell-shaped, white flowers in spring. Best in full sun. 1.2 × 1.2m/4 × 4ft

R. 'Yellow Hammer' A hardy, evergreen shrub with small leaves of dark green and carrying tubular-shaped, canary-yellow flowers in spring and often repeated in autumn. Position in full sun. 2 × 2m/6 × 6ft

Rhododendron 'Lem's Cameo'

Rhododendron luteum

Rhododendron moupinense

Rhododendron mucronulatum 'Cornell Pink'

Rhododendron 'Olive'

Rhododendron ponticum

Rhododendron 'Praecox'

Rhododendron racemosum

Rhododendron williamsianum white form

Rhododendron 'Seta'

Rhododendron 'Yellow Hammer'

Rhodohypoxis baurii

Rhus × pulvinata Autumn Lace Group

Rhus typhina (autumn foliage)

RHODOHYPOXIS

A genus of hardy to frost hardy perennials of clump forming habit. Short stemmed flowers in pink, purple, red or white for prolonged periods in summer. Well suited to the rock garden. For well drained soil in full sun.

R. baurii A frost hardy perennial producing basal leaves of dull grey-green over which are carried pale to deep red-pink flowers in summer. 10 × 10cm/4 × 4in

RHUS (Sumach)

Genus of hardy to frost tender, deciduous or evergreen shrubs, trees and climbers grown largely for their attractive leaves which, in the case of many species and cultivars, colour shades of flame in autumn. Panicles of inconspicuous flowers are produced in spring and are followed by fruits in autumn.

R. × pulvinata Autumn Lace Group A hardy, deciduous shrub of suckering habit carrying rich green leaflets colouring orange, red and purple in autumn. Panicles of yellow-green flowers in summer are followed by red fruits. 3 × 5m/10 × 15ft

R. typhina (Stag's horn sumach) A hardy, deciduous shrub of suckering habit. Deep green leaflets colour orange-red in autumn. Summer flowers of yellow-green are followed on female plants with crimson fruits. 5 × 6m/15 × 20ft

Ribes laurifolium

Ribes sanguineum

Ribes speciosum

RIBES (Flowering currant)

A genus of hardy to frost hardy deciduous, sometimes evergreen, shrubs grown mainly for their small, cup-shaped flowers and berry-like fruits. Included in the genus are *R. nigrum* (blackcurrant), *R. rubrum* (redcurrant) and *R. uva-crispa* (gooseberry). In the main best in full sun.

R. laurifolium A hardy, deciduous shrub of spreading habit with leathery leaves of deep green and producing racemes of green-yellow flowers in late winter and early spring followed by red fruits ripening to black. Thrives in part shade. 1 × 1.5m/ 3 × 5ft

R. sanguineum A hardy, deciduous shrub of upright habit with aromatic leaves of deep green and procucing racemes of pinkish-red flowers in spring followed by blue-black fruits. 2 × 2m/6 × 6ft

R. sanguineum 'White Icicle' Similar to *R. sanguineum* but with racemes of white flowers in spring. 2 × 2m/6 × 6ft

R. speciosum (Fuchsia flowered currant) A hardy, deciduous shrub of arching habit with spiny shoots, red when new, and leaves of shiny, mid-green. Deep red flowers with protruding stamens, in the manner of a fuchsia, are produced in mid to late spring followed by red fruits. 2 × 2m/6 × 6ft

Ribes sanguineum 'White Icicle'

Ricinus communis

Robinia kelseyi

Robinia pseudoacacia 'Frisia'

RICINUS (Castor oil plant)

A genus of a single species of half hardy, evergreen shrub of suckering habit valued for its large, attractive leaves and spikes of small, cup-shaped flowers Well suited to a conservatory or glasshouse or grown as an annual in full sun.

R communis A half hardy shrub of upright habit with shiny leaves of mid-green, red-purple or bronze and producing greenish-yellow flowers in summer followed by rounded, red-brown capsules. As an annual to 1.8 × 1m/6 × 3ft

ROBINIA

A genus of deciduous shrubs and trees grown mainly for their attractive foliage and for their hanging racemes of pea-like flowers in late spring and early summer. Well suited as specimens. Best in full sun and tolerant of poor, dry conditions.

R. kelseyi An upright shrub of suckering habit with leaves and leaflets of dark green and freely producing racemes of rose-pink flowers in late spring and early summer. 2.5 × 3m/8 × 10ft

R. pseudoacacia 'Frisia' (False acacia) A rapidly growing, columnar tree of suckering habit with foliage of golden-yellow, greening towards summer and colouring orange-yellow in autumn. Racemes of scented white flowers in summer are followed by brown seedpods. 15 × 8m/50 × 25ft

Rodgersia aesculifolia

Rodgersia pinnata 'Superba'

Romneya coulteri

RODGERSIA

A genus of rhizomatous perennials of clump forming habit grown for their striking basal leaves, sometimes tinged bronze, and for pyramidal panicles of star-shaped, white or pink flowers followed by darkly coloured fruits. For moisture retentive soil in sun or part shade.

R. aesculifolia A rhizomatous perennial with crinkled leaves of mid-green, and producing panicles of white or pink flowers in midsummer. 2 × 1m/6 × 3ft

R. pinnata 'Superba' A rhizomatous perennial with shiny, crinkled leaves of deep green, bronze when young, and producing panicles of bright pink flowers in mid and late summer. 1.2m × 75cm/4 × 2.5ft

R. sambucifolia A rhizomatous perennial with leaves of deep green, not dissimilar to those of an elder, and producing panicles of white or pink flowers in early and mid summer. 1 × 1m/3 × 3ft

Rodgersia sambucifolia

ROMNEYA (Tree poppy)

A genus of frost hardy, sub-shrubby perennials valued for their glaucous foliage and for their poppy-like, scented white flowers. For a position in full sun out of the reach of cold, drying winds. Mulch heavily in winter.

R. coulteri A frost hardy, sub-shrubby perennial with attractive large leaves of grey-green and producing white, cup-shaped flowers with deep yellow stamens in summer. 1-2.5m/3-8ft × indefinite spread

Rosa 'Albertine'

Rosa 'Amber Queen'

Rosa 'American Pillar'

Rosa 'Ballerina'

Rosa banksiae 'Lutea'

Rosa 'Blanche Double De Coubert'

ROSA (Rose)

A genus of hardy to frost hardy, semi-evergreen or deciduous shrubs and climbers consisting most often of upright, arching or scrambling thorny stems with leaves divided into variably shaped, frequently toothed leaflets. Roses are generally cultivated for their usually perfumed flowers, in a wide range of colour, size and shape, and for their fruits or heps. From the crossing of species, huge numbers of cultivars have been raised. These may be loosely classified into old and modern. The first includes Alba, Bourbon, Centifolia, China, Damask, Gallica, Hybrid Perpetual, Moss, Noisette, Portland and Sempervirens. The second includes Climbers, Floribunda, Hybrid Tea, Miniature, Patio, Polyantha, Rambler, Rugosa and Shrub. Roses are tolerant of a wide range of soils and situations. Best in damp but free draining, humus-rich soil in the full sun.

R. 'Albertine' A hardy rambler rose of vigorous habit with leaves of mid-green and rounded to cupped, double, scented pale salmon-pink flowers in midsummer. 5 × 4m/15 × 12ft

R. 'Amber Queen' A hardy floribunda rose with bronze-tinted leaves and cupped, double, scented amber-yellow flowers from summer to autumn. 60 × 60cm/2 × 2ft

R. 'American Pillar' A hardy rambler rose of vigorous habit with leaves of shiny, mid-green and cupped, single, carmine flowers with white eyes in midsummer. 5 × 4m/15 × 12ft

R. 'Ballerina' A hardy, dwarf polyantha rose with leaves of mid-green and a profusion of cupped, pale pink flowers with white centres from summer to autumn. 1.2 × 1m/4 × 3ft

R. *banksiae* 'Lutea' A frost hardy climbing species rose with small leaves of light green and rosette-shaped, double, scented lemon-yellow flowers in late spring. 12 × 6m/40 × 20ft

R. 'Blanche Double de Coubert' A hardy rugosa rose with leathery leaves of mid-green and flat to cupped, double, scented white flowers, followed sometimes with heps, from summer to autumn. 1.5 × 1.2m/5 × 4ft

R. 'Blush Noisette' A hardy noisctte climbing rose with leaves of matt, mid-green and cupped, double, scented pink-white flowers from summer to autumn. 2.2× 1.2m/7 × 4ft

R. 'Buff Beauty' A hardy shrub rose with leaves of darkest green and cupped, double, scented warm apricot flowers in summer. 1.5 × 1.5m/5 × 5ft

Rosa 'Blush Noisette'

Rosa 'Buff Beauty'

Rosa 'Complicata'

Rosa 'Céleste'

Rosa 'Comte de Chambord'

R. 'Céleste' A hardy alba rose with leaves of deep green and urn-shaped, double, scented pale pink flowers in midsummer. 1.5 × 1.2/5 × 4ft

R. 'Complicata' A hardy Gallica rose with leaves of grey-green and slightly cupped, single pink flowers, paler towards the centre, in summer. 2.2 × 2.5m/7 × 8ft

R. 'Comte de Chambord' A hardy Portland rose with leaves of mid-green and rosette-type, double, scented lilac-pink flowers from summer to autumn. 1.2 × 1m/4 × 3ft

R. 'Cornelia' A hardy shrub rose with leaves of deep green and rosette-type, double, blush-pink flowers, copper towards the centre, from summer to autumn. 1.5 × 1.5m/5 × 5ft

R. 'Empress Josephine' A hardy Gallica rose with leaves of grey-green and rounded, semi-double rose-pink flowers, flushed with mauve, followed by heps, in summer. 1 × 1.2m/3 × 4ft

R. 'Fragrant Cloud' A hardy hybrid tea rose with leaves of deep green and rounded, double, scented scarlet flowers from summer to autumn. 1 × 1m/3 × 3ft

R. 'Fritz Nobis' A hardy shrub rose with shiny leaves of deep green and rounded, double flowers of light pink in summer followed by heps. 1.5 × 1.2m/5 × 4ft

R. *gallica* 'Versicolor' A hardy Gallica rose with leaves of deep green and slightly cupped, semi-double, scented, pale rosy-pink flowers, blotched and striped cerise-pink, in summer. 1.2 × 1.2m/4 × 4ft

Rosa 'Cornelia'

Rosa 'Empress Josephine'

Rosa gallica 'Versicolor'

Rosa 'Fragrant Cloud'

Rosa 'Fritz Nobis'

Rosa glauca

Rosa 'Golden Showers'

Rosa 'Gertrude Jekyll'

Rosa 'Graham Thomas'

Rosa 'Iceberg'

R. 'Gertrude Jekyll' A hardy shrub rose with leaves of grey-green and cupped, single, scented flowers of deep pink from summer to autumn. 1.2 × 1m/4 × 3ft

R. *glauca* A hardy species rose with stems of maroon-red, leaves of grey-green and flat, single cerise-pink flowers followed by heps in summer. 2 × 1.2m/6 × 4ft

R. 'Golden Showers' A hardy climber rose with leaves of deep green and cupped, double, scented bright yellow flowers from summer to autumn. 3 × 2m/10 × 6ft

R. 'Graham Thomas' A hardy shrub rose with leaves of light green and rosette to cupped, double, scented flowers of golden yellow from summer to autumn. 1.2 × 1.2m/4 × 4ft

R. 'Iceberg' A hardy floribunda rose with leaves of light green and rosette to cupped, double, white flowers from summer to autumn. 1.2 × 1.2m/4 × 4ft

R. 'Ingrid Bergman' A hardy hybrid tea rose with leaves of deep green and high centred, double flowers of dark red from summer to autumn. 1m × 60cm/3 × 2ft

R. 'Madame Alfred Carrière' A hardy noisette climbing rose with leaves of light green and rounded, double, scented pale pink to white flowers from summer to autumn. 5 × 3m/15 × 10ft

R. 'Madamme Isaac Pereire' A hardy Bourbon shrub or climbing rose with leaves of deep green and quartered-rosette, double, scented purple-pink flowers from summer to autumn. 2.2 × 2m/7 × 6ft

Rosa 'Ingrid Bergman'

Rosa 'Madame Alfred Carrière

Rosa 'Madame Isaac Pereire'

Rosa 'Marchesa Boccella'

Rosa 'Mermaid'

Rosa 'Mountbatten'

Rosa 'Nevada'

R. 'Marchesa Boccella' (syn. R. 'Jacques Cartier') A hardy Portland rose with leaves of pale green and quartered-rosette, double, scented rose-pink flowers from summer to autumn. 1.2 × 1m/4 × 3ft
R. 'Mermaid' A hardy climbing rose with leaves of glossy, dark green and cupped to flat, single primrose-yellow flowers from summer to autumn. 6 × 6m/20 × 20ft
R. 'Mountbatten' A hardy shrub rose with leaves of bright green and rounded, double, scented mid-yellow flowers from summer to autumn. 1.2m × 75cm/ 4 × 2.5ft
R. 'Nevada' A hardy shrub rose of arching habit with leaves of pale green and flat, semi-double, scented cream-white flowers in early summer and again, but fewer, in autumn. 2.2 × 2.2/7 × 7ft
R. 'New Dawn' A hardy climbing rose of vigorous habit with leaves of glossy, mid-green and cupped, double, scented blush-pink flowers from summer to autumn. Tolerant of part shade. 3 × 2.5m/10 × 8ft
R. 'Paul's Himalayan Musk' A hardy climbing rose of vigorous habit with leaves of deep green and rosette-shaped, double pale pink flowers in summer. 10 × 10m/ 30 × 30ft
R. 'Pink Bells' A hardy ground cover rose of spreading habit with leaves of mid-green and pompon, double, bright pink flowers in summer. 75cm × 1.5m/2.5 × 5ft
R. 'Rambling Rector' A hardy rambler rose with leaves of grey-green and cupped to flat, semi-double, scented cream-white flowers in summer followed by red heps in autumn. 6 × 6m/20 × 20ft

Rosa 'New Dawn'

Rosa 'Paul's Himalayan Musk'

Rosa 'Pink Bells'

Rosa 'Rambling Rector'

Rosa 'Scharlachglut'

Rosa 'Sweet Dream'

Rosa 'Tequila Sunrise'

Rosa 'The Queen Elizabeth'

Rosa 'Variegata di Bologna'

Rosa × *xanthina* 'Canary Bird'

Rosa 'Roseraie de l'Haÿ'

R. 'Roseraie de l'Haÿ' A hardy rugosa rose with wrinkled leaves of light green and cupped to flat, double, scented purple-red flowers from summer to autumn. 2.2 × 2m/7 × 6ft

R. 'Scharlachglut' A hardy shrub or climbing rose with leaves of deep green and cupped, single, scarlet flowers followed by bright red heps in autumn. 3 × 2m/ 10 × 6ft

R. 'Sweet Dream' A hardy patio rose with leaves of mid-green and clusters of cupped, double, slightly scented apricot-peach flowers from summer to autumn. 45 × 30cm/1.5 × 1ft

R. 'Tequila Sunrise' A hardy hybrid tea rose with shiny leaves of deep green and rounded, double, scarlet-edged, golden-yellow flowers from summer to autumn. 75 × 60cm/2.5 × 2ft

R. 'The Queen Elizabeth' A hardy floribunda rose of vigorous habit with leaves of dark green and rounded, double mid-pink flowers from summer to autumn. 2.2 × 1m/7 × 3ft

R. 'Tuscany Superb' A hardy Gallica rose with leaves of dark green and cupped to flat, double, scented, maroon to purple flowers in summer. 1 × 1m/3 × 3ft

R. 'Variegata di Bologna' A hardy Bourbon rose with leaves of pale green and quartered-rosette, double, scented pale pink flowers, stippled purple-crimson, from summer to autumn. 2.2 × 1.5m/7 × 5ft

R. × *xanthina* 'Canary Bird' A hardy species rose of arching habit with leaves of grey-green and cupped, single, scented mid-yellow flowers in spring and a few at other times. 3 × 4m/10 × 12ft

Rosa 'Tuscany Superb'

ROSCOEA

A genus of hardy to frost hardy tuberous perennials grown mainly for their striking, orchid-like flowers, hooded with prominent lips. For moist but well drained soil in part shade. In cold areas mulch heavily in winter.

R. purpurea A mainly hardy, tuberous perennial with dark green leaves over which are carried purple, occasionally white or bicoloured, flowers in early and midsummer. 30 × 15cm/1ft × 6in

ROSMARINUS (Rosemary)

A genus of frost hardy, evergreen shrubs grown for their aromatic foliage and flowers, the leaves frequently employed for culinary purposes. Well suited to the herb garden. Best in well drained, poorish soil in full sun.

R. officinalis A frost hardy shrub of upright or rounded habit with linear leaves of dark green, felted white on the undersides, and producing whorls of tubular purple-blue to white flowers from mid-spring to early summer and sometimes again in autumn.
1.5 × 1.5m/5 × 5ft

RUBUS (Bramble)

A genus of hardy to frost hardy, deciduous or evergreen shrubs, sometimes herbaceous perennials, grown for their saucer to cup-shaped flowers, their foliage and, in some instances, their winter shoots. The genus includes R. fruticosus (blackberry) and R. idaeus (raspberry). Best in well drained soil in sun or part shade.

R. 'Benenden' A hardy, deciduous shrub of arching habit with thornless stems, peeling bark and leaves of deep green. White, rose-like flowers are produced in late spring and early summer. 3 × 3m/10 × 10ft

R. phoenicolasius A hardy, deciduous shrub with leaves of mid-green, white felted on the undersides, and producing clusters of pale pink flowers in midsummer followed by edible orange-red fruits. 3 × 3m/10 × 10ft

R. thibetanus A hardy, deciduous shrub forming thickets of prickly shoots carrying a white bloom in winter. Saucer-shaped, red-purple flowers are produced in summer over deep green leaves, hairy white on the undersides, followed by black fruits with a white bloom. 2.5 × 2.5m/8 × 8ft

R. tricolor A hardy, evergreen shrub of prostrate habit with arching, bristly red stems and shiny, deep green leaves, hairy white on the undersides. Saucer-shaped, white flowers are produced in summer followed by edible red fruits. 60cm/2ft × indefinite spread

RUDBECKIA (Coneflower)

A genus of hardy to half hardy annuals, biennials and perennials grown mainly for their daisy-like flowerheads

Rosmarinus officinalis

Rubus thibetanus

produced over a prolonged period in summer and autumn. Some perennials are treated as annuals for summer bedding.

R. var. sullivantii 'Goldsturm' A hardy perennial forming basal clumps of somewhat coarse, dark green leaves over flowerheads from late summer to mid-autumn. 60 × 45cm/2 × 1.5ft

RUSCUS (Broom)

A genus of hardy to frost hardy, rhizomatous evergreen sub-shrubs noted for their unusual leaf-like shoots upon which are carried inconspicuous, starry flowers and bright red fruits. Suitable for dry shade.

R. aculeatus (Butcher's broom) A hardy, rhizomatous sub-shrub of clump forming habit with shiny, dark green leaf-like shoots upon which, on female plants, are to be found red fruits from late summer to winter. 75cm × 1m/2.5 × 3ft

RUTA (Rue)

A genus of hardy to frost hardy, deciduous or evergreen shrubs, sub-shrubs and woody herbaceous perennials grown for their attractive, aromatic foliage and flowers. Tolerant of hot, dry conditions.

R. graveolens 'Jackman's Blue' A hardy, evergreen shrub of compact habit with distinct grey-green leaves and dull yellow flowers in summer. 60 × 75cm/2 × 2.5ft

Rubus 'Benenden'

Rubus phoenicolasius

Rubus tricolor

Rudbeckia var. sullivantii 'Goldsturm'

Ruscus aculeatus

Ruta graveolens 'Jackman's Blue'

SAGITTARIA (Arrowhead)

A genus of hardy to frost tender, marginal and submerged aquatic annuals and perennials valued for their leaves and panicles or racemes of saucer-shaped, white flowers. For moisture retentive soil or shallow water in full sun.

S. sagittifolia A hardy, marginal aquatic perennial with arrow shaped leaves and carrying racemes of white flowers, each petal with a dark spot, in summer. 1m × indefinite spread

Salix alba subsp. *vitellina* 'Britzensis'

Salix caprea 'Kilmarnock'

Salix elaeagnos

Salix hastata 'Wehrhahnii'

Salix alba 'Tristis'

SALIX (Willow)

A genus of deciduous trees and shrubs grown mainly for their varied habit, their attractive foliage, striking catkins and, in some instances, their coloured winter stems. Species include those of large proportions to those appropriate for a rock garden or trough. Best in damp, well drained soil in full sun. Intolerant of shallow chalk.

S. alba subsp. *vitellina* 'Britzensis' A vigorous, spreading tree, most often pollarded to restrict growth and encourage bright, orange-yellow winter stems, with pointed leaves of dull green and producing yellow, male catkins in spring. 25 × 10m/ 80 × 30ft

S. alba 'Tristis' (Golden weeping willow) A vigorous, spreading tree of weeping habit with slender golden shoots and narrow, bright green leaves. Both yellow male and green female catkins are produced on the same plant in spring. 15 × 15m/50 × 50ft

S. caprea 'Kilmarnock' (Kilmarnock willow) A small tree of weeping habit with yellow shoots and leaves of deep green, grey-green on the undersides. Long, grey male catkins are produced in spring. 2 × 2m/6 × 6ft

S. elaeagnos (Hoary willow) A shrub of upright habit with new shoots of grey, maturing to near brown, and leaves of deep green, grey when young, colouring yellow in autumn. Male catkins with yellow anthers in spring. 3 × 5m/10 × 15ft

S. hastata 'Wehrhahnii' A slow growing shrub of upright habit with darkly coloured shoots and leaves of bright green. Silver-grey catkins are produced in early spring before the emergence of new leaves. 1.5 × 1.5m/5 × 5ft

Salpiglossis 'Casino Purple Bicolour'

SALPIGLOSSIS

A genus of half hardy annuals or short lived perennials grown mainly for their funnel-shaped, brightly coloured flowers in shades of bronze, purple, red, violet-blue or yellow and employed mostly as summer bedding. Position in full sun in damp but well drained soil.

S. 'Casino Purple Bicolour' A half hardy annual of compact habit with leaves of bright mid-green and carrying purple and gold, funnel-shaped flowers from summer to autumn. 60 × 30cm/2 × 1ft

Salvia lavandulifolia

Salvia (Sage)

A genus of hardy to frost tender annuals, biennials, perennials and shrubs, often with aromatic foliage, and valued, particularly in the case of annuals and perennials, many of which are grown as annuals, for their brilliantly coloured flowers making them well suited to summer bedding schemes. Most prefer light, humus-rich, well drained soil in sun or dappled shade.

S. confertiflora A half hardy, woody based perennial with yellowish leaves, woolly on the undersides, and carrying spikes of orange-red flowers from late summer to mid autumn. 1m × 60cm/3 × 2ft

S. lavandulifolia A hardy, woody based perennial with woolly leaves of grey and carrying racemes of lavender blue flowers in late spring and early summer. 45 × 60cm/1.5 × 2ft

S. leucantha A half hardy, evergreen sub-shrub with crinkled leaves of mid-green, the undersides with white down, and carrying racemes of white and purple flowers from winter to spring. 60 × 60cm/2 × 2ft

S. officinalis 'Purpurascens' (Purple sage) A hardy, evergreen, shrubby perennial with leaves of light purple, touched red, and carrying racemes of lilac-blue flowers in early and midsummer. 75cm × 1m/2.5 × 3ft

S. patens A frost hardy, tuberous perennial with hairy leaves of mid-green and carrying racemes of deep blue flowers from midsummer to mid-autumn. 45 × 45cm/1.5 × 1.5ft

Salvia confertiflora

Salvia patens

Salvia leucantha

Salvia officinalis 'Purpurascens'

217

Salvia sclarea var. turkestanica

Salvia splendens

S. sclarea var. *turkestanica* A hardy biennial or short lived perennial with crinkled leaves of mid to grey-green and carrying tall spikes of pink and white flecked flowers on pinkish stems in summer. 1m × 30cm/3 × 1ft

S. splendens (Scarlet sage) A half hardy perennial, most often cultivated as an annual, with leaves of pale to dark green and carrying spikes of tubular, brilliant red flowers from summer to autumn. Best in full sun. 45 × 30cm/1.5 × 1ft

S. × sylvestris 'May Night' A hardy perennial of clump forming habit with slightly hairy leaves of mid-green and carrying spires of indigo-blue flowers in early and midsummer. 75 × 45cm/2.5 × 1.5ft

S. uliginosa (Bog sage) A frost hardy, rhizomatous perennial forming clumps of toothed, mid-green leaves and carrying racemes of clear, light blue flowers from late summer to mid-autumn. 2 × 1m/6 × 3ft

S. verticillata 'Purple Rain' A hardy perennial with slightly hairy leaves of mid-green and carrying racemes of violet-purple flowers in whorls in summer. 1m × 45cm/ 3 × 1.5ft

S. viridis A hardy annual of upright habit with hairy leaves of mid-green and carrying spires of whorled pink to pale purple flowers surrounded with similar or white bracts in summer. 45 × 23 cm/1.5ft × 9in

Salvia × sylvestris 'May Night'

Salvia uliginosa

Salvia verticillata 'Purple Rain'

Salvia viridis

Sambucus nigra 'Guincho Purple'

...*densis* 'Plena'

Sambucus racemosa 'Plumos...'

...ARIA (Bloodroot)

...a single species of
...us perennial valued for its
...hite or pink, cup-shaped
...a spring. For humus-rich well
...soil in part shade.
...*ensis* A rhizomatous perennial
...aves of pale green to grey-green
...roducing white, sometimes pink,
...rs in spring. 'Plena' is a double
...l. 15 × 30cm/6in × 1ft

SAMBUCUS (Eld...
A genus of perennials and a...
attractive foliage, their white to ivory fl...
Hard prune where necessary to restrict growth.
S. nigra 'Guincho Purple' A shrub of upright habit with leav...
maturing to purple-black and colouring red in autumn. Purple stems a...
flowers tinged pink in early summer followed by shiny, black fruits. 6 × 6m/
20 × 20ft
S. racemosa 'Plumosa Aurea' A shrub of arching habit with finely cut leaves of
bronze maturing to golden yellow. Creamy flowers in summer are followed by
shiny red fruit. Position out of the reach of full sun to avoid leaf scorch. 3 × 3m/
10 × 10ft

...NGUISORBA (Burnet)
...genus of rhizomatous perennials
...rown mainly for their spikes of
...ottlebrush-like flowers, in green-white,
...pink, red or white, carried on wiry
...stems. Best in moist soil.
S. obtusa A rhizomatous perennial
forming clumps of basal leaves with
deep pink, bottlebrush-like flowers from
midsummer to early autumn. 60 ×
60cm/2 × 2ft

Santolina pinnata subsp. *neapolitana*

Saponaria ocymoides

Saponaria officinalis 'Rosea Plena'

SANTOLINA (Cotton lavender)
A genus of frost hardy, evergreen shrubs
grown largely for their aromatic foliage
and small, button-like flowers in yellow
or white. Suitable as a low form of
hedging. Best in poorish soil in full sun.
S. pinnata subsp. *neapolitana* A frost hardy,
rounded shrub of bushy habit with
aromatic leaves of grey-green and
producing bright yellow flowerheads in
mid-summer. 75cm × 1m/2.5 × 3ft

SAPONARIA (Soapwort)
A genus of annuals and perennials noted for their open flowers mostly in shades of
pink. Smaller species are well suited to the rock garden or for cultivation in
containers. Best in full sun in neutral to alkaline soil.
S. ocymoides (Tumbling Ted) A low growing perennial of spreading habit with lance-
shaped, hairy leaves of bright green and carrying a mass of violet-pink flowers in
summer. 8 × 45cm/3in × 1.5ft
S. officinalis 'Rosea Plena' (Bouncing Bet) A vigorous perennial of upright,
spreading habit with leaves of mid-green over which are carried double, rose-pink
flowers from summer to autumn. 60 × 45cm/2 × 1.5ft

Sarcococca hookeriana var. *digyna*

Saxifraga apiculata 'Alba'

Saxifraga 'Boston Spa'

SARCOCOCCA (Christmas or Sweet box)

A genus of hardy to frost hardy, evergreen shrubs cultivated for their foliage, often fragrant flowers and fruits. Excellent as a low, informal hedge.

S. hookeriana var. *digyna* A hardy shrub of suckering habit with tapering leaves of deep green and clusters of creamy-white flowers in winter followed by black fruits. 1.5 × 2m/5 × 6ft

Saxifraga burseriana

Saxifraga 'Tumbling Waters'

Saxifraga × *urbium*

SAXIFRAGA (Saxifrage)

A genus of hardy to frost hardy, evergreen, semi-evergreen or deciduous perennials, biennials and some annuals of varied form and habit, many of which are well suited to cultivation in the rock garden, alpine house or in troughs and containers. Growing conditions are dependent on the species and include those thriving in full sun and those requiring deep shade.

S. apiculata 'Alba' A hardy, evergreen perennial forming low cushions consisting of tight rosettes of dark green, lance-shaped leaves. Cup-shaped, white flowers are produced in early spring. Tolerant of full sun. 10 × 30cm/4in × 1ft

S. 'Boston Spa' A hardy, evergreen perennial forming hummocks of grey-green foliage and producing rich, primrose-yellow flowers in spring. 10 × 15cm/4 × 6in

S. burseriana A hardy, evergreen perennial forming tiny rosettes of blue-grey leaves and producing cup-shaped, white flowers carried on reddish stems in early spring. Tolerant of full sun. 5 × 15cm/2 × 6in

S. 'Gaiety' A hardy, evergreen perennial forming mats of mid-green leaves and producing rose-pink flowers in late spring. 15 × 45cm/6in × 1.5ft

S. 'Tumbling Waters' A hardy, evergreen perennial forming rosettes of narrow, silver-green leaves and producing cup-shaped, white flowers in spring. Best in full sun. Avoid excess of winter wet. 45 × 30cm/1.5 × 1ft

S. × *urbium* (London pride) A hardy, evergreen perennial of vigorous, spreading habit forming rosettes of mid-green leaves and carrying starry, pink with white flowers on slender stems in summer. Suitable for shade. 30cm/1ft × indefinite spread

Saxifraga 'Gaiety'

SCABIOSA (Scabious)
A genus of hardy to frost hardy annuals, biennials and perennials grown mainly for their solitary flowers in shades of blue, pink, white or yellow, each with a distinctive pincushion-like central floret. Attractive to bees and butterflies.
S. caucasica A hardy perennial of clump forming habit with lance-shaped, basal leaves of grey-green over which are carried pale to lavender-blue flowers in mid and late summer. 60 × 60cm/ 2 × 2ft

SCAEVOLA
Genus of frost tender, short lived, mostly evergreen perennials and climbers cultivated in the main as conservatory plants or employed in containers as summer bedding. Best in full sun or light shade.
S. aemula (Fairy fan flower) A frost tender, evergreen perennial carrying leafy racemes of violet-blue or blue flowers in summer over basal leaves. 45 × 45cm/1.5 × 1.5ft

SCHISANDRA
A genus of deciduous or evergreen climbers valued for their cup-shaped flowers in pink, red, white or yellow and for their coloured fruits, only obtained when both male and female plants are grown together.
S. chinensis A deciduous climber with shiny leaves of deep green and carrying clusters of cream to pale pink flowers in late spring and early summer followed, on female plants, with red or pink fruits. 10m/30ft

SCHIZANTHUS (Butterfly flower)
A genus of frost tender annuals and biennials mostly grown for their orchid-like flowers in a wide range of colours. Best suited to containers or for cultivation in a conservatory or glasshouse.
S. 'Hit Parade' A frost tender annual of upright habit producing orchid-like flowers in a range of colours each with contrasting markings. 30 × 30cm/1 × 1ft

SCHIZOPHRAGMA
A genus of hardy to frost hardy, deciduous, self-clinging climbers grown mainly for their striking flowerheads, not dissimilar to those of a 'lacecap' hydrangea.
S. integrifolium A frost hardy climber with leaves of deep green and bearing faintly scented, cream flowers surrounded with bracts of a similar colour in midsummer. 12m/40ft

SCHIZOSTYLIS (Kaffir lily)
A genus of a single species of near evergreen, rhizomatous perennials grown for their late flowering spikes of open, cup-shaped flowers, not unlike those of a gladiolus. Best in damp soil in full sun.

Scabiosa caucasica

Schizanthus 'Hit Parade'

Schizostylis coccinea 'Sunrise'

Scaevola aemula

Schizophragma integrifolium

Schizostylis coccinea alba

Sciadopitys verticillata

S. coccinea alba A perennial forming clumps of narrow, strap-like leaves over which are carried white flowers in autumn. 60 × 30cm/2 × 1ft
S. coccinea 'Sunrise' Similar to *S. coccinea alba* but with flowers of salmon pink. 60 × 30cm/2 × 1ft

SCIADOPITYS
A genus of a single species of evergreen, coniferous tree valued for its peeling bark and shiny leaves carried in whorls at the tips of shoots. An excellent specimen.
S. verticillata (Japanese umbrella pine) An evergreen tree of conical habit with reddish, peeling bark and leaves of deep green, olive on the undersides. Male and female cones. 10–20 × 6–8m/30–70 × 20–25ft

Scilla messeniaca

Scilla mischtschenkoana

Scilla siberica 'Spring Beauty'

SCILLA

A genus of hardy to half hardy, bulbous perennials grown mainly for their racemes or corymbs of mostly blue, but additionally pink, purple or white flowers. Suitable for naturalizing or, in the case of tiny species, the alpine house.

S. messeniaca A hardy, bulbous perennial with strap-like leaves of shiny green and carrying racemes of light blue flowers in spring. 25 × 15cm/10 × 6in

S. mischtschenkoana A hardy, bulbous perennial with basal, linear leaves and carrying racemes of starry, silver-blue flowers with deeper stripes in late winter or early spring. 10 × 5cm/4 × 2in

S. siberica 'Spring Beauty' A hardy, bulbous perennial with basal, linear leaves and carrying racemes of bowl-shaped, blue flowers in spring. 20 × 5cm/8 × 2in

SEDUM (Stonecrop)

Genus of hardy to frost tender annuals, evergreen, semi-evergreen and deciduous biennials, perennials, sub-shrubs and shrubs of variable form and habit suited, according to specics, to a wide range of garden situations. Best suited to well drained soil in full sun.

S. album subsp. *teretifolium* 'Murale' A hardy, deciduous perennial of spreading habit with leaves of grey-green and carrying starry white flowers on pinkish stems in summer. 8 × 45cm/3in × 1.5ft

S. 'Autumn Joy' A hardy, deciduous perennial with leaves of glaucous-green and carrying flat flowerheads of rosy-salmon, tinged bronze, from late summer to mid-autumn. 45 × 45cm/1.5 × 1.5ft

S. spathulifolium 'Cape Blanco' A hardy, evergreen perennial of mat forming habit comprising rosettes of silver-green leaves, powdered with white bloom, and carrying starry, bright greenish-yellow flowers in summer. 10 × 60cm/4in × 2ft

S. spurium 'Dragon's Blood' A hardy, evergreen perennial of spreading habit with bronze tinted green leaves and carrying starry flowers of deep pink in late summer. 10 × 60cm/4in × 2ft

S. telephium subsp. *maximum* ' Atropurpureum' A hardy, deciduous perennial forming clumps of deep purple, glaucous leaves and carrying flat inflorescences of pink flowers in late summer and early autumn. 45 × 30cm/1.5 × 1ft

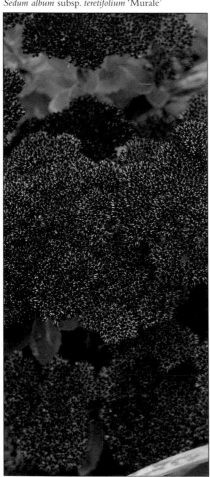

Sedum album subsp. *teretifolium* 'Murale'

Sedum 'Autumn Joy'

Sedum spathulifolium 'Cape Blanco'

Sedum spurium 'Dragon's Blood'

Sedum telephium subsp. *maximum* 'Atropurpureum'

SELINUM

A genus of perennials noted for their tall stems carrying finely cut leaves and umbrels of starry white flowers, occasionally flushed purple. Tolerant of many soils and situations.

S. wallichianum A perennial of clump forming habit with upright stems of reddish-purple and carrying tiny white flowers from midsummer to early autumn. 1.8m × 60cm/6 × 2ft

SEMPERVIVUM (Houseleek)

Genus of evergreen, succulent perennials forming rosettes of pointed leaves, sometimes covered with webs of white hairs, and producing stems of starry flowers in shades of purple, red, white or yellow. For poor soil in full sun. Protect hairy species from winter wet.

S.arachnoideum (Cobweb houseleek) An evergreen perennial forming rosettes of mid-green to red leaves covered in webs of white hairs. Reddish-pink flowers are produced on leafy stems in summer. 8 × 30cm/3 in × 1ft

S. 'Commander Hay' An evergreen perennial forming rosettes of shiny red-purple leaves, green at the tips, and producing greenish-red flowers in summer. 10 × 30cm/4in × 1ft

SEMIAQUILEGIA

A genus of often short-lived perennials, not dissimilar to *Aquilegia*, with divided leaves and spurless flowers in spring or summer. For neutral to acidic soil.

S. ecalcarata A short-lived perennial with leaves of mid-green, purplish on the undersides, and carrying pink to purple flowers in early summer. 30 × 20cm/1ft × 8in

Sempervivum 'Commander Hay'

Senecio cineraria

SENECIO

A genus of hardy to frost tender annuals, biennials, perennials, climbers, sub-shrubs, shrubs and small trees, often with white or silver leaves and mainly daisy-like flowers, mostly of yellow. Annuals are frequently employed as summer bedding.

S. cineraria A frost hardy, evergreen sub-shrub, generally cultivated as an annual, forming mounds of silver-grey leaves and carrying mustard-yellow flowers in the summer of the second year. Best in full sun grown as a foliage plant. 60 × 60cm/2 × 2ft

S. pulcher A frost hardy, deciduous or semi-evergreen perennial with leaves of mid-green and carrying purple-pink flowerheads in early to mid-autumn. 45 × 45cm/1.5 × 1.5ft

Sempervivum arachnoideum

Sequoia sempervirens

Sequoiadendron giganteum

Sidalcea 'Elsie Heugh'

Sidalcea 'Reverend Page Roberts'

SEQUOIA

A genus of a single species of evergreen, coniferous tree of rapid growth with whorled branches and foliage not dissimilar to that of yew.
S. sempervirens (Coastal redwood) A coniferous tree of conical habit with downward branches of red-brown bark and leaves of dark green, white on the undersides. Male and female cones. 30 × 9m/100 × 28ft

SEQUOIADENDRON (Wellingtonia)

A genus of a single species of evergreen, coniferous tree with narrow, wedge-shaped leaves and thick bark. Excellent as a tall specimen.
S. giganteum A coniferous tree of columnar habit with downward branches of red-brown bark and leaves of grey-green. Female cones. 25–30 × 7–10m/80–100 × 22–30ft

SIDALCEA (False mallow)

A genus of annuals and perennials forming clumps of mid-green basal leaves over which are produced stiff stems carrying hollyhock-like flowers in shades of pink, purple or white for prolonged periods. Best in light, neutral to acid soil in full sun.
_S_ 'Elsic Heugh' A perennial of upright habit carrying racemes of funnel-shaped, satiny, purple-pink flowers, the petals fringed, in summer. 1m × 45cm/3 × 1.5ft
_S._ 'Reverend Page Roberts' Similar to 'Elsie Heugh' but with pale rose-pink flowers. 1m × 45cm/3 × 1.5ft

Silene dioica 'Flore Pleno'

Silybum marianum

SILENE (Campion)

A genus of hardy to half hardy annuals, biennials and deciduous or evergreen perennials and, in the case of annuals, frequently employed as summer bedding. Most are tolerant of neutral to alkaline soil although _S. hookeri_ requires acidic conditions. Smaller species are well suited to the alpine house where they should be afforded sharp drainage.
S. alpestris A hardy, evergreen perennial with lance-shaped leaves of mid-green and carrying sprays of white or pinkish flowers in early summer. 15 × 20cm/6 × 8in
S. dioica 'Flore Pleno' A hardy, semi-evergreen perennial with lance-shaped leaves of grey-green and carrying double cerise flowers in summer. 15 × 20cm/6 × 8in

SILYBUM

A genus of annuals or biennials forming rosettes of thistle-like leaves, deeply cut and spiny, and producing purplish flowerheads surrounded by spiny bracts. For poorish soil in full sun.
S. marianum (Blessed Mary's thistle) A biennial producing lightly scented, purple-pink flowerheads from summer to autumn. 1.5 × 1m/5 × 3ft

Sinacalia tangutica

Sisyrinchium 'Blue Ice'

Sisyrinchium idahoense 'Album'

Sisyrinchium striatum

SINACALIA (Chinese groundsel)

A genus of a single garden species of deciduous perennial grown mainly for its deep green, divided leaves and panicles of bright yellow flowers.
S. tangutica A perennial of somewhat invasive habit with deeply cut leaves of dark green and producing yellow flowerheads from late summer to mid-autumn. Best in sun. 1.2 × 1.2m/4 × 4ft

SISYRINCHIUM

A genus of hardy to half hardy annuals and rhizomatous perennials, some evergreen, grown mainly for their clumps of linear leaves and star, cup or trumpet-shaped flowers in spring or summer. Best in full sun.
S. idahoense 'Album' A hardy, semi-evergreen perennial forming clumps of narrow, mid-green leaves with starry white flowers, with yellow throats, in summer. 12 × 15cm/5 × 6in
S. striatum A hardy, evergreen perennial forming clumps of stiff, grey-green leaves with open, cup-shaped, pale creamy-yellow flowers in summer. 1m × 25cm/ 3ft × 10in

Skimma × confusa 'Kew Green'

SKIMMIA

A genus of evergreen shrubs and trees, some of which are hermaphrodite, cultivated for their leaves, frequently scented flowers and red or black fruits produced on female and hermaphrodite plants.
S. × confusa 'Kew Green' An evergreen shrub of compact habit with aromatic leaves of mid-green and carrying panicles of creamy male flowers over a prolonged period in late winter and early spring. 1.2 × 1.2m/4 × 4ft
S. japonica 'Rubella' An evergreen shrub with faintly aromatic leaves of deep green, red-margined, and scented white male flowers, dark red in bud, in spring. 1.5 × 2m/5 × 6ft

Skimma japonica 'Rubella'

Smilacina racemosa

SMILACINA (False Solomon's seal)
A genus of principally rhizomatous perennials, not dissimilar to *Polygonatum* with most often arching stems and carrying racemes or panicles of starry, cream flowers followed by green fruits ripening to red. Best in part shade.
S. racemosa A rhizomatous perennial of clump forming habit with pointed, veined leaves of mid-green, colouring yellow in autumn, and carrying panicles of cream flowers in spring.
1m × 60cm/3 × 2ft

SMYRNIUM
Genus of biennials or monocarpic perennials grown principally for their umbels of unusual small, green-yellow flowers. Well suited for naturalizing in semi-woodland. For sun or part shade.
S. perfoliatum (Perfoliate Alexanders) A biennial of upright habit with bract-like leaves of yellowish green-yellow flow
1m × 60cm/3 × 2

Smyrnium perfoliatum

Solanum crispum 'Glasnevin'

Solanum jasminoides 'Album'

Solenostemon aromatica hybrid

SOLANUM
A genus of frost hardy to frost tender annuals, biennials, perennials and evergreen, semi-evergreen and deciduous shrubs, trees and climbers. Included within the genus is *S. tuberosum* (potato) and *S. melongena* (aubergine). Solanums are valued for their bell, trumpet or star-shaped flowers, in shades of blue, purple or white, and for their fruits. For the conservatory or glasshouse or, outdoors, in a sheltered position in full sun.
S. crispum 'Glasnevin' A frost hardy, evergreen or semi-evergreen climber with leaves of deep green and carrying scented, deep purple-blue flowers in summer followed by yellow-white fruits. 6m/20ft
S. jasminoides 'Album' (Potato vine) A half hardy, evergreen or semi-evergreen climber with shiny leaves of deep green and carrying scented white flowers in summer and autumn followed by black fruits. 6m/20ft
S. rantonnetii (Blue potato bush) A frost tender, evergreen shrub with leaves of mid to deep green and carrying trumpet-shaped flowers in various shades of blue in summer and autumn followed by red fruits. 1–2 × 1–2m/ 3–6 × 3–6ft

SOLDANELLA (Snowbell)
A genus of evergreen perennials with basal leaves, rounded or kidney-shaped, and carrying umbels of purple to white flowers in springtime. Well suited to the rock garden or alpine house.
S. alpina (Alpine snowbell) A perennial of clump forming habit with kidney-shaped leaves of deep green over which are borne funnel-shaped, violet flowers in early spring. 12 × 12cm/5 × 5in

SOLENOSTEMON (Coleus)
A genus of frost tender, evergreen perennials grown largely for their striking foliage and tubular blue, purple or white flowers. Well suited to cultivation under glass or as a houseplant.
S. aromatica hybrid A frost tender, evergreen perennial with toothed, hairy leaves of reddish-purple fringed bright green and carrying white flowers throughout the year.
60 × 60cm/2 × 2ft

Solanum rantonnetii

Solidago canadensis

Sophora microphylla

Sorbaria tomentosa var. *angustifolia*

SOLIDAGO (Golden rod)

A genus of vigorous perennials grown mainly for their stiff stems of veined, mid-green leaves and their racemes or spikes of golden-yellow flowers in late summer and autumn. Named hybrids are less rapid in growth.

S. canadensis A perennial of upright habit with leaves of mid-green and producing panicles of bright, golden-yellow flowerheads in late summer and early autumn. 1m × 45cm/3 × 1.5ft

SOPHORA

A genus of hardy to frost tender perennials and deciduous and evergreen trees and shrubs valued for their elegant foliage and pea-like flowers. Best in a sheltered position in full sun. Frost tender species may be grown in a warm glasshouse.

S. microphylla A hardy, evergreen shrub or small tree of spreading habit with leaflets of deep green carried on silky shoots and bearing racemes of deep yellow flowers, the petals pointing forwards, in spring. 8 × 8m/25 × 25ft

SORBARIA

Genus of deciduous shrubs of suckering habit grown for their attractive foliage and panicles of starry white flowers. For damp but well drained, neutral to alkaline soil in sun or part shade.

S. tomentosa var. *angustifolia* A shrub of spreading habit with slender, tapering leaflets of dark green and panicles of cream-white flowers in mid and late summer. 3 × 3m/10 × 10ft

SORBUS (Mountain ash, Rowan)

A genus of hardy to frost hardy, deciduous shrubs and trees highly valued for their ornamental foliage, often colouring in autumn, their corymbs of white, sometimes pink, flowers and for their colourful fruits. Sorbus are excellent as specimens and are tolerant of a wide range of soils and situations. *S. aria* thrives on both chalk and acidic soil.

S. aria 'Lutescens' (Whitebeam) A hardy tree of columnar habit with young leaves of silver-grey, maturing grey-green, and corymbs of white flowers in spring followed by brown-speckled, red berries. 10 × 8m/30 × 25ft

S. cashmiriana 'Rosiness' A hardy shrub or small tree of spreading habit with lance-shaped, deep green leaflets and corymbs of pink flowers in late spring followed by pink-tinted, white berries. 8 × 7m/25 × 22ft

S. commixta A hardy shrub or small tree of upright habit with tapering, lance-shaped leaflets of deep green, colouring flame in autumn, and corymbs of white flowers in late spring followed by orange-red berries. 10 × 7m/30 × 22ft

Sorbus aria 'Lutescens'

Sorbus aria 'Lutescens' (flowers)

Sorbus cashmiriana 'Rosiness'

Sorbus commixta

Sorbus fruticosa 'Koehneana'

Sorbus hupehensis

Sorbus sargentiana

S. fruticosa 'Koehneana' A hardy shrub or small tree of spreading habit with toothed leaflets of deep green and small corymbs of white flowers in late spring followed by mid-green berries, ripening to white, held on red stalks. 5 × 6m/15 × 20ft

S. hupehensis A hardy tree of columnar habit with leaflets of blue-green, colouring red in autumn, and corymbs of white flowers in late spring followed by pink-tinged, white berries. 8 × 8m/25 × 25ft

S. sargentiana A hardy, slow growing tree of upright habit with sticky red, winter buds, lance-shaped leaflets of deep green, colouring orange and red in autumn, and corymbs of white flowers in early summer followed by red berries. 10 × 10m/30 × 30ft

S. vilmorinii A hardy shrub or small tree of arching habit with leaflets of shiny, dark green and corymbs of white flowers in late spring and early summer followed by deep red berries ageing to pink then white. 5 × 5m/15 × 15ft

Sorbus vilmorinii

Spartina pectinata 'Aureomarginata'

SPARAXIS (Harlequin flower)
A genus of half hardy, cormous perennials cultivated for their spikes of funnel-shaped, colourful flowers in spring and summer. Well suited to a cool glasshouse or outdoors in well drained soil in a sunny, sheltered position.
S. tricolor A half hardy, cormous perennial forming basal fans of lance-shaped leaves and carrying orange, purple or red flowers, each with a darker central marking, in spring and early summer. 30 × 8cm/1ft × 3in

SPARTINA (Prairie cord grass)
A genus of a single species of perennial grass grown principally for its ribbon-like foliage and attractive flower spikes. For moist soil. Roots can be invasive.
S. pectinata 'Aureomarginata' A perennial grass with arching leaves of mid-green striped yellow and producing green flower spikes hung with purple stamens in summer. 1.8m/6ft × indefinite spread

Spartium junceum

Spiraea 'Arguta'

Spiraea japonica 'Goldflame'

SPARTIUM (Spanish broom)

A genus of a single species of frost hardy, evergreen shrub grown mainly for its racemes of pea-like flowers and dark green, broom-type stems. Tolerant of chalk. Best in full sun.

S. junceum A frost hardy shrub of upright habit with narrow, lance-shaped leaves, hairy on the undersides, and racemes of pea-like, brilliant yellow flowers in summer and early autumn followed by striking, flattened seedpods. 3 × 3m/10 × 10ft

SPIRAEA

Genus of deciduous or semi-evergreen shrubs grown principally for their profusion of saucer, cup or bowl-shaped flowers in shades of pink, purple, white or yellow in spring and summer. Smaller species are well suited to the rock garden. Best in full sun.

S. 'Arguta' (Bridal wreath) A deciduous shrub of rounded habit with arching stems and carrying narrow, toothed leaves of bright green. Saucer-shaped, white flowers are produced in a mass in spring. 2.5 × 2.5m/8 × 8ft

S. japonica 'Goldflame' A deciduous shrub of clump forming habit with young leaves of bronze-red, maturing to yellow then green, and producing bowl-shaped, pink flowers mid and late summer. 1 × 1m/3 × 3ft

S. nipponica 'Snowmound' A deciduous shrub of rounded habit with leaves of deep green, blue-green on the undersides, and producing bowl-shaped white flowers in midsummer. 1.2 × 1.2m/4 × 4ft

Spiraea nipponica 'Snowmound'

Stachys byzantina

Stachys macrantha

STACHYS (Betony)

A genus of hardy to frost hardy annuals, perennials and some evergreen shrubs grown for their attractive foliage and tubular, often hooded, flowers mainly in shades of pink, purple, red, white or yellow.

S. byzantina (Lamb's ears) A hardy perennial of dense, carpeting habit with lance-shaped leaves of white-woolly grey-green over which rise upright stems of woolly spikes of purple-pink flowers from early summer to early autumn. 45 × 60cm/1.5 × 2ft

S. byzantina 'Silver Carpet' Similar to the type but a non-flowering form and with leaves of intense silver-white. 30 × 60cm/1 × 2ft

S. macrantha A hardy perennial of upright habit forming rosettes of wrinkled, veined leaves of deep green and carrying spikes of hooded pink-purple flowers on tall stems in summer. 60 × 30cm/2 × 1ft

Stachyurus praecox

STACHYURUS

A genus of deciduous or semi-evergreen shrubs, sometimes small trees, grown mainly for their hanging racemes of small flowers appearing before the new leaves. Lance-shaped leaves are carried on shiny red-brown shoots.

S. praecox A deciduous shrub of spreading habit and carrying racemes of bell-shaped, light yellow flowers in late winter and early spring. 1–4 × 3m/ 3–12 × 10ft

STERNBERGIA (Autumn daffodil)

A genus of frost hardy, bulbous perennials grown for their crocus-like, usually goblet-shaped, mostly brilliant yellow flowers over narrow, basal leaves. For full sun in well drained soil.

S. lutea A frost hardy, bulbous perennial with leaves of dark green and goblet-shaped, deep yellow flowers in autumn. 15 × 8cm/6 × 3in

STEWARTIA

A genus of hardy to frost hardy, deciduous or evergreen shrubs and trees valued for their peeling bark, their foliage, colouring well in autumn, and their cup-shaped, white flowers with pronounced stamens. For neutral to acidic soil in sun or partial shade.

S. sinensis A hardy, deciduous tree of conical habit with peeling bark of red-brown, deep green leaves colouring red in autumn and scented, white flowers in midsummer. 20 × 7m/70 × 22ft

STIPA (Feather grass)

A genus of hardy to frost hardy, evergreen or deciduous perennial, very occasionally annual, grasses cultivated mainly for their attractive habit and feathery inflorescences. Best in full sun.

S. gigantea (Golden oats) A hardy, evergreen or semi-evergreen perennial of clump forming habit with leaves of mid-green and producing green-purple spikelets, ripening to gold, in summer. 2.5 × 1.2m/8 × 4ft

S. tenuissima A hardy, deciduous perennial of clump forming habit with leaves of bright green and producing buff coloured panicles in summer. 60 × 30cm/2 × 1ft

STOKESIA (Stokes' aster)

A genus of a single species of evergreen perennial of upright habit grown for its cornflower-like flowerheads in shades of violet-blue, pink or white. Best in acidic soil in full sun.

S. laevis A hardy, evergreen perennial forming basal rosettes of mid-green leaves and carrying violet-blue, pink or white flowerheads from midsummer to early autumn. 60 × 45cm/2 × 1.5ft

STRELITZIA (Bird of paradise)

A genus of frost tender, evergreen perennials valued for their exotic-looking inflorescences consisting of boat-shaped spathes topped with crest-like flowers.

S. reginae (Crane flower) A frost tender perennial forming clumps of tall stemmed leaves and carrying green spathes, tinged orange and purple, with orange flowers from winter to spring. 2 × 1m/6 × 3ft

STROBILANTHES

A genus of hardy and frost tender, evergreen or deciduous perennials cultivated for their frequently hooded flowers in shades of blue, purple, white or, seldom, yellow.

S. atropurpureus A hardy perennial of upright habit with leaves of dark green and carrying spikes of tubular indigo or violet flowers in summer. 1.2 × 1m/ 4 × 3ft

Stewartia sinensis

Stipa gigantea

Stipa tenuissima

Strobilanthes atropurpureus

Strelitzia reginae

STYRAX

A genus of hardy to frost hardy, deciduous or evergreen shrubs valued for their attractive habit and clusters of bell or cup-shaped, scented white flowers. Best in neutral to acidic soil in a position out of the reach of cold winds.

S. americanus (American snowbell) A hardy, deciduous shrub with leaves of deep green and producing bell-shaped, white flowers in early and midsummer. 3 × 2.5m/10 × 8ft

SYMPHORICARPOS (Snowberry)

Genus of deciduous shrubs cultivated for their tiny bell-shaped white to pink flowers but mostly for their fleshy fruits in blue, pink, purple or white. Tolerant of most soils and situations.

S. albus var. *laevigatus* A shrub forming thickets of arching stems with leaves of deep green and carrying racemes of pink flowers in summer. Rounded, pure white fruits follow the flowers, lasting well into winter. 2 × 2m/6 × 6ft

SYMPHYANDRA

A genus of monocarpic or short lived, rhizomatous perennials grown for their tubular or bell-shaped flowers. Best in full sun or light shade.

S. hofmanii A generally monocarpic perennial forming rosettes of basal leaves and carrying racemes of hanging, tubular creamy-white flowers in summer. 45 × 30cm/1.5 × 1ft

SYMPHYTUM (Comfrey)

A genus of rhizomatous perennials noted for their hanging, tubular flowers in shades of blue, pink, purple, yellow-white or white frequently employed as ground cover in shady and woodland areas. Leaves may be steeped in water to produce liquid manure. Some species may become invasive.

S. caucasicum A perennial of clump forming habit with hairy leaves of mid-green and carrying vivid blue flowers in summer 60 × 60cm/2 × 2ft

S. 'Hidcote Blue' A perennial of clump forming habit with hairy leaves of mid-green and carrying pale blue flowers, red in bud, in mid and late spring. 45 × 45cm/1.5 × 1.5ft

SYRINGA (Lilac)

A genus of deciduous shrubs and trees noted mainly for their pyramid-shaped panicles of small, scented tubular flowers in varying shades of blue, pink, purple and white. For neutral to alkaline soil in full sun. Well suited as specimens.

S. × *josiflexa* 'Bellicent' A shrub of upright habit with leaves of deep green and carrying scented, clear pink flowers in late spring and early summer. 4 × 5m/12 × 15ft

S. meyeri var. *spontanea* 'Palibin' A slow growing shrub of rounded habit with leaves of mid-green and carrying

scented lavender-pink flowers in late spring and early summer. 1.5 × 1.5m/5 × 5ft

S. vulgaris (Common lilac) A shrub or small tree of spreading habit carrying highly scented, single or double lilac flowers in late spring and early summer. 7 × 7m/22 × 22ft

Symphytum caucasicum

Symphytum 'Hidcote Blue'

Syringa × *josiflexa* 'Bellicent'

Syringa meyeri var. *spontanea* 'Palibin'

Syringa vulgaris

231

Tagetes erecta

Tagetes patula

Tanacetum densum subsp. *amani*

Tanacetum parthenium

TAGETES (Marigold)

A genus of half hardy annuals and perennials of which there are numerous hybrids and cultivars valued for their daisy-like or carnation-type flowerheads and employed mainly in summer bedding schemes and in pots and containers. Easily raised from seed which may be sown in situation. Best in full sun.

T. erecta (African marigold) A half hardy annual of compact habit producing double, ball-shaped flowerheads in a range of colours from pale lemon to deepest orange from late spring to autumn. 75 × 45cm/2.5 × 1.5ft

T. patula (French marigold) A half hardy annual of bushy habit producing mainly double flowerheads in a wide range of colours to include orange, red-brown, yellow or mixed from late spring to autumn. 30 × 30cm/1 × 1ft

Tamarix tetrandra

TAMARIX (Tamarisk)

A genus of deciduous shrubs and small trees grown mainly for their small, needle-like leaves, feathery in appearance, and plume-like racemes of tiny flowers in shades of pink. Well suited to coastal areas on account of resistance to wind. Best in full sun.

T. ramosissima A shrub or small tree of arching habit with pointed leaves carried on red-brown shoots and producing racemes of pink flowers in late summer and early autumn. 5 × 5m/15 × 15ft

T. tetrandra A shrub or small tree of arching habit with needle-like leaves carried on purple-brown shoots and racemes of light pink flowers in spring. 3 × 3m/10 × 10ft

TANACETUM

A genus of half hardy annuals, evergreen and deciduous perennials and sub-shrubs grown for their mostly aromatic foliage, sometimes silver, and button-type or daily-like flowerheads. Smaller species are well suited to the rock garden.

T. densum subsp. *amani* A hardy, largely evergreen perennial with finely cut leaves of grey-white and carring daisy-like yellow flowerheads in summer. Suitable for the rock garden. 25 × 20cm/10 × 8in

T. parthenium (Feverfew) A hardy, short-lived perennial of bushy habit with basal, aromatic leaves and carrying daisy-like yellow and white flowerheads in summer. 30 × 30cm/1 × 1ft

Taxus baccata

Taxodium distichum

Taxus baccata 'Aurea'

Taxus baccata 'Fastigiata'

TAXODIUM (Swamp cypress)

A genus of deciduous or semi-evergreen coniferous trees of conical habit valued largely for the brilliance of their autumn colour. Well suited as specimens. For moisture retentive, acidic soil in full or part shade.

T. distichum A deciduous, coniferous tree with lance-shaped leaves of pale green colouring rust in autumn, and green female cones, ripening to brown, and hanging red male cones. 20–40 × 6–9m/70–130 × 20–28ft

TAXUS (Yew)

A genus of evergreen, coniferous shrubs or trees valued for their red-brown bark, their mostly deep green leaves and, on female plants, their coloured fruits. Highly valued as specimens, for hedging or employed as topiary. Tolerant of a wide range of soils and situations.

T. baccata A tree of conical habit with spreading branches of deep green leaves widely employed as hedging. Yellow male cones in spring. 10–20 × 8–10m/30–70 × 25–30ft

T. baccata 'Aurea' A large shrub or small tree of conical habit with leaves of soft gold, reverting to greener tones when grown in shade. 6 × 5m/20 × 16ft

T. baccata 'Fastigiata' (Irish yew) A tree of columnar habit with leaves of deep green and producing single seeded, egg-shaped fruits. 10 × 6m/30 × 20ft

Telekia speciosa

Tellima grandiflora

Teucrium fruticans

TELEKIA

A genus of perennials of upright habit with coarsely toothed, basal leaves and daisy-like flowerheads. Best in damp soil in part shade. Afford protection from strong winds.

T. speciosa A rhizomatous perennial with aromatic leaves and carrying yellow, daisy-like flowerheads on tall stems in late summer and early autumn. 2 × 1m/6 × 3ft

TELLIMA (Fringe cups)

A genus of a single species of perennial grown mainly for its attractive foliage and racemes of tiny, bell-shaped flowers. Tolerant of dry soil and suited to a partially shaded situation.

T. grandiflora A perennial forming rosettes of scalloped leaves of light green and carrying racemes of green-white flowers from late spring to midsummer. 75 × 30cm/2.5 × 1ft

TEUCRIUM

A genus of hardy to frost hardy perennials and deciduous and evergreen shrubs and sub-shrubs grown largely for their aromatic foliage and tubular or bell-shaped flowers. Smaller species are well suited to the rock garden or for cultivation in troughs. Best in full sun.

T. fruticans (Shrubby germander) A frost hardy, evergreen shrub with lance-shaped, grey-green leaves and carrying whorls of light blue flowers in summer. 60cm × 4m/2 × 12ft

233

THALIA

A genus of half hardy to frost tender deciduous or evergreen, marginal aquatic perennials noted for their striking, tall stemmed, lance-shaped leaves and unusual violet flowers. For moisture-retentive soil or shallow water in a sunny, open situation.

T. dealbata A half hardy, evergreen, marginal aquatic perennial with leaves of grey-green and carrying panicles of violet flowers in summer. 2 × 2m/6 × 6ft

Thermopsis montana

THERMOPSIS

A genus of rhizomatous perennials grown mainly for their attractive foliage and racemes of lupin-like flowers in shades of purple or yellow. Tolerant of a wide range of soils and situations.

T. montana A rhizomatous perennial with leaves of mid-green and producing lupin-like butter-yellow flowers in late spring and early summer.
75 × 75cm/2.5 ×2.5ft

Thunbergia alata

THUNBERGIA

A genus of half hardy to frost tender annuals, evergreen perennials, some shrubs and climbers valued for their bright flowers in shades of blue, orange, red, white or yellow. Suitable for a warm conservatory or glasshouse or, treated as annuals outdoors, in full sun.

T. alata (Black-eyed Susan) A frost tender, evergreen perennial climber, most often treated as an annual, with leaves of mid-green and producing flowers of orange, yellow or sometimes white, with or without deep purple centres, from summer to autumn.
1.5–2m/5–8ft

Thalictrum aquilegiifolium

Thalictrum flavum subsp. *glaucum*

THALICTRUM (Meadow rue)

A genus of hardy to frost tender, rhizomatous or tuberous perennials grown mainly for their attractive, often ferny, foliage and tiny, petalless flowers in shades of lilac, pink, violet, white or yellow. For humus-rich soil in part shade.

T. aquilegiifolium A hardy, rhizomatous perennial with aquilegia-like leaves of mid-green and panicles of fluffy, pink, purple or white flowers in early summer.
1m × 45cm/3 × 1.5ft

T. flavum subsp. *glaucum* A hardy, rhizomatous perennial with veined, glaucous leaves and panicles of pale, sulphur-yellow flowers in summer. 1m × 60cm/3 × 2ft

Thuja occidentalis 'Rheingold'

Thuja orientalis 'Aurea Nana'

THUJA

A genus of evergreen, coniferous trees of conical or columnar habit largely cultivated as specimen trees, as hedging or, in the case of smaller cultivars, for the rock garden. Best in full sun.

T. occidentalis 'Rheingold' A small tree of conical habit with orange-brown bark and loosely held branches of golden-yellow leaves, tinged pink when young.
3 × 1.5m/10 × 5ft

T. orientalis 'Aurea Nana' A small tree of dwarf habit with leaves of yellow-green colouring bronze in winter. Well suited to the rock garden. 60 × 60cm/2 × 2ft

Thymus serpyllum 'Snowdrift'

Thymus vulgaris

THYMUS (Thyme)

Genus of hardy to frost hardy, evergreen perennials, shrubs and sub-shrubs many of which are of carpeting habit, are aromatic and some of which have a culinary use. Tubular-shaped, tiny flowers are usually in shades of pink, purple or white. Attractive to bees. Best in full sun.

T. serpyllum 'Snowdrift' A hardy subshrub of mat-forming habit with trailing stems of mid-green leaves and white flowers in summer. 25 × 45cm/10in × 1.5ft

T. vulgaris (Garden thyme) A hardy sub-shrub of spreading habit forming cushions of aromatic, grey-green leaves and purple to white flowers in summer.
25 × 45cm/10in × 1.5ft

TIARELLA (Foam flower)

A genus of rhizomatous perennials grown for their attractive leaves, often colouring in autumn, and panicles or racemes of starry white or pink-white flowers. Best in full or part shade.
T.cordifolia A rhizomatous perennial of vigorous habit with leaves of light green, bronze in autumn, and spiky racemes of cream-white flowers in summer. 30 × 30 cm/1 × 1ft

Tiarella cordifolia

TILIA (Lime)

Genus of deciduous trees grown for their attractive form, foliage and flowers. Tilia is well suited to growing as a specimen, in avenues or, with some species, pleached. Tolerant of acid soil.
T. × ecuchlora A tree of rounded habit with heart-shaped, shiny leaves of dark green, paler on the undersides, and yellow white flowers in summer. 20 × 15m/70 × 50ft

Tilia × euchlora

TIGRIDIA (Tiger flower)

A genus of frost tender, bulbous perennials with narrow lance-shaped leaves and grown largely for their unusual iris-like or bell-shaped flowers. Well suited to a cool conservatory.
T. meleagris A frost tender, bulbous perennial with basal leaves forming a fan and carrying spotted, bell-shaped flowers of pale pink to maroon in summer. 30 × 10cm/1ft × 4in

TOLMIEA (Pick-a-back plant)

A genus of a single species of spreading perennial noted for the way in which young plants are produced on the leaves and valued either as ground cover in shade or as a form of houseplant.
T. menziesii A perennial of clump forming habit with toothed, kidney-shaped leaves of lime-green and producing greenish-purple flowers in late spring and early summer. 30cm × 1m/1 × 3ft

Trachelospermum asiaticum

TRACHELOSPERMUM

A genus of frost hardy, evergreen climbers cultivated for their attractive foliage and small, scented flowers. Best against a wall in a sheltered position out of the reach of cold winds.
T. asiaticum A frost hardy, evergreen climber with shiny leaves of deep green and carrying scented creamy-white flowers in mid and late summer. 6m/20ft

TRACHYCARPUS

A genus of frost hardy, evergreen palms grown mainly for their fan-shaped leaves, bowl-type flowers and fruits.
T. fortunei (Chusan palm) A frost hardy, evergreen palm forming fans of deep green leaves and carrying panicles of small yellow flowers in early summer followed, in the case of female plants, with blue-black fruits. 20 × 2.5m/70 × 8ft

Trachycarpus fortunei

Tradescantia × andersoniana 'Osprey'

Tradescantia × andersoniana 'Purple Dome'

Tricyrtis formosana 'Stolonifera'

TRADESCANTIA

A genus of hardy to frost tender, evergreen perennials with often fleshy leaves and short-lived, saucer-shaped flowers. Less hardy species may be grown as houseplants, in a conservatory or in hanging baskets and containers.
T. × andersoniana 'Osprey' A hardy perennial of clump forming habit with leaves of mid-green, often tinged purple, and carrying large white flowers with triangular petals from early summer to early autumn. 45 × 45cm/1.5 × 1.5ft
T. × andersoniana 'Purple Dome' Similar to 'Osprey' but with flowers of rich purple. 45 × 45cm/1.5 × 1.5ft

TRICYRTIS (Toad lily)

A genus of perennials grown for their star, bell or funnel-shaped flowers. Best in humus-rich soil in shade.
T. formosana 'Stolonifera' A rhizomatous perennial with shiny leaves of deep green, spotted dark purple, and producing deeply spotted, star shaped white, pink or purple flowers in early autumn. 75 × 45cm/2.5 × 1.5ft

235

Trifolium repens 'Purpurascens'

Trillium grandiflorum

Trillium grandiflorum 'Roseum'

Trillium sessile

TRIFOLIUM (Clover)

A genus of annuals, biennials and perennials of creeping or upright habit with divided leaves and small, pea-like flowers in spring or summer. The genus includes species which are generally regarded as weeds.

T. repens 'Purpurascens' A rhizomatous perennial with divided leaves of dark purple-brown, edged with green, and small, white flowers in summer. 10cm/4in × indefinite spread

TRILLIUM (Trinity flower)

A genus of rhizomatous perennials of upright habit grown mainly for their veined leaves, often marbled purple or silver, and attractive cup or funnel-shaped flowers. For humus-rich, acid to neutral soil in full or part shade.

T. grandiflorum (Wake robin) A perennial of clump forming habit with leaves of deep green and carrying pure white flowers, fading to pink, in spring and summer. 45 × 30cm/1.5 × 1ft

T. grandiflorum 'Roseum' Similar to the species but with flowers of clear pink. 45 × 30cm/1.5 × 1ft

T. sessile A perennial of clump forming habit with variably marbled leaves of deep green and carrying mainly maroon-red flowers in late spring. 30 × 20cm/1ft × 8in

TRITELEIA

A genus of frost hardy, cormous perennials valued for their umbels of funnel-shaped flowers largely in shades of blue, purple-blue, white or yellow. For light, sandy soil in full sun.

T. laxa A frost hardy, cormous perennial with narrow basal leaves, dying away by flowering time, and dark purple-blue flowers, seldom white, in early summer. 75 × 5cm/1.5ft × 2in

TRITONIA

A genus of frost hardy to half hardy cormous perennials, not dissimilar to and closely related to crocosmia, cultivated for their spikes of cup or funnel-shaped flowers in a variety of colours. For light, free draining soil in full sun.

T. disticha subsp. *rubrolucens* A frost hardy, cormous perennial with lance-shaped leaves and carrying spikes of funnel-shaped, mid-pink flowers in mid and late summer. 60 × 5cm/2ft × 2in

Triteleia laxa

TROCHODENDRON

A genus of a single species of frost hardy, evergreen tree or large shrub cultivated mainly for its striking leaves, arranged in spirals, and its racemes of green flowers. For neutral to acidic soil.
T. aralioides A frost hardy tree or large shrub of columnar habit with leaves of shiny, deep green and petalless, bright green flowers in late spring and early summer. 10 × 8m/30 × 25ft

TROLLIUS (Globe flower)

A genus of perennials of clump forming habit grown mainly for their divided leaves and rounded or bowl-shaped flowers usually in shades of orange or yellow. Well suited to the bog garden.
T. chinensis 'Golden Queen' A perennial of clump forming habit with basal leaves of mid-green and producing bowl-shaped orange flowers in early to mid summer. 75 × 45cm/2.5 × 1.5ft

TROPAEOLUM

A genus of frost hardy to frost tender annuals and perennials of bushy, climbing or trailing habit grown mainly for their brightly coloured, largely funnel-shaped flowers. Widely employed in summer bedding, in containers or hanging baskets. Best in full sun.
T. majus 'Alaska' (Nasturtium) A half hardy annual of bushy habit with cream speckled leaves of light green and producing flowers in shades of cream, orange, red or yellow from summer to autumn. 30 × 45cm/1 × 1.5ft
T. tuberosum var. *lineamaculatum* 'Ken Aslet' A half hardy, perennial climber with leaves of grey-green and producing orange flowers from midsummer to autumn. 2–4m/6–12ft
T. speciosum (Flame creeper) A frost hardy, perennial climber with leaves of mid to dark green and producing vermilion flowers followed by rounded fruits from summer to autumn. 3m/10ft

TSUGA (Hemlock)

A genus of evergreen, coniferous trees grown for their attractive foliage, cones and their ability to withstand shade. Best in acid to neutral soil.
T. canadensis 'Pendula' A slow growing, evergreen shrub of mound forming habit with purple-grey bark and narrow, toothed leaves of mid-green. Female cones. 4 × 8m/12 × 25ft

TULBAGHIA

A genus of frost hardy to frost tender, deciduous, occasionally semi-evergreen, perennials valued for their strap-like leaves, sometimes grey-green, and graceful umbels of mainly purple or white tubular flowers. Well suited to a cool conservatory or glasshouse.
T. violacea A frost hardy perennial of clump forming habit with scented lilac flowers from midsummer to early autumn. 45 × 25cm/1.5ft × 10in

Trollius chinensis 'Golden Queen'

Tropaeolum majus 'Alaska'

Tropaeolum tuberosum var. *lineamaculatum* 'Ken Aslet'

Tropaeolum speciosum

Tsuga canadensis 'Pendula'

Tulipa 'Apeldoorn'

Tulipa 'Bellona'

Tulipa 'Black Parrot'

Tulipa 'Burgundy'

Tulipa 'China Pink'

Tulipa 'Duke of Wellington'

TULIPA (Tulip)

A genus of bulbous perennials cultivated mainly for the brilliance of their single or double flowers, largely egg, goblet or bowl-shaped, lily-like or occasionally fringed, in a wide range of colours which may be single, mixed or variegated, the outcome of a virus. For purposes of identification, tulips may broadly be divided into the following flower groups: Division 1 Single Early, Division 2 Double Early, Division 3 Triumph, Division 4 Darwin Hybrids, Division 5 Single Late, Division 6 Lily-flowered, Division 7 Fringed, Division 8 Viridiflora, Division 9 Rembrandt, Division 10 Parrot, Division 11 Double Late (peony-flowered), Division 12 Kaufmanniana, Division 13 Fosteriana, Division 14 Greigii Hybrids and Division 15 Miscellaneous. All are best in well drained soil in full sun.

T. 'Apeldoorn' A bulbous perennial tulip belonging to the Darwin Hybrids group with single flowers of bright cherry-red in mid-spring. 60cm/2ft

T. 'Bellona' A bulbous perennial tulip belonging to the Triumph group with single, scented, flowers of deep butter-yellow in mid-spring. 45cm/1.5ft

T. 'Black Parrot' A bulbous perennial tulip belonging to the Parrot group with single flowers of the deepest maroon-red in late spring. 60cm/2ft

T. 'Burgundy' A bulbous perennial tulip belonging to the Lily-flowered group with single flowers of dark burgundy-wine lightening to deep pink. 60cm/2ft

T. 'China Pink' A bulbous perennial tulip belonging to the Lily-flowered group with single flowers of mid-pink, tinged white at the base, in late spring. 45cm/1.5ft

T. 'Duke of Wellington' A bulbous perennial tulip belonging to the Single Late group with single white flowers in late spring. 60cm/2ft

T. 'Fantasy' A bulbous perennial tulip belonging to the Parrot group with single flowers of pink and rose red with green markings in late spring. 60cm/2ft

Tulipa 'Fantasy'

Tulipa 'First Lady'

Tulipa 'Fringed Elegance'

Tulipa 'Gaiety'

T. 'First Lady' A bulbous perennial tulip belonging to the Triumph group with single flowers of mid-pink in mid and late spring. 45cm/1.5ft

T. 'Fringed Elegance' A bulbous perennial tulip belonging to the Fringed group with single flowers of primrose-yellow, paler at the edges and greenish-yellow on the insides, in late spring. 30cm/1ft

T. 'Gaiety' A bulbous perennial tulip belonging to the Kaufmanniana group with single flowers of butter-yellow paling to near white, deep brown at the base and marked with dull red on the outer sides. 15cm/6in

T. 'General Eisenhower' A bulbous perennial tulip belonging to the Darwin Hybrids group with single scarlet flowers in mid to late spring. 60cm/2ft

T. 'Golden Melody' A bulbous perennial tulip belonging to the Triumph group with single flowers of deep lemon-yellow in mid to late spring. 45cm/1.5ft

T. 'Groenland' A bulbous perennial tulip belonging to the Viridiflora group with single flowers of light green with broad cream into pink margins in late spring. 45cm/1.5ft

T. 'Keizerskroon' A bulbous perennial tulip belonging to the Single Early group with single flowers of scarlet widely margined with yellow in mid-spring. 30cm/1ft

T. linifolia Batalinii Group A bulbous perennial tulip belonging to the Miscellaneous group with flowers of cream tinged pale green in early and mid-spring. 20cm/8in

T. 'Maréchal Niel' A bulbous perennial tulip belonging to the Double Early group with double flowers of bright yellow tinged with orange in mid-spring. 30cm/1ft

Tulipa 'General Eisenhower'

Tulipa 'Golden Melody'

Tulipa 'Groenland'

Tulipa 'Keizerskroon'

Tulipa 'Maréchal Niel'

Tulipa linifolia Batalinii Group

Tulipa 'Mariette'

Tulipa 'Monte Carlo'

Tulipa 'Noranda'

Tulipa 'Oranje Nassau'

Tulipa 'Purissima'

Tulipa 'Queen of Night'

Tulipa 'Mount Tacoma'

T. 'Mariette' A bulbous perennial tulip belonging to the Lily-flowered group with single flowers of deep rose-pink in late spring. 45cm/1 5ft

T. 'Monte Carlo' A bulbous perennial tulip belonging to the Double Early group with double flowers of rich yellow in mid-spring. 30cm/1ft

T. 'Mount Tacoma' A bulbous perennial tulip belonging to the Double Late group with double pure white flowers in late spring. 45cm/1.5ft

T. 'Noranda' A bulbous perennial tulip belonging to the Fringed group with single flowers of blood-red fringed orange at the outer edges in late spring. 45cm/1.5ft

T. 'Oranje Nassau' A bulbous perennial tulip belonging to the Double Early group with double flowers of blood-red tinged orange-red in mid-spring. 30cm/1ft

T. 'Purissima' A bulbous perennial tulip belonging to the Fosteriana group with single flowers of pure white in mid-spring. 30cm/1ft

T. 'Queen of Night' A bulbous perennial tulip belonging to the Single Late group with single flowers of deepest maroon, near black, in late spring. 60cm/2ft

T. 'Red Riding Hood' A bulbous perennial tulip belonging to the Greigii group with single flowers of brilliant scarlet in early spring. Leaves are striped dull maroon and green. 20cm/8in

T. saxatilis A bulbous perennial tulip belonging to the Miscellaneous group with scented, single flowers of lilac-pink, tinged yellow at the base, in mid and late spring. 30cm/1ft

Tulipa 'Red Riding Hood'

Tulipa saxatilis

Tulipa 'Spring Green'

Tulipa 'Scarlet Baby'

Tulipa sprengeri

Tulipa turkestanica

T. 'Scarlet Baby' A bulbous perernnial tulip belonging to the Kaufmanniana group with single flowers of scarlet, egg-yolk yellow at the centre, in early and mid spring. 20cm/8in
T. sprengeri A bulbous perennial tulip belonging to the Miscellaneous group with single flowers of orange-red, pale ochre at the base, in early summer. 45cm/1.5ft
T. 'Spring Green' A bulbous perennial tulip belonging to the Viridiflora group with single flowers of creamy-white with mid-green markings in late spring. 45cm/1.5ft
T. turkestanica A bulbous perennial tulip belonging to the Miscellaneous group with off-white flowers with yellow centres in early and mid-spring. 30cm/1ft
T. 'West Point' A bulbous perennial tulip belonging to the Lily-flowered group with flowers of clear yellow in late spring. 45cm/1.5ft

Tulipa 'West Point'

Tweedia caerulea

Typha angustifolia

TWEEDIA

A genus of a single species of frost tender, evergreen scrambling sub-shrub most often treated as an annual and grown in a cool glasshouse.
T. caerulea A frost tender, evergreen sub-shrub with twining stems and lance-shaped leaves of mid-green and flowers of sky-blue, ageing to purple, from summer to early autumn. 1m/3ft

TYPHA (Bulrush)

A genus of aquatic perennials for the margins of ponds and streams valued for their thin, basal leaves and poker-like flower spikes (bulrushes). Rhizomes may become invasive.
T. angustifolia An aquatic perennial with narrow leaves, sheathed at the base, and dark brown flower spikes in midsummer. 1.5m/5ft × indefinite spread

Ulex europaeus

Ulmus minor 'Dampieri Aurea'

ULEX (Furze)

A genus of evergreen shrubs, whose young leaves are rapidly replaced by green spines, and which are cultivated for their pea-like, yellow flowers. Suited to poor, acidic to neutral soil.

U. europaeus (Gorse) An evergreen shrub of upright habit carrying scented yellow flowers periodically throughout the year. Dark brown seedpods in summer. 2.5 × 2m/8 × 6ft

ULMUS (Elm)

A genus of deciduous, occasionally semi-evergreen, trees and very rarely shrubs grown mainly for their form, their foliage, often colouring in autumn, their bell-shaped flowers and fruits. In recent years all elms have been affected by Dutch elm disease which, in most cases, has proved fatal.

U. minor 'Dampieri Aurea' A deciduous tree of columnar habit with upright branches of shiny, bright yellow leaves and clusters of small red flowers very rarely in spring. 10 × 6m/30 × 20ft

U. procera (English elm) A deciduous tree of upright habit forming a dense crown in maturity. Dark green leaves, paler underneath, colour yellow in autumn. Small red flowers in spring are followed by winged green fruits. 40 × 15m/130 × 50ft

Uvularia grandiflora

Valeriana phu 'Aurea'

UVULARIA (Merrybells)

A genus of rhizomatous perennials grown mainly for their long, hanging, tubular to bell-shaped yellow flowers on tall slender stems. For humus-rich, well drained soil in full or part shade.

U. grandiflora A rhizomatous perennial with downward pointing leaves of mid-green, slightly hairy on the undersides, and tubular to bell-shaped yellow flowers in mid and late spring. 75 × 30cm/2.5 × 1ft

VACCINIUM (Blueberry)

A genus of hardy to frost hardy, deciduous, evergreen or semi-evergreen shrubs and trees cultivated for their attractive foliage, flowers in various shades and edible berries.

V. angustifolium var. *laevifolium* A hardy, deciduous shrub of spreading habit with shiny leaves of deep green, colouring red in autumn, and bell-shaped, white flowers in spring followed by edible blue-black berries. 60 × 60cm/2 × 2ft

VALERIANA (Valerian)

A genus of annuals, perennials, semi-evergreen sub-shrubs and, most often, evergreen shrubs. Those in cultivation, mainly herbaceous perennials, are grown for their attractive flowers carried over a prolonged period.

V. phu 'Aurea' A rhizomatous perennial forming clumps of basal leaves, soft yellow in spring maturing to mid-green by summer, with small, white flowers in early summer. 1m × 60cm/3 × 2ft

VANCOUVERIA

A genus of hardy to frost hardy, rhizomatous perennials, closely related to epimedium, and some of which are evergreen, valued for their attractive basal leaves and for their panicles of small flowers carried on thin, wiry stalks in late spring and early summer. For humus-rich, well drained soil in part shade out of the reach of cold winds.

V. hexandra A hardy, deciduous, rhizomatous perennial forming basal leaves divided into bright green leaflets and carrying white flowers on thin, upright stems in late spring and early summer. 45 × 45cm/1.5 × 1.5ft

Veratrum viride

VERBASCUM (Mullein)

A genus of hardy to frost hardy biennials, some annuals and perennials and a few sub-shrubs, some semi-evergreen or evergreen, from which are derived many hybrids. Verbascums are largely cultivated for their attractive basal leaves, frequently grey-green, and their most often, outward facing, saucer-shaped flowers held on tall, upright stems. Flower colour is varied and includes shades of purple, red, red-brown, yellow or white. Best in alkaline soil in full sun.

V. chaixii 'Album' A hardy, semi-evergreen perennial forming rosettes of hairy, mid-green leaves and carrying white flowers with mauve centres on white, woolly stems in mid and late summer. 1m × 45cm/3 × 1.5ft

V. olympicum A hardy perennial, often monocarpic, forming rosettes of mid-green leaves and carrying clusters of golden-yellow flowers on branched, white, woolly stems from early to late summer. 2m × 60cm/6 × 2ft

Veratrum nigrum

VERATRUM

A genus of perennials of vigorous habit valued mainly for their veined leaves of mid to deep green and their upright, tall stems of starry flowers in shades of green, red-brown, near black in some cases, or white followed by seedheads. Flowers are both unisexual and bisexual, carried together in the same inflorescence. Best in rich soil which does not dry out in part shade.

V. nigrum A rhizomatous perennial forming clumps of pleated basal leaves and carrying red-brown to near black flowers, the backs of which are striped green, on tall stems in mid and late summer. 1m × 60cm/3 × 2ft

V. viride (Indian poke) A rhizomatous perennial forming clumps of pleated basal leaves, hairy on the undersides, and carrying green to yellow-green flowers in early and midsummer. Tolerant of wet conditions. 2m × 60cm/6 × 2ft

Verbascum chaixii 'Album'

Verbascum olympicum

243

Verbena × hybrida

Verbena bonariensis

VERBENA

A genus of hardy to frost tender annuals, perennials and sub-shrubs noted for their square stems and valued for their small but brightly coloured flowers over a prolonged period. Of the numerous hybrids, many are employed in summer bedding schemes or used in containers or hanging baskets. Best in full sun.

V. bonariensis A frost hardy, short-lived perennial forming low, basal clumps of somewhat coarse, toothed leaves of dark green and carrying rounded heads of tiny, lilac-purple flowers carried on tall, branched stems from midsummer to mid-autumn. 2m × 45cm/6 × 1.5ft

V. × hybrida A half hardy perennial, most often treated as an annual, of upright or bushy habit with leaves of mid to dark green and producing most often white-eyed flowers in a wide range of colours to include pink, purple, red, white or yellow. 45 × 45cm/1.5 × 1.5ft

V. 'Sissinghurst' A frost hardy perennial of mat forming habit with leaves of deep green and producing magenta-pink flowers from late spring to early autumn, most in summer. 20cm × 1m/8in × 3ft

Verbena 'Sissinghurst'

VERONICA (Speedwell)

A genus of hardy to frost hardy annuals, perennials and some largely deciduous sub-shrubs valued for their small, outward facing flowers in shades of blue, pink, purple or white. Smaller species are well suited to the rock garden, for containers or the alpine house and should be cultivated in full sun in well drained soil. *V. beccabunga* should be grown at the margins of a pond or in wet soil in a bog garden. *V. austriaca* Corfu Form A hardy perennial of mat forming habit with grey-green leaves and carrying saucer-shaped, intense sky-blue flowers on upright stems over a prolonged period in summer. to 30 × 45cm/1 × 1.5ft

Veronica austriaca Corfu Form

V. gentianoides 'Tissington White' A hardy perennial of carpeting habit forming basal rosettes of lance-shaped, deep green leaves and carrying upright stems of cup-shaped, palest blue-white flowers in early summer. 45 × 45cm/1.5 × 1.5ft

V. peduncularis 'Georgia Blue' A hardy perennial of mat forming habit with shiny leaves of mid-green, tinged dark purple at times, and carrying saucer-shaped, Oxford-blue flowers from early spring to summer and occasionally in autumn and winter. 10 × 60cm/4in × 2ft

V. pinnata 'Blues Eyes' A hardy perennial of carpeting habit with leaves of mid-green and carrying spires of saucer-shaped, intense blue flowers in spring and early summer. 10 × 30cm/4in × 1ft

V. prostrata A hardy perennial of prostrate habit with leaves of bright green and carrying saucer-shaped, pale to deep blue flowers in early summer. 15 × 45cm/6in × 1.5ft

V. spicata subsp. *incana* A hardy perennial of mat forming habit with hairy leaves of silver-green and carrying spires of starry, purple-blue flowers in summer. 30 × 30cm/1 × 1ft

Veronica peduncularis 'Georgia Blue'

Veronica pinnata 'Blue Eyes'

Veronica gentianoides 'Tissington White'

Veronica prostrata

Veronica 'Shirley Blue'

Veronica spicata subsp. *incana*

VERONICASTRUM

A genus of perennials of upright habit grown mainly for their racemes of pink, purple-blue or white flowers well suited to contributing height to the summer herbaceous border.

V. virginicum f. *album* A perennial of upright habit with pointed leaves of dark green and bearing tall racemes of white flowers from midsummer to early autumn. 2m × 45cm/6 × 1.5ft

Viburnum betulifolium

Viburnum bodnantense 'Dawn'

Viburnum carlesii 'Aurora'

Viburnum burkwoodii

Viburnum davidii

Viburnum × juddii

VIBURNUM

A genus of hardy to frost hardy evergreen, semi-evergreen and deciduous shrubs, sometimes trees, valued for their attractive foliage, their flowers, sometimes scented, mostly of cream, white or pink, and their fruits of black, blue or red. Viburnums are tolerant of a wide range of conditions and situations but prefer to be grown in damp but well drained soil in sun or part shade. *V. lantanoides* should be afforded lime free soil.

V. betulifolium A hardy, deciduous shrub of upright habit with arching branches of shiny, deep green leaves and producing domed corymbs of small, white flowers in early summer followed by red fruits. 3 × 3m/10 × 10ft

V. bodnantense 'Dawn' A hardy, deciduous shrub of upright habit with leaves of deep green, bronze when young, and producing clusters of highly fragrant, tubular, rose-pink flowers on bare wood from early winter to spring. Occasional blue-black or purple fruits. 3 × 2m/10 × 6ft

V. burkwoodii A hardy, evergreen shrub of rounded habit with shiny leaves of deep green and producing domed corymbs of scented, tubular, white flowers, opening from pink buds, in spring followed by red fruits ripening to black. 2.5 × 2.5m/ 8 × 8ft

V. carlesii 'Aurora' A hardy, deciduous shrub of bushy habit with leaves of deep green, frequently colouring red in autumn, and producing domed corymbs of scented, tubular, pink flowers, red in bud, in spring followed by red fruits ripening to black. 2 × 2m/6 × 6ft

V. davidii A hardy, evergreen shrub of compact habit with veined leaves of deep green and producing flat heads of small, tubular, white flowers in late spring followed by steely-blue fruits where both male and female plants are grown together. 1 × 1m/3 × 3ft

V. × juddii A hardy, deciduous shrub of rounded habit with leaves of deep green, sometimes colouring red in autumn, and producing spherical corymbs of scented, pink flushed, white flowers, pink in bud, in spring. 1.2 × 1.5m/4 × 5ft

Viburnum opulus

Viburnum opulus 'Sterile'

Viburnum opulus 'Xanthocarpum'

V. opulus (Guelder rose) A hardy, deciduous shrub of vigorous habit with maple-like leaves of deep green, colouring red in autumn, and producing flat, lacecap-type heads of tubular, white flowers in late spring and early summer followed by fleshy red fruits. 5 × 4m/15 × 12ft

V. opulus 'Sterile' (Snowball tree) A hardy, deciduous shrub of rounded habit with maple-like leaves of deep green, tinted purple in autumn, and producing spherical heads of white or green-white flowers, sometimes becoming pink, in late spring and early summer. 4 × 4m/12 × 12ft

V. opulus 'Xanthocarpum' Similar to the species but producing translucent yellow fruits. 5 × 4m/15 × 12ft

V. plicatum 'Mariesii' A hardy, deciduous shrub of spreading habit with branches forming a series of tiers and with leaves of deep green, colouring red-purple in autumn. Rounded heads of saucer-shaped, white flowers are produced in late spring followed occasionally by fruit. 3 × 4m/10 × 12ft

V. rhytidophyllum A hardy, evergreen shrub of vigorous habit with veined, shiny leaves of deep green and producing rounded heads of small, tubular, cream-white flowers in late spring followed by red fruits ripening to black. 5 × 4m/15 × 12ft

V. tinus (Laurustinus) A hardy, evergreen shrub of compact habit with leaves of deep green and producing flat heads of small, white flowers from late winter to spring followed by blue-black fruits. 3 × 3m/10 × 10ft

Viburnum rhytidophyllum

Viburnum plicatum 'Marsiesii'

Viburnum tinus

Vinca major

Vinca minor 'Alba Variegata'

Viola cornuta

Viola 'Bowles' Black'

Viola hybrid

Viola hederacea

VINCA (Periwinkle)

A genus of hardy to frost hardy, evergreen sub-shrubs and herbaceous perennials cultivated largely for their often variegated leaves and for their attractive flowers, sometimes double, in shades of blue, violet, purple or white. Tolerant of a wide range of conditions and situations although most flowers are achieved in full sun.

V. major (Greater periwinkle) A hardy, evergreen sub-shrub of prostrate habit with arching stems of deep green leaves and carrying violet-blue or violet flowers from mid-spring to autumn. Inclined to become invasive. 45cm/1.5ft × indefinite spread

V. minor 'Alba Variegata' (Lesser periwinkle) A hardy, evergreen sub-shrub of prostrate habit with trailing stems of light green leaves, broadly margined pale-yellow, and carrying white flowers from mid-spring to autumn. 20cm/8in × indefinite spread.

VIOLA (Pansy, Violet)

A genus of hardy to half hardy annuals, biennials, evergreen, semi-evergreen and deciduous perennials with variable leaves, mostly of mid-green, and grown mainly for their often scented flowers in a wide range of colours, many of which are 'patterned'. The hybridization of many species has resulted in numerous cultivars, often loosely referred to as pansies.

V. 'Bowles' Black' A hardy annual, biennial or short-lived, evergreen perennial with velvet flowers of near black, each with a golden-yellow eye, from spring to autumn. Comes true from seed. 10 × 20cm/4 × 8in

V. cornuta A hardy, evergreen perennial with lightly scented flowers of lilac to lavender-blue or white from spring to summer. 7 × 20cm/3 × 8in

V. hederacea (Ivy-leafed violet) A frost hardy, evergreen perennial with lightly scented flowers in shades of cream, violet or white, sometimes white with violet patches, in late summer. Well suited to the alpine house in part shade. 10 × 20cm/4 × 8in

V. hybrid A hardy biennial or short-lived perennial with 'patterned' flowers of light and deep purple and yellow from early spring to summer. 20 × 20cm/8 × 8in

Viola labradorica

V. labradorica (Labrador violet) A hardy, semi-evergreen perennial with leaves of deep green, tinged purple when young, and pale purple flowers in spring and summer. 8cm/3in × indefinite spread
V. soraria 'Freckles' A hardy perennial with white flowers heavily speckled with lavender from mid-spring to early summer. 10 × 20cm/4 × 8in
V. 'Sorbet Mixed' A hardy biennial or short-lived perennial with bicoloured flowers in a number of shades to include cream, yellow, purple and violet in spring. 10 × 30cm/4in × 1ft
V. tricolor (Heartsease) An annual, biennial or short-lived, evergreen perennial with flowers in a number of shades of lavender, purple, violet, white or yellow, the upper petals mostly of deep purple, from spring to autumn. 10 × 10cm/4 × 4in

VITIS (Vine)

A genus of deciduous climbers, rarely shrubs, grown for their attractive foliage and fruits (grapes). Ornamental vines thrive best in neutral to alkaline soil in sun or part shade and are well suited to training over a pergola, trellis or against a wall.
V. coignetiae A deciduous climber of vigorous habit with large, heart-shaped leaves of deep green, veined on the upper sides, felted on the lower, colouring red and producing blue-black grapes in autumn. 15m/50ft
V. vinifera 'Purpurea' A deciduous climber with rounded, toothed leaves opening grey-hairy, maturing to plum and colouring to deep purple in autumn when small, purple grapes are produced. 7m/22ft

Viola soraria 'Freckles'

Viola 'Sorbet Mixed'

Viola tricolor

Vitis vinifera 'Purpurea'

Vitis coignetiae

Waldsteinia ternata

Weigela florida 'Foliis Purpureis'

Weigela 'Florida Variegata'

Wisteria floribunda

Wisteria sinensis 'Alba'

WALDSTEINIA

A genus of rhizomatous perennials cultivated for their attractive leaves and their saucer-shaped, yellow flowers in late spring and early summer. For full or part shade and well suited as ground cover. Tolerant of dry conditions.
W. ternata A semi-evergreen perennial of vigorous habit with divided, toothed leaves of mid-green and producing bright yellow flowers in late spring and early summer. 10 × 60cm/4in × 2ft

WATSONIA

A genus of half hardy, cormous perennials grown for their upright, sword-like leaves and their spikes of tubular flowers in orange, pink, red or white. Well suited to a cool conservatory.
W. borbonica A half hardy, cormous perennial of clump forming habit with branched spikes of bright pink flowers in summer. 1m × 10cm/3ft × 4in

WEIGELA

A genus of deciduous shrubs grown mainly for their bell to funnel-shaped flowers in shades of pink and red and also, but less often, white and yellow. Tolerant of a wide range of conditions and situations where soil is well drained.
W. florida 'Foliis Purpureis' A deciduous shrub forming arching stems of bronze-green foliage and producing funnel-shaped flowers of deep pink in late spring and early summer. 1 × 1.5m/3 × 5ft
W. 'Florida Variegata' A deciduous shrub of rounded habit with leaves of pale green, margined creamy-white, and producing funnel-shaped light pink flowers, deeper in bud, in late spring and early summer. 2–2.5 × 2–2.5m/ 6–8 × 6–8ft
W. 'Snowflake' A deciduous shrub of spreading habit with leaves of deep green and producing bell-shaped, white flowers in late spring and early summer. 1.2 × 1.5m/4 × 5ft

WISTERIA

A genus of deciduous climbers grown for their most striking, pea-like flowers carried in hanging racemes in spring and summer and followed by bean-like seedpods. Twining stems, growing in an anticlockwise direction, are particularly attractive in maturity when they take on a gnarled appearance. Well suited to training over a pergola, against a wall or into a tree. May be grown free-standing.
W. floribunda (Japanese wisteria) A vigorous climber with divided leaves forming numerous leaflets and carrying scented racemes of blue, violet, pink or white flowers in early summer followed by velvety seedpods. 9m/28ft
W. sinensis 'Alba' (Chinese wisteria) A vigorous climber with divided leaves forming a number of leaflets and carrying scented racemes of white flowers in late spring and early summer followed by velvety seedpods. 9m/28ft

XYZ

XANTHOCERAS

A genus of a single species of upright, deciduous shrub, seldom to be seen in gardens, and grown largely for its starry white flowers in late spring. Well suited for wall training. Best in full sun.

X. sorbifolium A deciduous shrub of upright habit with narrow, lance-shaped, toothed leaves of shiny, deep green and carrying white flowers in late spring as the new leaves emerge.
4 × 3m/12 × 10ft

Xanthoceras sorbifolium

YUCCA

A genus of hardy to frost tender perennials, some of which are monocarpic, evergreen shrubs and eventual trees grown for their mainly lance-shaped, often rosette-forming leaves and their panicles of mainly white flowers. Well suited as specimens. Best in full sun.

Y. filamentosa (Adam's needle) A hardy shrub forming clumps of near stemless, basal rosettes of stiff, deep green leaves, faintly margined white, and carrying upright panicles of white, tinged green, bell-shaped flowers in summer.
75cm × 1.5m/2.5 × 5ft

Y. gloriosa (Spanish dagger) A frost hardy shrub of upright habit carrying narrow, lance-shaped leaves of blue-green, later deep green, on a stout stem and producing panicles of white, sometimes flushed purple, bell-shaped flowers from late summer to autumn. 2 × 2m/6 × 6ft

Yucca filamentosa

Yucca gloriosa

ZANTEDESCHIA (Arum lily)

A genus of hardy to frost tender perennials valued for their attractive leaves and white or coloured spathes in spring and summer. For humus-rich, moisture retentive soil in full sun. *Z. aethiopica* may be grown as a marginal aquatic.

Z. aethiopica A frost hardy, rhizomatous perennial, sometimes evergreen, of clump forming habit with arrow-shaped, shiny, bright green leaves and producing white spathes with cream spadices from late spring to midsummer. Apply a heavy mulch in winter in cold areas. 1m × 60cm/3 × 2ft

Zantedeschia aethiopica

ZAUSCHNERIA (Californian fuchsia)

A genus of hardy to frost hardy, deciduous or evergreen perennials cultivated mainly for their mass of tubular to funnel-shaped flowers, mostly scarlet, carried in racemes in late summer and early autumn. Best in full sun out of the reach of cold winds.

Z. californica 'Dublin' A hardy, deciduous perennial with narrow leaves of grey-green and carrying racemes of tubular, orange-red flowers in late summer and early autumn. 25 × 30cm/10in × 1ft

ZIGADENUS

Genus of frost hardy, bulbous or rhizomatous perennials grown mainly for their upright, small, starry flowers in green-white or yellow-white in summer. For deep, moisture retentive soil in full sun or part shade although *Z. fremontii* requires full sun and may be best in a bulb frame.

Z. elegans A frost hardy, bulbous perennial with narrow, basal leaves of grey-green and producing spikes of starry, green-white flowers in mid and late summer.
75 × 8cm/2.5ft × 3in

Zauschneria californica 'Dublin'

ZINNIA

A genus of frost tender annuals, perennials and subshrubs, mainly grown for summer bedding schemes, and valued for their daisy-like flowerheads carried on long stems in a wide range of colours to include shades of lilac, orange, purple, red, white or yellow. Best in full sun.

Z. hybrid A frost tender annual of upright, bushy habit with leaves of mid-green and carrying daisy-like, broad petalled flowers in shades of orange, purple, red or yellow in summer. 60 × 30cm/2 × 1ft

Zinnia hybrids

Index of Common Names

Spanish bluebell. See *Hyacinthus hispanica*.
Spanish broom. See *Spartium*.
Spanish dagger. See *Yucca gloriosa*.
Speedwell. See *Veronica*.
Spider flower. See *Cleome*.
Spindle tree. See *Euonymus*.
Spleenwort. See *Asplenium*.
Spotted laurel. See *Aucuba*.
Spotted orchid. See *Dactylorhiza*.
Spruce. See *Picea*.
Spurge. See *Euphorbia*.
Squirrel tail grass. See *Hordeum*.
St. Bernard's lily. See *Anthericum liliago*.
St. Bruno's lily. See *Paradisea*.
St. Dabeoc's heath. See *Daboecia*.
Star of Bethlehem. See *Ornithogalum*.
Statice. See *Limonium*.
Stiff bottlebrush. See *Callistemon rigidus*.
Stinking hellebore. See *Helleborus foetidus*.
Stock. See *Matthiola*.
Stokes' aster. See *Stokesia*.
Stonecrop. See *Sedum*.
Strawberry. See *Fragaria*.
Strawberry tree. See *Arbutus*.
Strawflower. See *Helipterum*.
Stone cress. See *Aethionema*.
Sunflower. See *Helianthus*.
Sun rose. See *Cistus*.
Swamp cypress. See *Taxodium*.
Sweet alyssum. See *Lobularia*.
Sweet box. See *Sarcococca*.
Sweet cicely. See *Myrrhis*.
Sweet chestnut. See *Castanea*.
Sweet gum. See *Liquidamber styraciflua*.
Sweet pea. See *Lathyrus odoratus*.
Sweet pepper bush. See *Clethra*.
Sweet rocket. See *Hesperis matronalis*.
Sweet William. See *Dianthus barbatus*.
Switch ivy. See *Leucothoe*.

T

Tamarisk. See *Tamarix*.
Tea tree. See *Leptospermum*.
Tickseed. See *Coreopsis*.
Thorow-wax. See *Bupleurum*.
Thrift. See *Armeria*.
Thyme. See *Thymus*.
Tiger flower. See *Tigridia*.
Toadflax. See *Linaria*.
Toad lily. See *Tricyrtis*.
Tobacco plant. See *Nicotiana*.
Tree ivy. See *Fatshedera × lizei*.
Tree lupin. See *Lupinus arboreus*.
Tree of heaven. See *Ailanthus altissima*.
Tree peony. See *Paeonia delavayi*.
Tree peony. See *Paeonia suffruticosa*.
Tree purslane. See *Atriplex halimus*.
Trembling grass. See *Briza media*.
Trinity flower. See *Trillium*.
Trumpet vine. See *Campsis*.
Tulip. See *Tulipa*.
Tulip tree. See *Liriodendron*.
Tupelo. See *Nyssa*.
Turkscap. See *Lilium martagon*.
Turtlehead. See *Chelone*.

U

Umbrella pine. See *Pinus pinea*.

V

Valerian. See *Centranthus*.
Valerian. See *Valeriana*.
Venetian sumach. See *Cotinus coggygria*.
Violet. See *Viola*.
Viper's bugloss. See *Echium vulgare*.
Virginia cowslip. See *Mertensia pulmonarioides*.
Virginia creeper. See *Parthenocissus*.

W

Wallflower. See *Erysimum*.
Walnut. See *Juglans*.
Water hawthorn. See *Aponogeton distachyos*.
Water hyacinth. See *Eichhornia*.
Water lettuce. See *Pistia*.
Water lily. See *Nymphaea*.
Water plantain. See *Alisma*.
Water violet. See *Hottonia*.
Weeping beech. See *Fagus sylvatica* 'Pendula'.
Wellingtonia. See *Sequoiadendron*.
Welsh poppy. See *Meconopsis cambrica*.
Whitebeam. See *Sorbus aria* 'Lutescens'.
Whitlow grass. See *Draba*.
Whorlflower. See *Morina longifolia*.
Widow iris. See *Hermodactylus tuberosus*.
Widow's tears. See *Commelina*.
Wild onion. See *Allium cernuum*.
Wild rye grass. See *Elymus*.
Willow herb. See *Epilobium*.
Windflower. See *Anemone*.
Winter aconite. See *Eranthis*.
Winter jasmine. See *Jasminum nudiflorum*.
Winter's bark. See *Drimys winteri*.
Wintersweet. See *Chimonanthus*.
Wire-netting bush. See *Corokia cotoneaster*.
Witch hazel. See *Hamamelis*.
Wonga wonga vine. See *Pandorea pandorana*.
Woodruff. See *Asperula*.
Woodrush. See *Luzula*.
Wormwood. See *Artemisia*.

Y

Yarrow. See *Achillea*.
Yew. See *Taxus*.
Yellow flag. See *Iris pseudacorus*.
Yellow pond lily. See *Nuphar*.
Young's weeping birch. See *Betula pendula* 'Youngii'.

Acknowledgements

The producers are grateful to the author for permission to reproduce the photograph of *Aesculus × neglecta* 'Erythroblastos'; to Stapeley Water Gardens Ltd, London Road, Stapeley, Nantwich, Cheshire for permission to reproduce *Nymphaea* 'Gonnère' and *N.* 'Venusta'; and to Thompson and Morgan Ltd, Ipswich, Suffolk for permission to reproduce *Cobaea scandens*.